Eager Street

Praise for *Eager Street*

"The gangster's story is almost an ancient tale at this point, generations old, as certain and entrenched as the American ghetto seems to be. But this one is honestly told by a writer who has paid every possible cost to tell it, and who spares himself little, all things considered. *Eager Street* argues convincingly that in some worlds it is never a decision to destroy yourself and others, but merely the absence of a decision."

David Simon
Producer and Author
The Corner: A Year in the Life of an Inner-City Neighborhood

"Tray's memoir is a letter from my own home. The life he lived in the streets is one that I know, as well as the possibilities for claiming and nurturing our humanity despite the obstacles. Black men have the sense of the world as being set against them, and although it may in fact be that way for many of us, there is also the broad and bright spectrum of courage, and that courage is the door to beating back those obstacles and to claiming love of ourselves and love of life. Clear and unsentimentally honest, *Eager Street* truly represents a great deal of what took place in the latter twentieth century in East Baltimore, as well as elsewhere in America's African-American communities at that time in history"

Afaa Michael Weaver
Professor and Pushcart Prize-Winning Poet
The Plum Flower Dance

"These are difficult days and difficult times and truth is we have been conditioned for lies that lead us further into a reckless abyss. Tray Jones speaks truth to power and to the powerless. His work is uncut, unconditional truth and thus unconditional love. Read it and re-read it. Read the lines, read between the lines and behind the lies. Tray Jones speaks volumes to the nature of human triumph and failure; about fear, heartache, submission, defeat, and, ultimately, courage."

Tyrone Powers, Ph.D.
Professor and Author
Eyes to My Soul: The Rise or Decline of a Black FBI Agent

Eager Street

A Life on the Corner
and Behind Bars

Arlando "Tray" Jones

Apprentice House
Baltimore, Maryland

© 2010, Arlando "Tray" Jones

Library of Congress Cataloging-in-Publication Data
Jones, Arlando, 1968-
Eager street : a life on the corner and behind bars / Arlando "Tray" Jones.
p. cm.
ISBN 978-1-934074-18-3
1. Jones, Arlando, 1968- 2. Prisoners--Maryland--Biography. 3. Prisons--
Maryland. I. Title.
HV9468J66 2007
365'.6092--dc22
[B]
2007031932

Printed in the United States of America
First Edition
Paperback Edition ISBN 978-1-934074-45-9

Jacket photos credit: Margo Weiner
Cover design: Elizabeth Watson, John Likoudis, and William "Mike" Tirone
Internal design: Elizabeth Watson, Margo Weiner, and William "Mike" Tirone

Special thanks to Michael Cook for editorial assistance.

Published by Apprentice House
The Future of Publishing...Today!

Apprentice House
Communication Department
Loyola University Maryland
4501 N. Charles Street
Baltimore, MD 21210
410.617.5265 • 410.617.5040 (fax)
www.ApprenticeHouse.com • info@ApprenticeHouse.com

This book is dedicated to all those who loved me well enough to make me loving and lovable: Kim, Leola, Karen, Viola, Iola, Joyce, Tracey, Mrs. Testerman, and, of course, my Baby-Boo.

If not for chivalry and a recognition of Drew Leder's humility, I would dedicate this book to him. For I owe him a debt I couldn't begin to repay. That said, thanks Drew. You are my hero, though where I come from a hero ain't nothing but a sandwich.

Contents

Foreword

What you are about to read is the life-story of a young man. A very young man. Arlando Jones's account of growing up in East Baltimore, sinning and sinned against in more ways than any child should be, takes us only to age sixteen. This detailed account of early life provides much of the sociological value of this document, and its fascination. We are given an answer to such questions as: What is it like growing up in the inner city surrounded by addiction, chaos, and crime? How do you learn to become a drug dealer? A murderer? How...and why?

Beyond its sociological value, this is also a coming-of-age story with universal resonances. A child struggles to find his family, identity, sexuality, friends, and future. We've all been there. Of course, not all of us have had to cope with the extreme adversity of Tray's situation, twisting and distorting those searches. Not all of us can identify with the criminal choices he makes, the consequences of which have been severe for him and those he harmed.

Yes, he was a criminal, but was he a child? The law said otherwise when he was sentenced as an adult to serve life plus twenty. Was he ever a child? He grew up so fast, too fast, because he had to.

Sometimes life can be like that child's toy where you stick your fingers in either end and the harder you try to pull them out, the tighter the webbing closes around you. Tray reached out for money, sex, power, success, all ways of reaching for freedom. As he pulled harder it all closed tighter and tighter, finally shrinking down to a prison cell.

When I first met Tray (his nickname derives from the fact he's Arlando Jones, III) he was twenty-seven years old, serving his sentence in the maximum security Maryland Penitentiary. I was volunteer-teaching a philosophy course meant to last six weeks but finally continuing for eighteen months. Tray appeared to me bright, handsome, articulate, self-possessed. True, he had an oversized ego, but was also quick to poke fun at it himself. Good sense of humor. Engaging smile. A true lady's man, or so he was quick to claim (and I believe it). But beneath the bright shiny surface—part real, part pose—was a thoughtful and motivated guy.

A lot of people in prison are just serving time. Tray wanted time to serve him. Through a prison college extension program (since abolished, as have been so many others around the country), he had completed a bachelor's degree in Applied Psychology with a minor in Management Science. He had been chosen as the inmate representative to interface with prison administrators. He served as co-leader of Project Turnaround, an organization that brought at-risk kids into the prison to "scare 'em straight."

When we read and discussed the writings of Socrates, Epictetus, Lao Tzu, and many, many others, Tray and his fellow students were not just playing mind-games. These men, most of them lifers, were seeking ways to better understand their lives, change them, do it over, get it right. This was the acid test to which each philosophical system was subjected: Will it work here in prison? Surrounded by bars and barbed wire, will this help set me free?

Tray was an enthusiastic contributor to these discussions, some of which were captured in our book, The Soul Knows No Bars: Inmates Reflect on Life, Death, and Hope (Rowman and Littlefield, 2000). The course and events there recorded are now over a decade ago. Since then he and I have stayed in touch through continual correspondence and intermittent phone calls. This has enabled me to chart the broad outlines of his stationary journey. Tray has been married and, sadly, divorced. He has deepened his philosophical studies. He has inquired into religion, at one point developing a Christian identity, and then working with yogic practices involving meditation, chanting, study, and service. (For several years now he has progressed through a Siddha Yoga correspondence course provided by the group's Prison Project.)

Tray has had his ups, but also his downs. Occasional battles with prison guards. Stretches of solitary confinement, sometimes for reasons at first unexplained or an infraction of which he was later cleared. Denial by the parole board. Frustrated attempts to have his case legally reopened, with hopes, so far unmet, for reduction of sentence.

Through it all Tray has remained surprisingly cheerful. "Life is good!" His letters or phone calls are filled with witticisms and ironic reflections, along with requests for books and information. He has internalized the spiritual view that we are not the victim of outer circumstances but create our own experience. We choose joy or misery when we choose what to think, how we interpret our reality. Tray chooses to interpret his life circumstances as an opportunity for soul-growth. He refuses to succumb to outer restraint or inward darkness though both shadow his long days and nights in prison.

When we sentence someone to life we assume an identity between the teenage criminal and his later selves, all the way up through the old man he will become. But are we that unitary? The now thirty-eight-year-old Tray telling his story may not be the same person as the boy he writes so eloquently about.

And who is that boy? A drug dealer and murderer, we know he is very different from you and me. (Some call such people subhuman, evil, superpredators, animals.) But is he that different? Could we imagine making the same choices he made if we had grown up in his world?

Questions abound as we read this powerful book, questions I will not seek to answer but merely clarify. Who is to blame here? Tray, who must finally be held responsible for his destructive choices? The family and "friends" who so let him down? The scourge of drugs? A society that neglects and scorches its underclass, that chooses to build weapons instead of schools?

Is someone like Tray then a victim of his world, or a victimizer? We like to divide the universe into black and white categories but do they work? Victims become victimizers who spawn new victim/victimizers as violence and despair go around in a circle

How to break that circle? Through imprisonment? The United States, with more than 2.2 million inmates, now houses one-quarter of all the world's prisoners. There are more prisoners, for example, in the state of California then in the nations of France, Germany, Great Britain, the Netherlands, Singapore, and Japan all put together.

If not prison, our one-size-fits-all "solution," then how else to intervene with social problems, and kids in trouble? Head Start programs, and better funding for public education? Drug treatment? Job training? Boot camps? Conflict resolution training? Urban renewal? Moral renewal? And how might we accomplish the latter—the cultivation of compassion, responsibility, and justice in our country and in ourselves?

Though it may not seem like it, I understand the writing of this book as a part of Tray's moral renewal. Take responsibility and you strengthen your ability to respond to the challenges around you. Illuminate your personal darkness and it lessens. Share your story and you may speak as well for wordless others. Written in a penitentiary, the book somewhat takes the form of the penitential memoir, a tradition stretching back to St. Augustine who confessed the sins of an ill-spent youth as part of his soul's ascending journey.

Yet Tray's memoir doesn't exactly take that form. It ends when he is still a young man. Though I have tried to give a glimpse of his subsequent, and fruitful and, yes, spiritual journey of decades, this is not Tray's focus here. He's telling the story of a kid who lived harshly in a hard world.

Nor does he spend a lot of words reflecting philosophically and penitentially on his wrongdoings. We may wish for more such pronouncements, and feel this bespeaks a moral lack on the part of the author. Maybe so. Or maybe Tray is chiefly guided by a different moral principle—that of simple honesty. The book's working title was "This is My Story." Perhaps that's finally what Tray is trying to do—tell his story honestly without excessive commentary, justification, self-accusation, or self-glorification. It's a shocking story, perhaps. Reprehensible? Understandable? Tragic? An indictment of our society, or of Tray and his street-mates?

You, the reader, will decide what it all means and what to do about it.

Dr. Drew Leder
Professor, Department of Philosophy
in Maryland

Preface

I am eager to share with readers a world that few get to experience or to learn about. While pop-culture paints a life of criminality as glamorous and alluring for the purpose of video and music sales, I will expose the harsh realities—hanging out on the ghetto street corners, normalizing crime, betrayal, and treachery. In my pursuit for family, identity, and esteem, I unwittingly perpetuated a vicious cycle of poverty, imprisonment, and pain.

Some may wonder why don't I express remorse for the wrongs I committed or endeavor to invoke sympathy for the wrongs committed against me. Fair enough! I just want to tell my story in a way that gives authentic voice to a powerless, marginalized, disenfranchised people. I want it to be known that folks who desire happiness will eagerly pursue whatever course they believe will bring it.

Where I lived, in East Baltimore, and hung out, on Eager Street, we did our very best to comprehend the incomprehensible and to bring order to the chaotic. Folks with little to no education, coping with drug addition, alcoholism, crime, and unrelenting poverty tried to find dignity and worth in life.

We all came to a place that made sense to us, the ghetto street corners. We conducted commerce there, picked up a joke or two to laugh about, or to dally in wanton sexual affairs. It all led to poor health, premature death, or imprisonment. But without strong, positive role models to guide a fatherless and motherless boy to adulthood, my fate was sealed.

If you sympathize with my plight, cool. If you hold me in contempt, I understand. Just don't be indifferent! And know that my experience isn't unique. My life experience is a common occurrence. Our society abandons or ignores children like me. Fortunately, God doesn't. The vicious cycle being perpetuated on Eager Streets around the world can be challenged by having a hard and honest look at it.

A life on the corner and behind bars is an excruciatingly painful life that entails loss, debauchery, and hopelessness. With eagerness and all the wisdom that suffering has brought me, I share with you my life.

Arlando "Tray" Jones, III
November 2007

I Danced to the Music

Chapter 1

Every man born will experience at least one great challenge. That challenge will have its ups and downs, highs and lows. No one can avoid life's inevitable great challenge. Therefore, no one is likely to be measured or judged by the challenge he faces. Each man is only measured or judged by the way he responds to his great challenge.

My life's great challenge is that I was born into a set of circumstances that more than encouraged me to be a criminal, it demanded it. There was no wavering between thoughts of wanting to be good and wanting to be bad. I started stealing from the local convenience stores in my neighborhood when I was about six or seven years old, and I didn't give a damn. If I wanted something and I did not have the money to buy it, I stole it. I knew it was wrong, unethical. I grew up in a home where I was taught to distinguish right from wrong, but I was instructed that nothing could be more wrong than going without when you possessed the talent to secure whatever it was you desired. Survival was the rule of the day. And by all accounts, I am a survivor. I have survived whippings, prison, and gun battles—and I am not finished surviving yet. Whatever it takes, I've got to survive until life lets me live. For surviving is for cockroaches. Humans should be allowed to live.

I was created to be better than circumstances ever permitted me to be. For the most part, I did not steal because I wanted to; I stole because I had to. And when petty thievery no longer satisfied my needs, I sold dope. I saw the devastation that dope was causing to the folks in my neighborhood. But I didn't care. Poverty was devastating me more, or at least, that is how I saw it.

My former wife, Francine, and other loved ones blame Fat Larry for my awful situation. They say, "It's because of that sorry fat mothafucka you're in prison serving life for murder." But it wasn't his fault. It was my fault for granting Larry so much influence over me. I admired Larry, and I loved him. He was the first real nigga who showed a young nigga, me, love. When I was out there struggling, trying to scrape a few coins together to treat myself to a decent meal, he scooped me up and showed me how to earn some real dough. He taught me how to make a dollar without sweating too hard and struggling so much only to come up empty at day's end. Despite it all, I ain't mad at Larry, even though he double-crossed me. He betrayed the rules of the game, the rules that he taught me—and he has totally neglected me since I have been in prison. But when I think about it objectively and honestly, the nigga did tell me, "It's a rotten-ass game, Tray, and only the rotten niggas are gonna make it out here." He told me, "The drug game is for rotten niggas." It's true, good people have no place in the drug game. It will eat them alive—totally destroy them. I should know. It destroyed a lot of my family and friends. It has come damn close to destroying me. It very well might have destroyed me, but I am not going to count myself out just yet. I am serving a life sentence; I truly think what's left of my life can be salvaged. Thus, I am not destroyed. God is still smiling on me. I don't know why, because I used to be just like all the other pushers in the game. I smiled in folks' faces, referred to them as friends and shot them in the back—sometimes literally. I convinced young girls to snort coke and dope because I was told that females performed better sexually while under the influence of that "thang."

I knew then and I know now that it is wrong to get a person to use drugs for the first time. I was witnessing what drug addiction was doing to my Aunt Kim. I saw what it had done to my cousin, Terrell. I watched how alcohol had reduced my mother from being one of the most attractive and productive sisters in Baltimore to a nothing drunk, incapable of taking care of her one and only son, me. I knew the pain and humiliation that my Aunt Kim had to endure because of her addiction.

She was reduced to doing unbelievable things just to keep shot money. Kim loved her children, all three of us. Yalanda, Kieshawn, and me. But being a dopefiend never permitted her to demonstrate that love to us in meaningful ways. The money, time, and attention that it would take to love three children, one of whom wasn't hers biologically, would have interfered with her blast. And nothing, and I do mean absolutely nothing, stands in the way of a dopefiend getting his/her blast.

I came in contact with the cruelest realities of drug addiction and poverty quite early in life. I am just fortunate enough to have received gentleness and kindness in my life before I had to deal with the hardships and cruelties. I still ended up psychologically scarred; but, the initial nurturing love given me by my mother, grandmother, and aunts enabled me to be lovable and loving. It made me able to face the many hardships without growing bitter and resentful.

I guess what I am really trying to express is: I was not a motherless child, though I have been made to feel that way more times than I care to remember. That's probably why it was easy for me to become Fat Larry's trigger-man. If any nigga had to be hit, Larry always knew he could count on me to get it done. My absolute loyalty belonged to Larry, and him alone. Proof of that dedication was shown time and time again in those all too frequent, "Tray, look here, that bitch ass nigga gotta go. I mean he gotta go with the quickness." I would never ask why was I selected to murder some man. I never even pondered the rightness or the wrongness of the matter. If Larry wanted it done, that was enough for me. The Pope wasn't the only man infallible and in possession of sovereignty. Larry was that nigga, too. Besides, my association with him, and serving at his pleasure, kept me living better than I had ever lived.

Prior to Larry coming into my life, I had never experienced having my very own bedroom. Now, not only did I have my very own bedroom, I had my very own telephone line installed in my room. Imagine the picture: king-size brass bed, thick brown wall-to-wall carpet, forty-inch floor model color television set—and no curfew. I got home when I got home. And home was, indeed, a luxurious place.

While I rolled with Fat Larry, I lived in luxury, drove in luxury, and did everything else in luxury. Further, and I would say above all, my association with Fat Larry gave me ghetto status. In other words, if Fat Larry was "that nigga," I was that nigga sitting next to "that nigga." The dopefiends and gold diggers alike bestowed upon me the kind of attention, admiration, and affection that made it possible for me to forgive the abject neglect I received from home.

I was angry with my grandmother for becoming an alcoholic—a pure and unadulterated drunkard. I resented her. More importantly, I was ashamed of her. For reasons I still can't figure out, I was not ashamed of my

Aunt Kim. She was shooting dope. She had the ugly tracks up and down her arms and legs to prove it. But she was cool with me. I could live with that. Besides, Kim was the one who loved me and provided for me more than anyone. Therefore, I could forgive and excuse damn near anything she did—or didn't do.

At a truly profound level, my Aunt Kim and I knew that we were in too deep. We both knew intuitively that life had robbed us of our innocence much too early and that we were burdened by too many responsibilities too soon in life.

The respect I held for Aunt Kim played itself out in some of the most morbid and twisted ways thinkable. For instance, I came into my grand-mother's home one early morning to find Kim doubled over the bathroom toilet vomiting. I asked her with genuine concern, "What's wrong, Kim?"

Irritably, she shot at me, "What the fuck you think?"

I knew instantly that she was ill—in desperate need of a heroin fix. I did not want to provide her with any narcotics. Kim was my guardian—my mother and father. She knew that I could easily provide her with a blast. I controlled damn near all the dope on Eager Street at that time. But she could not ask me for any drugs. It just wouldn't be right. And Kim had pride, she had dignity and the last thing she would ever want was for a child of hers to provide her with dope. But I could not bear seeing Kim ill, so I went down to Eager Street and caught up with one of her road dogs, this no-good busta named Poochie.

When I came upon Poochie, the nigga was happy as any dopefiend could be. I guess his good fortune could have been no greater than to have me, one of the neighborhood's biggest drug dealers come to him at six or seven o'clock in the morning, on a Sunday, the day that most dopefiends dread because it's the hardest day to hustle up shot money. (Most of the stores that a fiend shoplifted from were closed on Sundays—back in those days.) He was obviously in need of a favor.

"Poochie, Kim up at my grandmother's ill. So check it, I'm gonna give you a big joint. Go give Kim half. But don't let her know it's comin' from me—and don't shoot that shit in my grandmother's house, neither. And if you put some shit in the game, I'm gonna put my foot up your ass."

From my perspective, I was giving Poochie one helluva deal. I was giving him $55 worth of good heroin, and all he had to do was walk two blocks and share it with my beloved Aunt Kim.

The nigga told me, "Bet, Tray. Good lookin' out! I ain't know where I was gonna get my blast this 'ere mornin'."

I instructed Poochie to wait on the corner of Eager and Durham Streets. I let him know that one of my runners would come and give him the dope in a matter of minutes. I located one of my runners, Freddy. I instructed him to give Poochie a bag of dope. I went back to my grandmother's house expecting to see Poochie come to the door at any moment to collect Kim to offer her the free dope. I waited and waited. The nigga didn't show up. I told Kim what I had done, and we looked at each other in total amazement. Not because I would endeavor to aid my beloved through such a deceptive method, but because someone like Poochie or Freddy would disobey my clear instruction.

Kim was genuinely concerned that something awful might have happened to her friend, Poochie, and her dope. So, she rushed to the corner for some answers.

It did not take her long to discover that Poochie had done the unthinkable; he had run off with my dope.

The Way You Deal with the Devil

Chapter 2

Two weeks after Poochie had run off with the narcotics I had given him, I was walking down Eager Street with Annette, one of my many girl-friends at the time. Ms. Liz called me over to her.

"Tray, come 'ere."

I sensed from Ms. Liz's tense expression that something really important was on her mind. For Ms. Liz was one of those older no-nonsense women from my grandmother's generation. She was in her late fifties or early sixties. She reared many children—some were hers and some were not. It was all good, though. Ms. Liz was a mama figure. She commanded respect from all the neighborhood children and most of the adults. Personally, I was cautious around Ms. Liz; she had exclusive permission from my grandmother to exact corporal punishment upon me whenever she felt it necessary.

I can only recall Ms. Liz slapping me up the side of my head once; but, it was a damn good one and I did not want to experience it again. She was a strong, heavy-handed woman. I approached her with humility and caution. Besides, I respected and loved Ms. Liz, I am sure, as she did me.

"Yes, Ma'am."

"Why y'all beat Poochie damn near to his death?"

I could not meet Ms. Liz's hard-eye stare. But my voice was firm. Annette was with me, and I could not have Ms. Liz make me look like a sissy in her presence. "I ain't do nothin' to Poochie, Ms. Liz."

"Boy, don't stand here in my face and tell no bare-faced lies!"

Ms. Liz was one of my mother figures. She had fed me when I was hungry and given me comfort when I needed it. Moreover, she was one of the few women who disciplined me when I was young. But at that moment, on that summer day, on Eager Street, in the presence of my girlfriend, I surely did not want any discipline for my transgression, real or imagined. Therefore, I exited the situation the best way I could. I subtly eased my hand into my pocket and switched my pager button off and back on, and when the pager went "beep beep..." I quickly withdrew it from my pocket and feigned an important call. "Ms. Liz, that's Larry. I gotta go. I be right back, okay?"

"You make sure you bring your ass back, too, 'cause I ain't finish with what I gotta say."

Annette and I walked in silence up to Madison Street and Rutland Avenue where I had parked. I supposed she knew me well enough to know that I had been thoroughly punked by Ms. Liz, and if she spoke about the matter too soon, I would say all the saving-face things to her that I could never say to Ms. Liz.

Annette knew how to play me. Ms. Liz had made me feel like a child. So, to redeem my manhood, Annette offered a perfect opportunity.

"Tray, you gonna take me shoppin' today?"

I didn't immediately answer; I really didn't have an answer. Annette was a player. She was using me and a few other hustlers who had the ready money to take her shopping on a moment's notice. I often felt used by her. But she was an attractive young woman, and it served my ego quite well to have her among my girlfriends. She was my chocolate wonder. A slender girl with the perfect shape. She had a nice round butt, flat stomach, angel-like facial features, with a smile bright enough to light any room she entered. I think Annette's most notable physical attribute was her smile. Perfectly white even teeth highlighted with a golden tooth toward the side.

I couldn't say "no" to Annette for many reasons, even when I knew I should. I truly enjoyed being with her and sex with her was fantastic. She had a quick wit and beautiful sense-of-humor. She was also on gangster times. My lifestyle didn't frighten her, and she was not intimidated by anyone.

I finally asked Annette, "Why can't one 'em other niggas take you shoppin'?"

"Cause I ain't askin' nobody else to take me but you right now. You gonna take me or not?"

Annette is a player. She knew that it was a cardinal sin for a man-child in my esteemed position to demonstrate jealousy and insecurity by denying her a shopping trip because of her infidelity. It was understood, though never spoken, that Annette was my girl when she was with me. When she wasn't, it was her loss—or mine. It depends on whose ego is being challenged.

"Where you wanna go?" She had me, no doubt. But I have no regrets. When I came to prison a few years later, under a life-plus-thirty-five-year sentence, Annette was there for me, providing for me in ways that no amount of money could.

"Let's go out Golden Ring, first. I wanna check out Linda-Lind."

She was beaming with pride, and I wanted to simply give her whatever money she wanted so that she could go shopping alone. I hated shopping with women. But I had promised to take Annette shopping, personally, for her summer wardrobe. I knew that there was no escaping that promise. If I failed to do what I told her I would, as far as material matters were concerned, she would confront me in a far more aggressive manner than Ms. Liz.

Six months prior, I had called Annette in the early morning hours, at about eight o'clock. I had to catch her before she left for school. I wanted her to spend the day with me in the hotel while I cut and capped up some cocaine. Larry had copped a half a kilogram of coke the night before, and he wanted me to package it for street sale. It was not important that I rush. I could get a girl and go to the hotel to have a working party. Seemed simple enough. But after reaching Annette and convincing her to skip school for the day, I changed my mind without informing her. I decided to take Lacrisha instead.

Now, Lacrisha is another very attractive woman. A true dime. She spoke proper English—she was what we called "a county girl." Moreover, Lacrisha was cousin to Ada, Fat Larry's wife. For two years or so, I had been desperately trying to get Lacrisha. I tried to buy her—went bowling with her and everything. I mean, I truly courted this woman—and I do mean *woman*.

Lacrisha was twenty-two and I was barely fifteen. She was definitely attracted to me, but the age difference played a role in her hesitation to give me those draws. So happens on this particular morning, after I had made arrangements to pick up Annette, Lacrisha appeared at our house, which was not uncommon. She was family. What was uncommon was she was ready to be with me sexually. For when she asked me, "What's up?" looking all sensual and smelling all sexy, I knew I was going to hit that that day. I had an intuitive notion about the entire thing.

I had been plotting and scheming for about two years to have Lacrisha, and here she was in my bedroom in the early morning hours, asking me, "What's up?" in a provocative manner.

Anyway, I totally forgot about Annette. Well, not really, I simply disregarded her. It was typical of me, in my arrogance. In this instance, it caused me one helluva embarrassing scene.

I went to the hotel with Lacrisha. After I told her I had to go to the "cuttin' table" for Larry, she wanted to go. I suspect she was fascinated by the whole underworld adventure. I was fascinated by the prospect of having this fine "county girl" in a hotel room with me all day. For it was unthinkable that a woman could be in a hotel room with me all day and not let me have sex with her.

When Annette ran down on me that day in February of 1983, the world was truly a cold place.

"Motherfucka, I know you ain't have me waitin' out there on no bus stop waitin' on your punk-ass all day," Annette said to me as she approached me.

I could see that she was totally seething with anger. But it did not matter. I was standing on High Hat's Corner in full dope dealer regalia. Full length, all black leather coat, thick gold chains, diamond rings, and all the finery that indicated I was a reigning dope boy—and damn proud of it. "Annette, don't start no dumb shit. I had somethin' to take care of."

"You could've called me or somethin'."

There was no way I was going to go back and forth with Annette. I was very important on Eager Street. I thought it utterly beneath my station to argue with some woman about my changing plans without consideration for her. Besides, Moochie-Baby, Black, my cousin Terrance, and a whole host of other corner niggas were present. I had to end this confrontation with Annette in a style that was exceedingly satisfying to my ego.

"Bitch, I'll get with ya later," I said to her as I turned to walk farther up the block, to indicate to her and everyone who was looking on and listening that the conversation was over.

No sooner than I took a few steps, did I hear Black yelling at me, "Watch out." I turned around just in time to see a half pint liquor bottle hurdling directly toward my head. Grateful to my dog for calling me in time, I immediately gave him an assignment.

"Get that bitch, Black."

Black, along with everyone else, was too busy laughing at this spectacle to interfere. So, I had to do what any self-respecting man would do, if caught in this ugly situation. I instantly grabbed this offended and genuinely angry woman in an attempt to subdue her because she was obviously searching for some other object to assault me. But Annette wasn't having any of that. She was hurt, angry, and, no doubt, embarrassed. She was determined to reduce me to the same dismal state. "Get the fuck off me," was her angry retort once I finally grabbed hold of her.

"Stop actin' crazy, girl," were the only words I could manage. But obviously, it wasn't enough to calm the situation.

"Let me go and I'm gonna show you what crazy is." True to her word: no sooner than I released Annette from my grasp, instructing her to go about her business, did she start at me. Punching me in the face with closed fists and endeavoring to kick at my private area. I could not contain her without striking her. But I could not do that. I was taught early in life: that at no time is it okay for a man to hit a woman.

This disturbance could not continue. It was humorous to those not involved. But dope was sold on High Hat's Corner. This dumb stuff that Annette and I were engaged in would bring the police. So, I had to bring it to a close.

"Black, come on man, get dis bitch." I was desperate.

Black was my ace, my best friend in all the world. We considered each other brothers. No bond between two men could have been stronger. We understood each other at a truly profound level. He knew I would not strike Annette. The only female I have ever hit in my entire life was Kieshawn, my Aunt Kim's oldest daughter—my sister. And that was after she had initiated the physical confrontation.

Black, on the other hand, had absolutely no qualm with kicking anybody's butt who needed it kicked. If he could whip you and you deserved whipping, he would give you a whipping.

"Black, get the fuck off me." This had been going on for about fifteen to twenty minutes. The bottle throwing, loud cursing, and wrestling. But Annette wasn't satisfied. She started at Black for having the audacity to interfere. What a terrible mistake. Black and I didn't share identical principles when it came to the virtue of striking women. Annette should have known that. We all grew up together and lived around each other our entire lives.

No sooner than Annette raised her hand to strike Black, once she wrestled herself from his tight grasp, did he slap her across the face with a thunderous blow. The blow was so powerful it knocked Annette to the ground. It reduced her to a bundle of fear. Her anger was gone. All that remained was fear. Black was not me.

"Bitch, go 'head 'bout your business," he bellowed to Annette. "I ain't gonna tell you no more."

I must give it to Annette. She was hurt by Black's powerful blow and obviously afraid. She knew of his reputation. Black could really fight. He hit real hard and only a damn fool would want to fight him. He carried his 6'2" 220 pound frame well. At eighteen years of age, jet black, he was quite the intimidating force. Yet, Annette was going to try to beat him in a physical fight.

Yeah she was crazy. But I could not permit this. I got in between the two; I pulled Annette toward me and urged her to come with me.

"Come on girl," I instructed as I aided Annette to gather herself.

"Nigga, you don't be puttin' your hands on me," Annette shouted at Black as she made a half-hearted attempt to pull away from me to charge at him.

"Bring your dizzy ass on." Annette realized that this was a no-win situation, so she relented and came along with me.

That was six months ago, and we have been together ever since—with an understanding of what it's like to be a hustler's girlfriend. I provide her with material trinkets, and she services me sexually without any emotional complications or public embarrassments. Fair exchange ain't a robbery.

The arrangement was totally degrading to both of us. We frequently engaged in the most personal action that two humans can engage in, yet, there was no intimate connection. "You have sex with who you want to, and I will do likewise. Just make yourself available when I want to be with you. And yeah, although I know you are seeing other dudes, don't let me catch you." All I had to do was keep risking my life everyday to keep a cash flow coming.

A Luxury Once Tasted Soon Becomes a Necessity

Chapter 3

I grew up at 1815 East Eager Street, in a household headed by my paternal step-grandfather, Richard Griffin. He was the only man I ever called "Daddy." The day he died was one the saddest days of my life.

Daddy was a man of conviction. He was also a walking contradiction. He was involved with illegal gambling. He wrote the numbers prior to there being a state-sponsored lottery. He also tricked with the young neighborhood women. I guess Daddy had to have sex, too.

From Daddy I learned the value of hard work. I also learned that you have an absolute right, hell, a duty to enjoy the fruits of your labor. Daddy used to tell me that it was never right to go into another man's pocket and steal from him. He told me, "Son, if'n you gonna get somebody's money, make sure d'em done gave it to ya, and glad they did." Daddy hated thieves and liars. He said that a thief and a liar was one and the same. For if you lied, you stole, and if you stole, you lied. Moreover, a thief and a liar could never be trusted. Thieves and liars are pure and unadulterated cowards and parasites. They managed their lives by humbling themselves and going behind folks' backs doing one dastardly deed after another. Their weaknesses are demonstrated by their inability to work hard.

Daddy may have been deeply involved in a criminal activity, but he was a hard working man. He maintained us in the prettiest house on that ghetto block. Our home was always freshly painted. The plumbing was never in disrepair, as many of the other houses on our block were, and we were proud to call 1815 East Eager Street home.

Whenever I talk to Aunt Viola about her father, Richard Griffin, it sparks many feelings of nostalgia. For Daddy was an extraordinary man. He married my paternal grandmother, Florence Redd-Griffin, in the early 1950s when she had three children: my father, Arlando Jones, Jr., my Aunts Arlene Jones and Joyce Ann Redd, and from that union, they produced my beloved Aunt Viola. Their marriage was a happy one, albeit fraught with its shares of difficulties and tragedies, such as my father's murder by the Baltimore City Police followed by Mama Florence's chronic illness that rendered her, ultimately, bed ridden.

Throughout it all, Daddy hung in there with his family. He gave us equal love and affection up until the day he died, at the ripe old age of 89.

By the time I was born in '68, in the summer month of July, Daddy had already gained a wealth of wisdom from sheer experience. I was truly blessed to have received his nurturing love and guidance. I attribute my love and appreciation of women to Daddy. He taught me that women are treasures to behold and appreciate.

Daddy was known for trickin'; he would buy some pussy so quick your head would spin. I remember sitting up in the room with Daddy watching the baseball game; the Orioles were playing some team. One of my aunts were having a party in the basement. Mama Florence was long deceased. My Aunts Arlene, Joyce, and Viola were teenagers, and they hung out with fine teenage women. Anyway, I was in the room with Daddy enjoying myself. I was far too young to attend the teenage party occurring in the basement. I was only about five or six years old in 1973 or '74. And Daddy was seemingly too old. So, we were stuck with each other until Jackie came up to ask Daddy, "Hi you doin', Mr. Richard?"

"I'm all right, girl," Daddy replied. "Come on in and sit yo'self on down."

I knew at this point that I was going to be asked to leave the room at any moment. I had been in that situation before. Besides, I was not naïve. Daddy was about to get a trick. If I played my cards right, I would get a good peek. I may have been too young to attend my aunts' party, too young to even turn a trick, but I'll be damned if I was too young to watch grown folks do the nasty.

"What y'all doin'?" Jackie asked me as she gently and playfully ran her fingers through my hair. I liked Jackie; she was always nice to me. She had this gentle, very feminine manner about herself. She was very attractive. I wanted to "do it" to her real bad. But I did not have the courage, at five or six years of age, to ask her. I would have to leave that up to Daddy. For now, I would simply sneak a peek.

"We ain't doin' nothin' but watchin' this sorry ole game," I said to Jackie as she gazed directly into my eyes, causing me to blush.

Jackie had to know the effect she had on me. She had to have overheard me telling Squirt, at least a thousand times, I was going to eventually fuck her. I made it a point to let Squirt know it every time he let me know that he had already fucked half the women in my family, including my mother, when she, according to him, was on Baltimore Street selling herself for $25.

Anyway, Daddy was hungrily looking at Jackie. Taking in her young, firm teenage body. No doubt being enchanted by her golden smile and fine light skin.

"Boy, you know this is a good game," Daddy blurted in my direction. But the game and me were the last things on his mind.

We all sat there in silence for a moment, pretending to be watching the baseball game. But none of us were actually focused on the game. I pretended to be tired or bored with their company and exited the room. I went down stairs to the first floor of our three story home to find it completely empty. Everyone was in the basement where the party was in full swing. I started to go down there. But I did not want to get slapped up side the head for being in the way. Besides, I had to get back upstairs to watch Daddy "do it" to Jackie. That was my plan, and I damn sure wasn't about to abandon it for a slap up side my head that would probably hurt.

My timing was near perfect. When I got up to Daddy's bedroom, the door was closed shut. I tried to ease it open without making a sound; but, it was locked. I had to resort to peeking through the keyhole.

I was an accomplished peeper. I was not daunted by the locked door and my limited view. I knew that Jackie and Daddy were in bed together from the grunts and moans, and other sounds. The nasty was being done, and knowing that was good enough for me. If I held my position, I knew I would see Jackie's entire nude body when they finished and prepared to dress.

Daddy was well into his eighties; he wouldn't be long at all. Experience had taught me that the deed would be over in minutes. I waited and sure enough, five to ten minutes after I had posted up to peek at Daddy and Jackie do the nasty, they finished. I saw Jackie rise up from the bed buck-ball ass naked—looking as good as any pin up girl in a magazine. I was truly blessed to live under the roof of a grandfather who loved to trick with young girls and three aunts who kept the young girls coming in.

It should not have been too shocking that I developed into the kind of hustler who would turn a trick at the drop of a dime. I was affectionately known to my friends and closest acquaintances as "Trickin' Tray."

"No matter how tryin' life become, a man can always be comforted by the tender touches of a woman" was what Daddy taught me—in a round-about way. What he taught me most directly was how to be responsible. "No excuses, boy. If you did it, own up to it," was his battle cry. Real men needed no alibi to hide behind. If you had a duty, perform it to the best of your ability and if you came up short go back at it until you accomplish what you set out to do.

I had a responsibility to my grandfather's business. He ran the neighborhood numbers, the lottery for black folks before the state took the business over. Anyway, I had four stops to make every day after school. I had to stop at Polly's Cut Rate on Chase Street, Mr. Charles Barber Shop farther down the very same street, then around the corner to Rutland Avenue to see Ms. Hazel at Star's Cleaner, and the final stop, my favorite, Bill Davis's Penny Store. At each stop, I simply picked up an envelop full of numbers. No money, just the numbers that were being played by hundreds of folks every day.

I had to make sure Daddy had the numbers before four o'clock in the afternoon. He had to make sure everything was recorded before the actual "shoe" came out. If someone hit the number, he or she wanted to be paid on the spot. No excuses or alibis.

I got out of school at two-thirty in the afternoon. Therefore, I had an hour and a half to make my rounds and get the numbers home. If I was late, he would be gravely disappointed in me. And to disappoint Daddy was punishment enough.

Daddy was the most easy going man I have ever come across in my life. He was full of energy and laughter. I can't recall ever seeing Daddy actually get angry. I saw him get annoyed, but he always seemed to remain calm in the most tense situations. Daddy was exceedingly charming; for him to punish any of his children, all he had to do was display the slightest disappointment.

Another Loss Love

Chapter 4

Daddy had spoiled all the children under his care. He was an excellent provider. Perhaps, to a fault. He denied his daughters nothing in terms of material possessions. I guess the "street numbers" was a lucrative business. Hell, now that I think about it; I should have been paid more than $2 a day for my daily after-school trips. I sacrificed much playing time to satisfy my responsibility to Daddy's business. I guess that's why he never expressed a great anger on the days when I would simply say "fuck it" and go play with friends. If numbers did not reach their intended destination, so what, I was only a kid. I was simply doing what Daddy told me to do.

When Daddy died, things really changed drastically. We were all used to Daddy taking care of us, paying whatever bills that needed paying, sending for our weekly groceries, giving out the weekly allowances for purchasing clothes or whatever. We were hopelessly dependent upon Daddy. His death rendered us sad, alone, and incapable of supporting ourselves.

I was only a child, so, I had every expectation of continued support. But my aunts, Arlene, Joyce, and Viola were truly in trouble. Viola was the youngest of the girls. When Daddy died in July of 1977, Viola was about 21 years old. Joyce was about 23 and Arlene, the eldest, was nearly 25. None of them had completed school or ever worked. They didn't have to—Daddy was the man for real. None of his children had to do anything they didn't want to do. Hence, none of his children had a true life-skill at the time of his death. Of course, we felt extremely important and special. But high self-esteem doesn't pay bills or put food on the table. My home at 1815 East Eager Street started to fall on hard times after Daddy's death. The utilities were turned off because of unpaid bills. The refrigerator and cabinets were no longer overflowing with food. Things just got real raggedy for my aunts on Eager Street. It took them quite some time to learn how to take care of themselves.

Fortunately enough for me, my maternal grandparents on Madison Street and Aunt Kim were around to care for me. My mother was still alive, too. But the role she played in my development was rather insignificant. Kim was my "mother" for all intents and practical purposes. It was Kim or Mama (my maternal grandmother) who cared for me or disciplined me. My mother, Karen Jones, was a hopeless drunk. Partying and entertaining friends were her primary concern. A young son was too demanding and too complex for her lifestyle, I suppose.

Don't get me wrong. I love my mother, and I know she loved me. We had a few tender moments. However, Karen was just a kind relative of mine who came around every now and again to buy me a pair of shoes or some other much-needed item. When my mother died in the spring of '79 (or was it '78?), I received the news as if a stranger had died.

I will never forget the day. I was in school. The intercom came on in my classroom and announced: "Arlando, come to the office, please." It was the vice principal's voice.

I knew I had not done anything wrong that day, so why was the vice principal fucking with me. Kim had brought me back to school from suspension just two days prior. I was keeping my nose clean because I knew if I got into more trouble so soon after being returned to school, Kim would hit the roof, and I would get a whippin'.

I could not figure out for the life of me why the vice principal was summoning me to the office. I gave up and simply marched myself to the office.

Once I got there, Mrs. Dickerson, the school's vice principal, greeted me with a look that was solemn—sad, in fact. I knew that something tragic had occurred.

"Come on in, Sugar," Mrs. Dickerson said to me as she guided me into her comfortable office. "Sit down."

I was positioned into one of the chairs usually reserved for parents when kids like me messed up enough to warrant a visit to the school by a parent or guardian.

Now, you really had to do something bad to warrant a visit from your parent up to Elmer A. Henderson Elementary School on Wolfe and Biddle

Streets. For the teachers had permission to whip our asses if we misbehaved. Therefore, there was seldom need for me to see the inside of the principal's or vice principal's office. If I misbehaved, one of the teachers corrected me by whatever method he or she deemed appropriate. If I kept the school's administration and my parents out of the matter, I considered myself fortunate.

So here I was, in Mrs. Dickerson's office, in the stuffed black leather chair that Mama and Kim sat in on a couple of occasions, to hear what the vice principal had to tell me.

Mrs. Dickerson's soft and gentle eyes began to water. "You have some bad news in your family," the tears were choking her throat. "I have to take you home."

It was unbearable. I had to know what Mrs. Dickerson knew. "What's the matter Mrs. Dickerson?" The tears were beginning to form in my eyes, too. And I didn't know why. Mrs. Dickerson was a strong women, a typical black matriarch. She was not large in physical stature. She was a petite woman, with graying hair, and a smooth caramel complexion. She appeared regal and sophisticated; she commanded respect.

Her loss of emotional control frightened me. I managed to ask, "I have to go home?"

"I'll take you."

I wanted to leave right away. Moreover, I wanted to be alone. In my mind I just knew that something awful had happened to Mama.

"I'll get home okay."

"You sure?"

I made an affirmative nod, and exited the office and the school. I was totally oblivious to my surroundings. I couldn't really see anything or hear anything outside my own head. I had not really recovered from the loss of Daddy, and I felt like Mama was gone, too. Mrs. Dickerson was not an emotional woman. I had never seen her portray any emotions, other than anger towards the students for one reason or another.

I understood that my grandmother and Mrs. Dickerson were friends. They had attended school together as children, the old Paul Lawrence Dunbar, when schools were segregated. Every time I misbehaved in school, Mama would get a call, that is, if Mrs. Dickerson didn't feel like correcting me herself. Something must to have happened mighty awful to Mama to get such an emotional reaction from Mrs. Dickerson. That was my reasoning.

I was walking up Wolfe Street in a complete daze. The sun was bright on that May day and many folks were out on their front steps. No one spoke to me, which enhanced my sense of fear. We all knew each other in that neighborhood, and it was truly disturbing that I could be out in the streets before school was out, and no one would mention it. But I guess everyone knew what I was to find out in only a few moments more.

• • •

It only took me about ten minutes to walk the five blocks from school to my grandmother's house on Madison Street. When I came through the front door my Aunt Kim embraced me. Her eyes were puffy from crying and her voice was strained. Her sister had just died—my mother.

"Tip is gone, Tray," Kim told me without any preliminaries.

I knew exactly what she meant. At ten, I was already acquainted with death, probably more than I had a right to be. I lived on Eager Street, where death was a constant occurrence.

"My mother is gone," I was shocked. "What you mean, Kim?"

"She passed away this morning, baby. I'm so sorry." Kim was grief-stricken. Tippy was my mother's nickname. Only her family and close friends called her that. Everyone else called her by her Christian name, Karen.

I didn't know how I was supposed to respond. In my heart, I felt overwhelming relief. I thought Mama was gone. To me, Tippy was simply a good family member. We had no maternal connection. I had no maternal connection to anyone. I was a motherless child for the most part. I was cared for and loved, but I have never experienced that special bond that a child feels for a mother.

Mama and Kim were the closest I ever got to that connection. My other aunts were cool. But they were my aunts, they were more like my big sisters than a mother, or even aunts for that matter. I suppose Mama Florence cared for me as if I was her very own child; but I hardly remember her. I was barely four when she died.

Now I had to see Mama Pittman, my maternal grandmother. I had to be assured that she was alive. I knew I couldn't bear losing her—or Kim. But Kim was right there with me, holding me close to her. I knew she was okay.

"Where is Mama?" I demanded to know. "I wanna see Mama."

"She upstairs restin'." The voice belonged to my Aunt Shirley, my grandmother's youngest sister.

I pulled away from Kim's grasp and headed toward Mama's room. Aunt Shirley tried to stop me, but I was determined to see Mama. "Don't go up there, boy," Aunt Shirley was yelling in my direction as she reached for me. "Leola has been through a lot today."

"Me too—leave me alone." When Mama was around, I could sass whoever I pleased. Mama wouldn't let anyone whip me in her presence. In her eyes, I could do no wrong, She was my boo and I was hers. I had no doubt about that—at any time in my life.

I reached Mama's bedroom door with Aunt Shirley on my heel. I pulled the door open, and as soon as I saw Mama lying there in bed, I cried out, "Mama," in sheer relief.

Aunt Shirley and Kim stood there, and I rushed toward Mama's open arms. Mama embraced me warmly and all Aunt Shirley could say was, "Come on, Tray, let Ola rest."

I was not going anywhere, and that was perfectly okay with Mama. "I'm all right, Shirley. Let us be."

I laid there in bed with Mama for quite some time. We both cried. She because of overwhelming grief at the loss of her eldest child, and I because Mama was in such pain. I did not feel a sense of loss over my mother's death. I understood that Tippy was my mother, and I did love her. But it was not an abiding love that would leave me feeling empty inside because she was gone. Hell, I seldom saw her. While I was living at 1815 East Eager, at the home of my deceased father, she would come by every so often to hug me and say hello. But for the most part, she spent her time there chatting with Joyce or Viola or Arlene.

There were a few times when my mother did, indeed, spend moments with me. For instance, there sticks out one memorable time when Viola and all the others at the Eager Street house were going out for the night. I think they were going to attend a Jackson Five concert at the Baltimore Civic Center. I doubt Daddy was going to the concert. But whatever was going on, it resulted in my mother being my baby-sitter for the night.

We had a terrific time together. Well, at least, I really enjoyed her company that night. We played a board-game called Candy Land, talked about my activities in school and my friends. She gave me a bath, which made me feel very uncomfortable. No one bathed me. I was not a baby; I was a kindergartener.

"Mom, I don't need you givin' me no bath," I had protested the impending offense.

She exercised pure charm, "Tell ya what," Tippy was not going to give up this chance to bond with her only child. "Let me help you take your bath, and we can pop some popcorn and watch Ghost Host Theater together."

My mother had pushed the right button that night. If she was going to let me stay up all night to watch Ghost Host Theater, I most certainly would let her aid me in taking my bath.

Lying there in bed with my grandmother, grieving over my mother's death, brought up that warm moment I had spent with her years before. How she went upstairs and prepared the bathtub full of sweet smelling bubbling water; how she called me up to bathe me.

It was truly a tender moment. She told me that she loved me and that I was just like my father, very handsome and smart. She told me that someday I would be a heart breaker—the girls were going to fall hopelessly in love with me.

"What about my ugly wino lips, Mom?" I asked. I always felt insecure about my red lips.

She smiled at me and told me that my lips were far from ugly. In fact, my lips were my beauty mark. "When you get older, watch how all the girls gonna wanna be kissin' all over you," she insisted. "Now come on and get out the water—wino lips," she joked.

After I was dried and got into my favorite pajamas, my mother and I went into the kitchen and popped some popcorn, made a full pitcher of Kool-Aid, and deposited ourselves on the couch in front of the television just in time to hear Billy Lagosha announce, "Good Evening, welcome to Ghost Host Theater. Tonight you will be watching…." I can't recall the exact movie, but I do recall the warmth I shared with my mother that night. It was the only such moment that we shared.

Now, here I was with Mama crying over her premature death, not knowing why I was crying. I most certainly did not feel sad. I felt nothing. The occasion was a somber one, and the appropriate thing to do was to cry like everyone else. After all, Karen Jones was my mother.

"Mama, how my mother die?" I was curious.

This was a hard topic for my grandmother. Her daughter had just died that very morning. Shortly after sending me off to school, the call came in from Johns Hopkins Hospital instructing my grandmother to come there quick. Her daughter, Karen, needed her. Of course, that was an understatement. Karen Jones was already dead by the time my grandmother got to the hospital—less than fifteen minutes after receiving the call. All Mama could do once she reached the hospital was find out how and why her daughter had died.

She discovered the answer, and now had a duty of explaining it to me as best she could through her grief.

"Your mother had pneumonia, Tray," she begun saying as she sat up in bed with me still resting in her bosom. "She didn't know she had it, and it messed with her heart and lungs."

It was too painful for Mama to talk about. So, I was not going to make any further inquiries. I was just going to continue to lie there, in Mama's embrace, because I sensed my being there made her feel better.

Tears That Wouldn't Come

Chapter 5

My mother's funeral is virtually a blur to me. I recall getting into the limousine and the procession of cars starting off from my grandmother's house. I can even recall reaching the funeral home, March's. When we got inside, I took my place on the bench in the first row, along with Mama, Aunt Shirley, Kim, Uncle Beau (my grandmother's eldest brother), and Daddy Pain (Mama's second husband, my mother's step-father).

The mood, I suppose, was solemn. The preacher gave a passionate eulogy that was dynamic, I guess. It had everyone in the place crying, except me. The preacher made me mad. He talked about my mother like he knew her.

"Karen was a beautiful child," the preacher eulogized. "Her family and friends loved her. She brought laughter…" He went on and on. I just wanted to get out of there. I didn't want to be around all these folks who were obviously grieving for my mother in a way that I could not. I was not experiencing their loss. This woman who I knew to be my mother was not connected to me in any meaningful way. I knew that she should have been, and that made me feel guilty. Here I was, at my mother's funeral, among family and friends who loved her enough to cry over her extremely prema-ture death, and I couldn't manage a tear. The tears would come much later, when I was in the Maryland Penitentiary, convicted of first and second degree murders and sentenced to serve the balance of my natural life in the Maryland Division of Correction.

Fat Delores sung this gospel song entitled "One Day at a Time Sweet Jesus." It moved the entire group attending the funeral, even me. I recall being transfixed on Delores as she sung. I had no ideal the song she was singing would later have the effect of making me cry like an irritated infant each time I heard it.

I was happy when the funeral was finally over. We drove to the cemetery and put my mother into the ground. Uncle Beau asked me, "Do you want to say a few things to your Mom before we leave?" I shook my head no. I wanted to ask him, "What the hell am I suppose to say to her? She can't hear me." I held my tongue. I wasn't going to insult him. I understood the emotionalism of the moment. Folks were trying to be nice to me because I lost my mother. No one knew that Karen's death was a greater loss to him or her than it was to me.

Everyone was more understanding of Mama's mood than mine. Plans were made to have the folks mourning my mother gather at the home of my cousins Melvin and Carolyn. Mama went straight home after the burial, where I wanted to go. But I was stuck with the family. If the house had not been raided by the Baltimore City Police Department's Narcortic Division, it would've been a typical "after funeral occasion."

My cousins, Melvin and Carolyn, sold weed, the harmless drug. Nothing major, just enough to make ends meet.

"Get the fuck on the floor," the narcotics officers were yelling as they came through the front and back doors. "Don't do nothing stupid."

"What the fuck?"

"Why ya doin' this crazy shit?"

"Ya rottin' mothafuckas," Carolyn was infuriated, her voice was the only one that could be distinguished in the cacophony of angry voices. "This is a funeral goin' on in here. You mothafuckas could've waited."

"Yeah, yeah, we gotta warrant to search this place," the narcotic detective said.

"Officers," Uncle Beau was going to try to control the situation. "My niece was just buried today. We are here to mourn her passin'."

A uniformed police officer stepped up. He appeared to be compassionate. "We saw all the traffic coming in and out of this house today, and we thought a lot of drug activity was goin' on."

I was burning with anger. I wanted to snatch a gun from one of the many police who were gathered in the house among us and shoot as many of them as I could. This was too much. These motherfuckers killed my father, and now here they were again, preventing me from closing it out with my mother. Damn! It's no wonder I decided not to be on the side of Baltimore City's finest. I hated them. While they were searching the house looking for drugs, my family and I were kept in the living room.

To say that we were angry would be an understatement. Personally, I was ready to die—and kill. This was an insult; a fundamental attack to our dignity. We were closing out the loss of a member of our family. To raid the house at that particular time was mean and pure devilish. With all the hard drugs, like dope and cocaine, that were sold in that neighborhood, the police could have and should have picked a better place to raid.

Despite the diplomatic petition made to the cops to delay the raid for compassionate reasons, they aggressively searched the house. A very small quantity of marijuana was found and my cousins, Melvin and Carolyn, were carted off to jail.

The fat white uniformed police, with two bars on his lapel, the one the cops referred to as "Captain," explained to us that Melvin and Carolyn were the only ones going to jail. He was telling us, "This house is a known drug location. Technically, we can lock everyone up in here 'cause drugs have been found on the premise."

I couldn't take no more of his shit. I had to be heard.

"We just said bye to my mother, and y'all funky mothafuckas won't even let us do that," I was yelling, and tears were flowing. "I hate y'all and I hope y'all die." I meant every word.

My Aunt Kim grabbed me before I did something stupid. I felt like having a physical confrontation. I needed to kick somebody's ass or have mine kicked.

The captain obviously understood the depth of my grief. Perhaps more than I did. He ordered his subordinates out of the house. Of course, when they left, they took Carolyn and Melvin with them—in handcuffs.

I hung around the house with Melvina, Niece, and Wayne, Melvin's and Carolyn's three children. I really liked Melvina. I considered her to be one of my favorite female cousins. She was three years older than I. At thirteen, she was a knock-out. Damn near all the niggas around the way wanted to make Melvina their girl. Whether they wanted to love her or simply fuck her is a matter for debate. I know she was not considered too easy to get. She often boasted about her ample breast and onion ass. There were no questions in Melvina's mind, or many others for that matter, that she was a dime. Her honey complexion and fine features were an absolute sight to behold. And her personality was magnetic. She had charm and a wonderful sense of humor. She had her bitchy ways, but who doesn't? So I won't highlight that aspect of her character.

Niece was everything Melvina was not. Niece and I were the same age, ten going on twenty-one our next birthday. We stayed at each other's throat. I promised her an ass whippin' every day. But I never fulfilled the promise. I didn't want to have to kick Melvin's butt, too. For she was, no doubt, Daddy's little girl—and knew it.

Anyway, I stuck around to help Melvina out. Clean up the house and deal with the shitty attitude of Niece if need be. Wayne was no problem. He was only six or seven years old; he wasn't old enough to rebel against authority.

Alone on the back porch, after cleaning up the house, Melvina went down to the basement and got us some weed to smoke. The police had not found it all. In fact, they did not find much of anything. The police simply found the piece that Carolyn and Melvin had been smoking earlier that day. The pound and a half in the basement went unnoticed by Baltimore City's finest.

We were sure that Melvina's mother and father would be home before morning, or midnight even. Therefore, we decided to smoke a few joints to relax our nerves. The day had been quite trying for both us.

For at the moment, we were both orphaned. She in one respect, and me in another. At some level Melvina and I were connected. We were both called upon to be more mature than our chronological years generally allowed. Like I said, "Melvina was a dime." Her mother and father taught her how to hustle so she would not need a man for anything. She was taught that good looks were a dime a dozen, and could be dangerous in the ghetto. For in the 'hood, if she did not earn her keep, and relied upon the hustlers for money and other material things, she would be fucked-out, coked-out, and burned-out, looking for a hand-out before her eighteenth birthday.

Relaxed by the euphoria brought on by smoking good marijuana, Melvina and I were prepared to make sense out of our circumstances.

"Tray, this is some fucked-up shit," Melvina begun. "My mom and dad are in jail and both yours is dead."

"Yeap." The truth needed no support.

"Tip got burned-out, but I don't now why your father ain't here no more," she went on. "How your father die?"

I really didn't want to talk about my parents. But I knew Melvina well enough to know that I had to answer her questions or curse her out for getting too deep into the matters that affected my heart. "Nigga just ain't here.

Police killed him; caught him slippin' in a caper." I had hoped that would satisfy her curiosity, but it didn't.

"You gonna be like your daddy?" She asked.

I didn't know my father. How could I answer that question. It was not fair; it was irritating. Therefore, I answered her in a manner that would fully reflect my irritation.

"How in the fuck I'm suppose to know who I'll be like?"

"You better hurry up and know who in the fuck you'll be like." One of Melvina's qualities wasn't to be lady-like. Her speech came right out of the garbage can. She cursed like a sailor.

"Why I gotta know who I'm gonna be like?"

"Look at our fucked-up situations," Melvina was emotional. "Your Mom died 'cause this shit around her done burned her out and my mother and father is in jail right after comin' from her funeral."

My cousin was trying to impress upon me some valuable lesson I wasn't prepared to accept. I couldn't understand. She glimpsed my future. She knew that I had been flirting with the fast life. On more than one occasion, Melvina had seen me hanging down on Eager Street with the drug boys.

He's Gonna Be a Bad Boy

Chapter 6

My childhood was one of ghetto privilege. What I mean by that is I never went to bed hungry. I was never physically abused by a step-father or anything heinous like that. There were always nice toys under our Christmas Tree each year. The home I grew up in was always warm and comfortable. Yes, I was ghetto-privileged. Many of my childhood friends can't boast the same claim. I was reared in a community where abject poverty was everywhere. Many of my homies didn't have adequate clothing or shelter. Some even experienced physical abuse from alcoholic parents. But not me. The greatest tragedy in my childhood, from my perspective, was that I was permitted to develop my own moral code. It was up to me to figure out what was right or wrong. I seldom got punished or received parental chastisement for whatever choice I made.

After Daddy died, and then my mother, things began to change for me in the most dramatic ways. There were never enough things anymore. My clothes were beginning to wear out and become raggedy. My grandmother seemed to start drinking far more than I recalled her doing before. I was accustomed to being among the best dressed students in school, if not the best dressed. I always had a buck or two in my pocket. It would have been beneath me not to be able to afford a pack of Now & Later candy for my homies and me, not to mention a pretty girl. Poverty did not settle well with me. I understood that my family was poor, but we always had the basic comforts. I could not accept the sudden change.

I hooked up with my dear friend Squirt, an accomplished thief at thirteen. He was always in need of an accomplice. We started hittin' the stores on Monument Street and in the Old Town Mall. We stole small things, underwear and cosmetic items. That kind of stuff was easier to sell on the streets and easy to steal. On most days, Squirt and I would make about ten or fifteen dollars, not much. But enough to keep the lint out of our pockets. Squirt lived on Eager Street where my aunts still lived. I spent a lot of time there—on the block. Hell, even if Squirt and my folks had not lived there, I would have still come to Eager Street regularly, that was the spot. All the hustlers and major players hung out there, or at least came through frequently. Since Squirt and I were in the business of stealing and selling underwear at a ridiculously low price, Eager Street was the best place to market our booty. Hustlers needed drawers, too. And they didn't mind a discount.

I recall the time I first met Eggy Scott, a ghetto legendary nigga. He was known for his quick temper and ferocious fighting skills. The 'hood had it that Eggy didn't take "no shit from nobody"—woman, man, or child. In fact, Eggy was out of prison on an appeal bond for knocking a dopefiend broad's eye out. Her name was Brenda Mae or something like that.

Anyway, Eggy was on his way into High Hat's Bar, the player's spot. Squirt and me were down to our last six or seven packs of drawers when I spotted Eggy.

"Yo, ask Eggy if he wanna buy these draws." I was a better salesman than Squirt; we both accepted that. But he was asking me to approach Eggy because he didn't want to. I didn't either, but I was getting tired of selling drawers. We had been at it all day, and it was summertime, very hot and humid. The sooner we get rid of the last of the underwear, the sooner we could go do something more entertaining.

"Yo, Mr. Eggy," I called out as I came toward the legend. "You wanna buy some draws and undershirts—dirt cheap?"

Now, Eggy was an intimidating man. He was not tall in stature; but he was stocky and muscular. He had these narrow menacing eyes that seemed to say, "Leave me alone." But he did not tell me to leave him alone. He asked me in his low, very deep voice, "What 'n the fuck I want some draws for?"

I was the salesman. I had to answer all questions. "Everybody need clean draws, Mr. Eggy; 'pose you gotta go the hospital or sumthin'?"

Eggy grinned at that. I knew I had a sale, so I pushed ahead, as any good salesman would, "One of the nurses might be wantin' to hit you off. If your draws ain't right, she gonna think you ain't right, either. So you gotta keep your draws tight. And you know that's right, Mr. Eggy."

Squirt had eased up beside me. He sensed that everything was going well between Eggy and me because Eggy was laughing at my sales pitch.

"Boy what size y'all got?" He was going to buy some drawers.

"We got your size—large. Right?"

"Where 'n fuck y'all get this shit from anyway?"

We all knew that the question did not require an answer. "Give us a dime and take all seven packs," Squirt finally spoke up.

"We got seven packs left, three draws and four undershirts."

"Cool, Eggy, just give us the dime," Squirt was closing the deal. "And everything's yours."

"Bet," he said as he reached into his pocket and pulled out a bank roll big enough to choke a horse. "The smallest thang I got is a twenty." He handed it to me with a simple instruction, "Take that shit 'round to my mother's. I ain't carryin' it 'round."

I knew where Eggy's mother lived. How he knew I knew was beyond me. I guess he was aware of his fame—or infamy. In either case, I had an extra ten dollars to split, and I was satisfied with that. I was going to make the home delivery and go find a way to enjoy my day's earnings.

Squirt and I took Eggy's stuff around to his mother's house, then we decided to go around to the playground. It seemed like everyone was outside sitting on his or her front steps. At the playground, at Elmer A. Henderson, our homies were playing a pick-up game of basketball. Squirt and I went over to the basketball court where they were to see if we could play.

Greg chose me immediately. He told Squirt that he would have to wait until the next game. Squirt was not having it. He and Greg didn't like each other. They fought each time they crossed paths. It was an insult to Squirt to choose me over him, when everyone present knew that Squirt played better ball than I—and perhaps better than everyone on the court.

"Nigga, what the fuck you mean I gotta wait 'til next game?" Squirt was livid with anger.

"Look man, we already started playin'," Greg was pretending to be diplomatic. "Soon as this game is over, you can play the next one."

This was truly ridiculous. On the basketball court, there was no such thing as a superior player having to wait until the next game in order to play. Just as Greg told Low-Low that his services were no longer necessary in order to make room for me to play, he could have told some other player to make room for Squirt. Black or Kirk or Wayne, on the opposing team, could have made room for Squirt, too. Moreover, Squirt and I could have simply sat on the bench to await the start of a new game. But it was summertime and niggas like starting shit when it's hot.

Squirt and I were considered nice with our hands, we could fight. Greg and Black could, too. And we rarely, if ever, passed up the opportunity to test each others' skills. I know Squirt and I were up on adrenaline.

"Bitch ass nigga, I ain't waitin' for no next game," Squirt squared off with Greg. "I'm playin' now."

Greg was a little taller than Squirt. At twelve, Greg was taller than all of us. A skinny kid, lanky but athletic. Before Squirt fully completed his statement, Greg threw the basketball directly toward his head. Squirt ducked the basketball, but he caught a hard straight right punch directly to his mouth. It was on. Squirt went underneath Greg and stole his legs from under him. Greg went down to the ground in a backward motion. His head hit the asphalt court with a nasty thud. I was thinking, damn, I know that nigga got one helluva headache. And he did. Greg laid there for a few seconds as Squirt tore into him. Punching him in the face a couple times.

When Squirt realized that Greg wasn't fighting back, he stopped punching and pulled away from him. He stood over Greg, as we stood around in spectator fashion, and told him in a most calm manner, "Next time I wanna play, punk, pick me."

"Soon as I catch my breath, I'm gonna be needin' to pick my foot out your black ass." Greg wasn't going to take that ass whipping laying down. No pun intended.

"Squirt, man, that nigga lettin' 'em cobwebs in his head fuck with him," Fat Kirk was endeavoring to be a peacemaker. "Let this shit ride."

"Let shit ride," Black chimed in. "Squirt came up here startin' shit— fuck that nigga up, man."

Greg was getting up from the ground, obviously feeling better. Squirt was wiping the blood from his lip, which had begun to swell from that thunderous punch he had caught. With both combatants prepared to go additional rounds, Greg and Squirt tore into each other. I can't say with certainty who won the fight, it was just a good fight.

I do recall that once the fight was over, it was truly over. We sat around and boasted. Bragged on who we thought had won. I thought that Greg had whipped Squirt. But I wasn't going to say that. It sort of came out when Wayne and I started arguing with each other. I was saying, "All my man had to do was step in close 'cause he's shorter than Greg—he would've fucked him up."

"I don't care what he could've done, he done got his ass whipped."

Wayne offended Squirt by saying that he got whipped. And since Squirt was not in any shape to fight anyone else, I had to defend his honor. It is the code. We walk together, we fight together. "Nigga, you couldn't do it." I was with my man, Squirt. Unfortunately, Squirt did not realize that I was on his side. I guess that ass whipping was confusing his thoughts.

"Nigga, ain't nobody do shit to me." Squirt was talking to Wayne and me. "I'll whip both y'all punk asses."

Even at the tender age of ten or eleven, I knew that Squirt was hurting, embarrassed; therefore, I maintained my focus on Wayne. "You keep runnin' your mouth, I'm gonna see 'bout you getting' your ass whipped."

"You and what army?" Wayne wanted to know.

Without hesitating, I threw a right cross that caught Wayne in the lip. Fighting words had been uttered; naturally, a fight ensued. I felt that it would be best for me to get off the first punch. I was an aspiring pugilist. I had been boxing at Mr. Mack Lewis's gym for about two years at that time. Wayne, Black, Squirt, Fat Kirk, and Greg may have been a year or two older than me, and a couple inches taller, but my heart was bigger than any of theirs when it came to fighting. I liked to fight. I could fight, and I knew it.

The punch caught Wayne off guard. But it did not take him long to recover. We exchanged a host of blows. The matter culminated with Slyvester, Squirt's oldest brother, coming over to the basketball court, along with my cousin Terrance, separating us. Slyvester and Terrance ordered us to be friends, or at least act friendly—before they whipped all of us.

Slyvester and Terrance were much older than we were. Plus, they were twice our size, Although we prided ourselves on being good with our hands; none of us was going to challenge these two guys.

"Y'all niggas don't be telling us what to do," we spoke in unison.

"Y'all keep that dumb shit goin' on," Terrance was threatening, "and I'm gonna show y'all how a ass whippin' go."

"Come on y'all ," Black was taking control of the situation. "Fuck them faggies."

We traveled farther down the school yard to the adjoining baseball field and out of the sight of Terrance and Sly. None of us wanted to continue fighting. We were, after all, friends. Fighting each other was simply a part of our recreational practice. There was never any actual malice in our heart when we fought. We kicked each other's butts seeking bragging rights for a day or two.

Welcome to the Game
Chapter 7

The neighborhood I grew up in was riddled with crime and violence. There were open air drug markets all over the place. Not too many days passed without there being a shoot-out. In fact, I can recall a local newspaper, *The Baltimore Sun*, labeling our neighborhood "Dodge City." All the known stick-up boys who plied their trade on Eager Street managed to get themselves killed. Too many to name, would-be con men, tricksters, perished on Eager Street. Eager Street was where it all happened. It made you or it killed you.

I felt safe growing up on Eager Street despite all the crime and violence. For no one was ever shot by accident. Every nigga who "caught it" on Eager Street knew exactly why he "caught it." There were street codes, unwritten rules that were strictly adhered to. For example: drugs were sold at certain spots in the neighborhood—usually, in or around certain bars or carry-out restaurants. There were spots in our neighborhood where drugs were not sold. Generally, those spots were where children played or the older folks in the community hung out. Around my old neighborhood drugs were not sold above Ashland Avenue toward the south of Eager or Chase Street to the north of Eager. Eager Street, from Broadway up to Patterson Park, was a thoroughfare for drug activity. That code somehow managed to keep children from being sexually molested or accidentally shot. That code made it possible for the elderly folks in my community to sit on their steps during the hot summer days, even walk around their community whenever they felt the urge, without fear of being hit in the head and robbed for their Social Security money. The code made it possible for the neighborhood children to play touch football in the street without getting shot. The code was a beautiful thing when it was adhered to. It allowed life to be managed in the ghetto—a totally chaotic and irrational place.

When I watch the news or read the paper and see children or old people being violated, I wonder, what ever happened to the code? It was such a beautiful thing. When I was coming up through the hustling ranks, I was taught never to violate a vulnerable person. In other words, old persons who were struggling to make ends meet were not to be preyed upon. I was taught not to take narcotics to school or around folks who were not about what I was into. Perhaps I grew up in a time when ethics, or least a sense thereof, were respected. There were certain things that men just did not do. Namely, allow children into the drug trade.

I recall my initial attempts to sell drugs. I caught hell from the older drug dealers. They fought to keep me out. But I was determined to come in. Nothing was going to stop me.

I convinced Squirt, my hustling partner, to hook up with me to buy a half-pound of weed so we could break it down into nickel bags to make a huge profit. I was tired of shoplifting from area stores all day, then selling our booty only to end up with enough coinage to carry us through a single day.

The idea was not revolutionary. Many of my friends were already acquainted with weed. We were already smoking it; it was the harmless drug. Before going to a block party or a house party, Wayne, Squirt, Fat Kirk, Greg, and I would always pool our money together to purchase a bag of weed, or two, to heighten the occasion. We would make our purchase from various spots. But usually, we bought it from my cousins, Carolyn, Melvin, and Melvina. I could always get a deal from them; they were my family. Everyone smoked weed, even the old folks—unless they were hopelessly self-righteous.

Anyway, after Squirt and I decided that we were going into the weed business, we had to come up with a way to get our capital together. For we did not want to work for anyone. We probably could have gotten weed on consignment. We both knew enough dealers to get a "ghetto summer job," but we wanted our own thing. We were entrepreneurs at heart. We decided to hit a few stores everyday until we raised the $200 needed to buy a half-pound of weed. We figured we could raise the money in two or three days if we did not spend any money and stayed focused.

Squirt and I stayed focused, and after a week of stealing cosmetics and underwear, we had two hundred dollars. I wanted to buy the weed from my cousins, but Squirt wanted to cop from this guy named David.

Squirt and I went around to Duncan Street, a little alley street where David had his weed shop set-up. We hardly expected to see him standing out there on the corner with all his dealers around him. But there he was on this hot summer day. I will never forget how it went down.

Squirt and I had walked straight down Ashland Avenue to Duncan Street. We had counted out our money at my grandmother's house, where we would not be disturbed. Once we finished and decided that we would cop our weed from David, not my cousins, we went to hook up with David. I naturally assumed that Squirt had an established rapport with the man, since he was the one who suggested that we take our hard earned money to him.

"There he go," Squirt poked me in the rib as he pointed toward David. "Right there."

"I see him," was my retort. "Go holla at him."

Squirt looked puzzled by my response. I imagine it was because I was the one who generally brokered our deals. He would come up with all the grand ideas, but it was I who had to ultimately carry them out. But in this instance, I felt apprehensive. I hardly knew David. I saw him around the neighborhood, purchased a few five dollar bags of weed from his dealers when he was present, but that was it. I did not even recall ever selling him any drawers, and I sold underwear to nearly everybody in that neighborhood.

"Yo, you do the rappin'," Squirt was putting me on the spot. "You good at it."

We were too close to David and his crew to debate the matter any further. And appearance is everything. If Squirt and I looked liked two confused, square ass kids who didn't know what we were doing, we would most certainly get cheated out of our money. That's how it goes. When a mark who's too good to be true comes along begging to be cheated out of his money, you can't pass it up. It may never happen again in your lifetime. It is similar to missing Haley's Comet. If you miss it, you just missed it. You probably won't ever get the opportunity to see it again.

"Dave," I spoke with a confidence I certainly did not feel. "Let me holla at you for a minute."

David didn't seem to be surprised by my request. I suspect a man in David's profession gets requests of this nature all the time. He asked me,

"What's on your brain, Shorty?" escorting me off to the side and out of the hearing range of the others on the corner.

"Yo," I began in a business-like tone. No formalities or pleasantries needed to be exchanged. "I'm tryin' to get down with a half-pound."

"Damn, little nigga, you and your man tryin' smoke y'all brain out or what?"

David's matter-of-fact tone let me know he was pure business. He wanted some assurance that I was serious about making such a large purchase. For it probably did not look like Squirt and I could afford to spend two hundred dollars on some weed simply to smoke. We were not dressed raggedy. We were dressed in the latest fashion, coaching shorts, B.V.D. Tee Shirts, Puma tennis shoes and Nikes. But we were not adorned in expensive jewelry that indicated ghetto's wealth and player's status.

I understood David's statement was an inquiry. How I responded would determine whether or not he dealt with us, and if he did, in what manner. Would he treat us fair or play us on the scale? For we were not yet "Triple Beam niggas." We had no experience with the scale. It had to show.

"Man, we ain't tryin' to smoke. We tryin' to get some riches." I hoped this satisfied his inquiry.

"I need two-fifty."

This nigga was trying to play me. Since when did a half-pound cost $250? I had to let David know that I was not completely ignorant. "Two-fifty," I was incredulous. "Ain't that higher than a mothafucker?"

David smiled his gold teeth at me, truly amused at my reaction to his price. "Shorty, I'm gonna let you rock some high-power shit."

"That's good and all that, but two-fifty," I was going to do my best to bring the price down to the standard two hundred dollars. "We ain't workin' with that kind of loot."

"Put your man on point," David was confident we had reached an agreement. "Tell him to wait here 'til we get back."

Trust is not a thing often rendered in the drug culture. But in this instance, it was appropriate to follow David. He was a major player. For him to take me off somewhere and knock me over the head and kill me for a couple hundred bucks was unthinkable. From every indication David gave, he and I were going to do business; he liked me. I was getting a break, an entrance into the game.

I called Squirt over to where David and I stood. David walked back over to his friends and told them that he would be back in an hour or so. I told Squirt, "Yo want me to go with him somewhere."

"What 'sup?" Squirt was anxious to know what type of deal was brokered.

"I don't know, yet. But he talkin' some two-fifty shit."

"He know we ain't got nuthin' but a deuce?" Squirt was starting to look a little disappointed.

"Naw, but he gonna know in a minute." I hoped that my confidence would ressure him. "Give me the money and wait here 'til we get back."

Without protest Squirt went into his pocket and handed me our hard-earned money, all two hundred. I signaled to David and he led me down Ashland Avenue to Collington Avenue where he was parked. We walked in silence. No words needed to be spoken; we were making a drug deal that was going to benefit each of us. Besides, I felt that if I spoke before questioned, I would reveal my naivete.

It was summertime 1980, the streets were full. Folks were outside sitting on their front stoop, children were in the street playing "Hop Scotch" or shooting "Skillet Tops." I was getting into the Lincoln Continetal with one of the devil's agents, selling my youth and my soul—for a very cheap price.

When we got into the car, David decided to ask me, "What's your name, man," he appeared somewhat embarrassed. "I be seeing you around and I know you cool. If you wasn't we wouldn't be here. But I forgot what they call you."

"Tray," I was a fellow hustler, the nigga should have known my name. "Like the shit you eat off."

"Tired of sellin' draws, huh?" This cat was, indeed, the devil's own. He knew my story.

"Yeah, you got that right," it was time I let David know I only had two hundred bucks. "Look man, I only got a deuce."

David didn't say anything. He simply continued on to our destination. But I could not bear the silence, I lacked the discipline—then. "You now that's all we usually pay."

"No problem," David finally decided to give me a clue as to what kind of deal we had brokered.

"What you buy, I am gonna give you."

True, I was a rookie. But I understood a thing or two about consignment. David felt confident of my ability to move his product. He wanted to lock me down. The only problem I anticipated was that Squirt did not like being employed by anyone.

Well, actually, that was not a problem for me. Squirt told me to do the talking, to make the deal. I did, and if he didn't like the deal I had serendipitously brokered, then fuck him. I liked the deal.

David and I talked about a few important matters. I told him that Squirt was my hustling partner. We split everything right down the middle—including risks. He was cool with that. I told him that I would sell the weed down on Eager and Durham, all around that area. David was cool with that, too. He just wanted assurance that I would not bring the weed past Chester Street. He did not want me to compete with his other dealers. Plus, the deal he was offering me was a secret. I was not to tell anyone about our special deal. I was the only one getting it.

I asked David why was I so special, and he told me some sentimental stuff, "When I started in this here game, I was just like you. That's why I dig you right off the top."

David went on to tell me not to trust anyone. Not even him. He told me it doesn't matter whether I sell weed, dope, or coke, "Niggas get cruddy when money is involved." He told me that if I expected to get some real money from this venture, I had to stop smoking the weed. He sagely informed me, "You can't get no money off anything you love." It doesn't matter what it is, if you love it, you can't get rich off it. "You can't pimp a bitch for her riches if you love her. You can't sell narcotics if you lovin' this shit," he told me.

We came to a stop at an apartment at Parkside Garden. It was a luxurious place by ghetto standards. Wall-to-Wall carpet, a grand entertainment center, brand new furnishing, and a sexy dressed red-bone broad who inspired an instant erection.

When David stuck his key in the door to get us into the apartment, she appeared almost magically. He introduced her as Vivian. She was a petite woman, about five feet tall. If she weighed better than a hundred pounds, I would have been utterly surprised. Her shape was beautifully proportioned. She wore only a "teddy," some kind of night shirt, as if she was prepared for bed. Damn, she's a fine ass red-bone was all I could think. I could not think. I was too busy trying to sneak a peek under that short outfit she was wearing.

David had to know I was captivated by his woman's beauty. I could hardly keep my tongue in my mouth. But he gave no indication that he even cared. I sat down on the thick leather couch and Vivian sat directly across from me to give me a perfect view of her fabulous figure. David turned some music on, some hip-hop jams, and exited the room. He went to one of the back rooms, and when he returned ten minutes later, he had a shopping bag full of weed.

I wanted to ask him if Vivian was a part of this great new relationship he and I were embarking upon. But common sense compelled me to keep my mouth closed on that matter. I sensed, intuitively, that Vivian was being used to test me. However, I was going to steal as many peeks under her "teddy" as she would have allowed.

David had Vivian rolled a couple joints, and we all smoked the weed, talked about inconsequential matters like music and fashion, and what were the best night clubs to attend. We seemingly got so close in that short period that Vivian felt comfortable enough to give me a "shot-gun." She put the marijuana cigarette into her mouth at the fire end, while I put the other end into my mouth, and she blew the smoke into my face and mouth.

The weed was really good. But Vivian's presence, no doubt, enhanced the quality of it. David knew my answer before he asked the question, "You like that?"

It was like on cue; when David asked me about the quality of the weed, shifting our casual moment to business, Vivian exited the room. "Yeah, I dig it all." I wanted to be as vague about matters as David had been. I was learning. I enjoyed Vivian, the shot-gun she had given me, the weed, the hospitality, the ride in the Lincoln, and the deal he was offering. But I could not say all that. If he did not know that he had impressed me, I was going to leave it that way. The last thing I wanted to do was to come off looking like some wet-behind-the-ear, impressionable sucker.

"You want the deal?" David wanted to know.

I paused for effect. I did not want to appear anxious. I wanted David to feel like we were doing each other a favor. "Yeah, let's do this."

I handed David the two hundred dollars that Squirt and I had raised. Without counting it, he threw it on the side table and handed me the shopping bag full of weed. "Here, this is the whole 'P.' You owe me three bills."

"Bet."

"Cool," David gathered his keys. "Let's roll."

David told me when I finished, I could find him on Duncan Street, at some time during the day. If he was not there when I came looking for him, just hang around, he would eventually show up. He told me that if I sold the weed quickly and kept his money straight, I would make plenty of money.

Arlando "Tray" Jones

The End Begins

Chapter 8

David dropped me off on the corner of Madison Street and Patterson Park. It would have been foolish of me to go on Duncan and Ashland, where Squirt was waiting for me, carrying a large brown shopping bag that contained a pound of marijuana. I asked David to tell Squirt to meet me at my grandmother's house. He told me that he would. I walked the four blocks westward on Madison Street to my grandmother's house.

When I arrived, my grandmother and step-grandfather were lounging in the living room. I detected from their mannerisms and the discarded liquor bottles that Mama and Daddy-Pain had been drinking heavily. Mama was slumped over the couch, her clothes and hair were disheveled and Daddy-Pain looked pretty much the same.

I had become accustomed to this scene. Ever since my mother died, maybe a year or so prior, Mama had started drinking noticeably heavy. It seemed like she was totally drunk before noon most days. I mean, Mama had always drank liquor. That was nothing, but now she stayed drunk. Daddy-Pain was always inebriated. I don't recall ever seeing Daddy-Pain sober. He was an accomplished alcoholic. Daddy-Pain would tell us, "I ain't no alcoholic. I'm a drunk. Alcoholics gotta go to them damn meetin's."

Daddy-Pain, no doubt, made a good point. He and my grandmother were together long before I was born. I knew that he was not my biological grandfather because every time he and my mother or he and grandmother argued, it would come out. My mother used to often tell Daddy-Pain, "You ain't my father," and Daddy-Pain would always shoot back, "I ain't none of y'all daddy. That's why y'all so fucked up."

I loved Daddy-Pain deeply. He worked and drank himself to death. For as long as I live, I will never figure out how he did it. He would be drunk by the time I got out of school at 2:30 in the afternoon, and he would continue to drink throughout the day, and would be up for work by six o'clock in the morning. I am amazed that he did it. Moreover, I am amazed and grateful that he managed, along with Mama, to keep a roof over our heads and food in our stomachs.

When I came into the house carrying the shopping bag with the weed in it, no one noticed me. I often went unnoticed during those times. Kim was usually out chasing her blast and Mama and Daddy-Pain were usually drunk. Food was always in the refrigerator and the house was heated. But it was a truly lonely place to be. Each of us living at 1805 E. Madison came and went pretty much as we pleased—Mama, Daddy-Pain, Kim and me. Kim's daughter, Kieshawn, was very young. Kim generally dropped her off with her paternal grandmother, Ms. Rose. For the most part, I was left alone, to commit my vices. The only time I received parenting was when my actions came to the attention of school officials or the police.

When I came into the house, I told Daddy-Pain, "Squirt will be here lookin' for me in a minute. I'll be in the basement."

"Okay," he responded. Daddy-Pain was always nonchalant. He did not care about most things. Half the time he wasn't even home. He paid the bills, occasionally cooked the dinner meals, but basically went about his personal affairs. Mama did likewise, only she was home most the time. She no longer worked at Church Homes Hospital where she performed housekeeping duties. She simply stayed home to drink herself into an early grave.

I went down to the basement and pulled out the brown coin bags and Scotch Tape that Squirt and I would need to package our marijuana. By the time I had taken out the paraphernalia, Squirt arrived. We poured the weed out and spread it over some old newspaper. "Damn," Squirt exclaimed. "That's a lot of smoke."

"Boy, you know I be handlin' my business," I said with pride.

"Yeah, but what's the deal?" Squirt wanted to know the terms of the deal I had brokered with David. "Did we make out?"

"I think so." I was going to explain the deal to Squirt, and attempt to convince him of the beauty of it. "Yo mashed us with the whole pound. He said what we buy, we get fronted." Squirt looked a little perplexed. I had to offer him more details to clear up his confusion.

"The nigga took me out to his crib, yo. He had this dime in the room with us givin' me all kinds of play." I gave him a complete description of how David had entertained me. I didn't leave anything out. I even told him about the shot-gun. "Yo, when she was blowin' the weed in my face, I ain't even care if she was a dick-sucker."

I convinced Squirt that we had brokered a great deal. We both felt that if we sold the weed quickly and got back to David, we would be able to buy jewelry, clothes, and cars just as fancy as David's. First thing we had to do was build up a big clientele. We decided the best way to do that was to make our nickel bags bigger than the competition's bags.

Squirt and I sat down in the basement for two or three hours packaging up our narcotics for street sell. When we were finished, it was dark outside, nearing nine o'clock. We had packaged over $900 in five-dollar bags. We split the inventory in half. Squirt knew that he had to come up with $150 because we owed David $300.

We both anticipated earning close to $300 apiece. The plan was that we would work our product up and down Eager and Durham. We were going to circle our whole neighborhood advertising our product to all the "potheads." We had even isolated a few bags to serve as samples. Our weed was the best thing around. We smoked a couple joints to be certain prior to leaving the house.

Squirt and I hit the strip on a high. We were both experiencing the euphoric sensation of the marijuana we had smoked. We were in an extremely humorous mood. We told everyone we passed on the streets, "Got that power weed." Some ignored us, but a significant number stopped and purchased our product.

The exchanges were almost always the same. Squirt and I would walk up to someone who we suspected smoked weed, which was damn near everyone out and about in the 'hood at that time of night, and announce, "Got that power weed."

If he or she asked, "How's the weight?" we had a potential sale. If he or she asked, "How's the weed?" we knew for certain we had a sale.

Within a few hours of opening up shop, Squirt and I had sold the five-dollar bags we had brought with us. We felt it wise to carry only ten to fifteen bags with us at a time.

I can't recall how long we stayed at it that first night. But I do recall selling close to $300 worth of weed, It was a weekend night, Friday or Saturday. Everyone was out looking for some good weed, and it did not take long before word got around that Squirt and I had the best weed in the 'hood.

Within twenty-four hours of copping the pound from David, Squirt and I had the $300 we needed to cop again.

We still had weed left to sell, but we had decided that we would pay David off the top. The first $300 we got was to go to him. We wanted to impress our connect. It was the least we could do, for he had impressed the hell out of us. Well, at least, he had impressed the hell out of me.

It did not bother me that everything in David's life was trivialized. His woman, his fancy apartment, his car, his jewelry, and his friends were ephemeral byproducts of his lifestyle. He befriended me without even knowing my name, or even caring whether or not I even had a name. In David's life, the life that was to become mine, everything is short lived. Today's friend is tomorrow's foe. The apartment, car, and jewelry were his until his next arrest. The pretty woman was his until he ran out of money or another came around with just a little more than he. It was all understood by those in the game who were not naïve. There was absolutely no need to attach yourself to anything. The narcotic trade trivialized everything and everyone. If you valued your life, if folks instilled in you early that your life had intrinsic worth and value, you avoided that lifestyle—no matter where you lived or how your environment was situated.

A Day in the Life

Chapter 9

"Man, when David comin' 'round?" I was growing impatient. "We been layin' 'round this cut damn near all day."

Squirt and I had come around to David's spot more than two hours ago looking for him. We were anxious to see David to let him know that we were able to move the weed very quickly. He was nowhere to be found, although his dealers were all out there on the corners of Duncan and Ashland and Duncan and Eager selling his product.

"Nigga, why don't you just lay and be cool," Ray-Ray, David's spokesman, was advising me. "You niggas can rock the rest of y'all shit while you wait."

Ray-Ray did have a point. Since Squirt and I had been waiting on David to appear, we had damn near sold out of the weed we had. I had to run back and forth to my grandmother's house twice to pick up more weed. Squirt had to go home three times to get more. Hanging around Duncan Street, David's spot, was not all that bad. I just wanted to pay David off, get some more weed, package it up, and work on building Eager and Durham Street into a marijuana marketplace like Duncan and Ashland and Duncan and Eager Streets were.

I understood enough about business to know that I had to have enough supply to encourage a demanding market. David had allowed me to see what real money could purchase, and I was ready for my share. I needed to see my connect to impress him with the fact that I had sold a pound of weed in less than a day. I was proud of my accomplishment; I felt confident that I would be able to get two pounds. He did say that what I bought he would give me on consignment.

Squirt and I had a good run from the gate. We made more money in twenty-four hours than we had made our entire lives. And, we were having fun doing it. I had been sexually propositioned at least three times in the twenty-four-hour period. I was considerably good looking. At twelve years of age, I was slender in build, athletic. My caramel colored brown skin was smooth, my even white teeth allowed my smile to enchant. I was only five-feet-five inches tall, but I was hardly finish growing. I was good looking with promise of becoming even better looking. However, my good looks were not why I received the sexual propositions.

Roslyn had come to me without any pretense. "Tray, I ain't got no money, but I wanna smoke some weed." She was wearing some very tight, cut-off jeans shorts. Her t-shirt could hardly contain her large breasts that were battling to burst through the fabric … to give me a hearty look.

I wanted to do it to Roslyn, lord knows. I was about twelve years old and she was about nineteen or twenty. She had buck teeth, and was not very pretty. In fact, Roslyn was an ugly woman—if you based attractiveness solely on facial features. Fortunately, I recognized other attributes in a woman. For example: I liked women who dressed sleazy and had no problem with using their sexuality for material gain. I liked women who were not complicated. They simply told you what they wanted from you and what they were willing to give for it. In other words, I liked a loose sleazy woman. If she fit the profile of what the niggas in my 'hood called a "freak," I wanted her.

Roslyn was no doubt a "freak bitch." She did not have an appealing face, but she had a voluptuous body. Everything on Roslyn was tight. Her breasts did not sag, her butt was not flat or droopy, and her dark skin was fine and shiny. She was definitely a sensuous woman, and I wanted to be with her. At twelve, I wanted to be with damn near every woman I saw. I guess I was going through that puberty thing.

"Roslyn," I was not shy when it came to asking for a woman's sexual favor. "If you smoke my shit for free, I wanna fuck."

Roslyn rubbed my face in a most sensual manner and instructed me to come around to her house, at eleven o'clock, after her mother left for work. I was okay with that. In fact, I was going to wait until midnight. I did not want to risk running into Ms. Jackie, Roslyn's mother. It seemed to me that Ms. Jackie was an evil woman. She was mad at every man who ever "did it" to Roslyn or wanted to "do it" to her.

It was commonly known throughout the neighborhood that once Ms. Jackie went to work, Roslyn would sneak some boy or man into their house for sex in order to get whatever gift she sought. That night, she sought marijuana, and it so happened to be my good fortune to have some. A whole pound, in fact. I was willing to share all my sample bags with Roslyn if she was willing to share with me what she had shared with Sly, Bobby, Ricky, Mike, Teddy, Billy, Romey, Timmy, and the many others who I cannot name.

I went around to Roslyn's house a little after one o'clock in the morning. Without any preliminaries or pretense of courtship or romance, Roslyn disrobed. She rolled a few joints of weed, smoked them, kissed me on my body and ultimately put me inside of her.

That was earlier that day, hours ago. Now, I was out here on the corner selling the last of my weed and enjoying the camaraderie of Ray-Ray, Lonnie, Richie, Monk, and Squirt, David's crew. The neighborhood was embracing us. The girls were adoring us, and the police took notice of us, although they did not bother us. We were empowered. We belonged to something that awarded us esteem. Well, at least, that is how I felt. But I am willing to venture that we all felt pretty much the same. The hidden feelings of shame, guilt, and disenfranchisement that brought us all to the corner to be merchants of death and destruction were repressed and unimportant.

I did not yet understand that it was impossible to bring harm, death, and destruction to others without bringing it to myself. I did not yet understand that what I was engaged in was even wrong. I could appreciate the fact that selling weed, or any kind of narcotic, was illegal. If the police caught you, you went to jail. Sometimes you got out immediately, and sometimes you didn't. It all depended upon the luck of the draw. From my life's perspective, it was better to be a drug dealer than not to be. I either sold drugs or experienced constant lack because of poverty.

Everyone in my neighborhood was poor. But my family's poverty was growing dismal. We often had our utilities cut off because we could not pay the bills. It seemed like something would always pop up to prevent my family from having everything we needed to be reasonably comfortable. Daddy-Pain got drunk and let one of the young girls trick him out of his pay check. Kim spent the gas and electric money on her blast. Mama misplaced the grocery money while in a drunken stupor. At 1805 E. Madison Street, I soon learned, it was every man for himself.

My paternal grandfather, Daddy, had already taught me a thing or two about survival. I was not totally disadvantaged when I went to stay with my mother's people. I was not some naïve twelve-year-old kid unable to navigate uncaring, cruel, and unloving terrain. Daddy used to tell me, "Stop your cryin' and do what ya gotta do." There was never time enough to create an excuse or moan over circumstances. If there was something that had to be done, get it done.

I had to keep food on my table, clothes on my back, and shelter over my head. Issues such as what was right and what was wrong were not going to stand as an excuse for me to lack anything. Plus, I was spoiled. Whatever I asked for, I was accustomed to getting. The fact that my primary sources of support had died prematurely was no reason for me not to have items of necessity or desire.

I hung around David's spot for about three hours before I decided to leave. Squirt was willing to stick around and wait for David until hell froze over. He was hoping for a trip and treat from David like the one I had received. I told Squirt that I felt that that royal treatment was a one time deal. Squirt did not care. He was hard-headed like me. "Yo, Squirt, I ain't gonna hang 'round here waiting on that nigga." I was trying to convince Squirt not to start off our business relationship with David by kissing his ass—excessively. "It ain't like he holdin' on to our money."

Squirt was basking in the glory of being out there with David's crew, being a part of that major economical mechanism. "Yo, I'm gonna lay." It was pointless trying to convince Squirt to leave the weed corner. "I'm gonna knock down my last four bags and keep three hundred with me. I can make the move for us."

I was nonchalant, "Cool, tell yo we got five hundred so we can get the two." I embraced Squirt in our traditional "one love thug hug" and told him he could catch me down on Eager and Durham. I wanted to build our clientele like David had built his. I was going to sell the last ten or fifteen bags I had down at my spot. Well, it was not my spot yet. I was working on it. If I applied ample attention and provided a quality product on Eager and Durham, it would be my spot. At the moment, I was still a fledgling drug dealer. It would be another year or two before I was able to reign supreme and declare a spot. I did not yet appreciate the fact that what I could not defend, I did not have a right to.

Feelings Are Only Feelings, But Business Is Business

Chapter 10

Squirt was unable to make the deal with David. Squirt had waited for David to show up until nine or ten o'clock that night, eight hours. And the dude refused to do business with him. David made it clear to Squirt that I was the only one who he would be dealing with. He understood that Squirt and I were partners; however, he would exchange money and narcotics only with me.

I felt rather honored when Squirt came to me to inform me that, "Yo, that nigga trippin'." Squirt was utterly disgruntled about David not wanting to do business with him. Squirt had waited on David for eight hours. I mean, he laid out there on the corner for David like some freak bitch.

Personally, I did not feel sorry for Squrit, I tried to convince him not to start off our relationship with David by kissing his butt. I had heard through the grapevine that David was a punk. He made a lot of money from dealing in illegal narcotics, but he was soft. Stick-up boys had robbed him and his dealers, and he never retaliated. A sure sign of a punk-ass nigga.

It is often said that "politics create strange bed fellows." Drug dealing does likewise. I did not really like David. I had only done business with him once. I had only, at this point, been in his presence once. However, I knew that I did not like him. He was superficial, a phony ass type nigga. I wanted his girl. I wanted his money. I wanted his car. I wanted to be held in the high esteem that he seemed to be held in. The only thing David had that I did not want was his reputation for being a "punk ass nigga." If someone robbed me—took my hard earned blood money— there certainly would be retaliation.

I was pleased that David would not deal directly with Squirt. That meant that Squirt would be dependent upon me to keep the connect going. I had some leverage. I did not quite know what leverage meant, and I was unsure as to how I was going to use mine. I just knew that I really liked having money in my pocket and girls wanting to have sex with me for a fee that I could afford.

"So Squirt, is the nigga gonna lay for me to get up there?" I was not about to walk the four blocks to David's spot if he was gone. "I ain't tryin' to be waitin' on that sucker like I'm some bitch or sumthin'." I intended for my remark to offend Squirt. Why, I don't know. I sensed that he was hurt because David would not do business with him, and I wanted to poke at him. It was how my personality was constructed, I guess. I enjoyed being annoying. Besides, Squirt was one of the many who used to make fun of me about my mother. He teased me because my mother was a prostitute. He teased me because my grandmother was an alcoholic. He teased me about every shameful and embarrassing aspect of my life.

Squirt and I "joned" each other our entire lives. We played the dozens, and exchanged quite a few vicious blows over hurt feelings. But deep down inside, Squirt and I loved each other. My mother, grandmother, and Aunt Kim have whipped his ass for his transgressions just as Ms. Lawcy, Squirt's mom, had whipped mine.

Where I come from, if your mother was able to whip me for misbehaving, then you and I were family. Moreover, Squirt had stayed overnight at my home just as many times as I had stayed overnight at his. I peeped every female in his household just as he peeped every female in mine. Squirt was my dog, I loved that nigga.

David offended my dear friend. I was teasing Squirt about it, but I was not going to let David get away with hurting my friend's feelings. I had told him that Squirt and I were partners; we shared everything. What he did to Squirt, he did to me.

I would deal with Squirt's hurt feelings later. For now, business had to be conducted. Squirt and I were completely out of weed. We had sold the last of our supply and we had told our clientele that we would have more weed in a few hours. We urged our customers not to spend their money with anyone else. We assured everyone who came to purchase weed from us that, "If you wait you won't be disappointed."

"Yo waitin' on you now," Squirt was hurt over how David had treated him, but business was business. "You want me to lay up your house or roll with you?"

"Roll with me." I was no fool, I was not going to carry two pounds of marijuana around by myself. I wanted to split our stash in half. If the police or the stick-up boys ran down on me or Squirt, either he or I would not have everything. I was a neophyte at selling drugs, but I was no fool. I could always think, plot, and scheme. I was a legitimate product of my environment.

Squirt and I met with David. He sold us a pound of weed and gave us a pound on consignment. When we met up with David on Duncan Street, he took Squirt and me into a house on the block. There wasn't anything remarkable about this house. It was a typical two story, red brick ghetto dwelling. The inside of the house was poorly furnished and the only occupants were David's dealers. No one actually lived there, and it showed. The tables and trash cans were littered with discarded carry-out food containers. There were no dishes in sight or anything that would suggest that someone lived there on a permanent basis. It was a stash-house. Trusted members of David's crew would take turns at staying in the house watching over whatever inventory of marijuana happened to be there.

It was evident I was not going to get a V.I.P. treatment this time. This was going to simply be a no-nonsense business transaction. I handled my end well and David was living up to his commitment. I counted $700 out to David. That was significant enough to satisfy the $300 I owed for the weed already given to me on consignment and $400 to pay for a pound. I could not fathom paying $500 for a pound.

"Tray, my pounds go for five bills," David was preparing to be stupid. "I thought you understood that."

"I understand your shit cost more than everybody else's," I shot back.

David grinned his multiple gold teeth and said, "Shorty, I'm sittin' on fifty pounds of the best weed in town; pay me what I ask, and you gonna be a rich nigga."

I had $300 more in my pocket, and I am sure Squirt had just as much as I did, or more. I shot Squirt a quick glance, offering him a chance to speak up and take his rightful place as my partner. "Pay the man his extra hundred—let him beat us." Squirt spoke well for the occasion.

"Ah baby-boy, why you sayin' that?" David was talking business with Squirt.

"Cause we can get a pound for four hundred anywhere else."

"Go somewhere else and get a deal better than I'm givin' up—with better weed." David's retort was ugly and quite intimidating. It rendered Squirt speechless and defeated.

I had heard through the grapevine that David was a punk ass nigga. I was not going to let him get away with intimidating my partner. He may feel that he could do that shit to me. "Nigga, you know muthafuckin' well pounds go for four bills." I was summoning my anger. "You just chargin' us this crazy ass price 'cause you think we can't go nowhere else."

Shocked by my outburst, David wanted to know, "Why you talkin' to me like you mad?"

"David, you ain't gotta put up with these little nuffin' ass niggas," Ray-Ray had David's back. Just as I had Squirt's back.

"I am mad, man," it was time to be diplomatic. "Me and my man can push the weed. But we ain't tryin' get carried like bitches."

David and Ray-Ray started laughing. Squirt and I looked puzzled. We did not know what David and Ray-Ray found so funny. Squirt asked, "What's so funny?"

"All that heart you dumb mothafuckas got," Ray-Ray was explaining the humor to us. "Y'all talkin' war talk but ain't neither one of y'all ready to go to war."

I analyzed the situation. Here Squirt and I were, in David's stash-house, surrounded by at least three of his loyal crew members (Ray-Ray, Monk, and Jerry). They probably had guns around. Squirt and I did not have anything that even looked like a gun. It was time to think like a smart man, or a bright kid.

"David, I want money," I was humbled. "Not war."

David told me I had made a wise choice. In fact, he was so pleased with the choice I made he elected to charge Squirt and me $450 for the pounds. I thanked him and told him that was the least he could do since he had treated Squirt like a bitch.

"How I treat your man like a bitch?" David genuinely wanted to know.

The mood had lightened, and we were jovial. "Man, Squirt waited 'round all day to hook up with you, and you refused to deal with him."

"I do my business my way."

"Yeah, but your way didn't let my man meet Vivian."

We all laughed at that, and ultimately concluded that David used Vivian to impress all prospective business associates. David did not love Vivian. She was simply a pretty young woman that shared his apartment and served as an ornament. If anyone present in that room were to enhance his economic station above David's, Vivian would be his. She was ghetto-fabulous and trashy in terms of morals. Our chosen lifestyle did not afford us the privilege to have a woman of high morals. Most women with high morals in our lifestyle ended up thrown into trash dumps with a hypodermic needle protruding from their arm. Others ended up coked-out, doped-out, fucked-out, begging for a hand-out before she reached her twenty-first birthday.

It happened to my mother, my Aunt Kim, and countless other women who entered the ghetto games with too many morals to stand a chance to make it. Fat Larry said, "Only rotten mothafuckas survive the dope game." I have heard those very same sentiments echoed time and time again. I have personally witnessed the good die young, the bad best the good, and the ugly consume the beautiful. How I ignored high morals baffles me. I decided right from wrong based on what served us as opposed to what didn't.

You Can't Change the Rule in the Ninth Inning

Chapter 11

The summer of 1980 marked a major turning point in my life. I was separating myself from my immediate family, and it seemed as if they were separating themselves from me. My grandmother and Daddy-Pain were consumed by their drinking. My Aunt Kim had had another daughter, my sister Yalanda, the previous year. Kim had also hooked up with this guy named Calvin. They seemed to be very much in love with each other and intent on making their relationship work.

Kim and her beau rented a house up in the 1800 block of Durham Street, and I moved in with them. It was Calvin, Kim, Kieshawn, Yalanda, and me. It was assumed that if Kim took care of me, I would have more parental supervision. I was running wild at Mama's. I came and went as I pleased, and I had virtually no adult supervision.

Moving to another location with Kim and her new boyfriend was not going to change me. I had been selling weed all summer long, and I was pleased with the money I was making. Moreover, I was getting more sex than an adolescent had a right to. I was set to rebel against any kind of parental authority Kim and Calvin planned on invoking upon me.

There is no doubt in my mind and heart that Kim loved me more than any mother could love her very own child. In fact, Kieshawn often complained that Kim treated me better than she did her. I can't say for certain whether or not Kieshawn's complaint had merit. For Kim and I have always had a special bond. No words could adequately express the depth of love I have for her, and the gratitude I feel toward her for the effort she put forth to rear me and protect me from the hardships I eventually faced. I understand that Kim was burdened by her own life issues. She was a high school drop out, addicted to heroin, and had two children of her own to care for. But never once did she make me feel like I was a burden. Kim freely gave me everything that she had in love, food, shelter, and moral values. She taught me how to properly bathe and groom myself. She demanded that I go to school so that "my dumb ass could at least learn how to write a letter home when they locked my hard-head ass up."

I truly appreciated Kim's love and attempt to be my parent. I know she was genuinely sincere. But I was not going to give up my lucrative income to all of a sudden be her well-behaved and good-mannered son. Plus, I didn't really like her boyfriend, Calvin. That sucker was selling just as much weed as I. In fact, he was taking money out of my pocket. Potheads that I considered as my clientele often purchased Calvin's weed over mine.

I definitely did not like the fact that this sucker was messing with my aunt. It pissed me off that he was essentially my parent, for Kim was my legal guardian at this point.

It was not long after we all had moved into 1800 N. Durham Street that Kim and Calvin laid out the new laws to me.

"Tray, all that hangin' out all times of night got to stop." Kim was being adamant and authoritarian. "You been runnin' 'round doin' what you wanna do when you wanna do it, and that gotta stop, now."

Calvin's punk-ass just sat there and nodded in agreement with Kim.

"I don't blame you for doin' what you been doin'," she was continuing. "Ain't nobody been there for you and you had to take care yourself. But I'm here now."

"Kim, you all right?" I was shocked that she was speaking to me in this manner. "You trippin' ain't you?" I grinned.

Without warning, Kim slapped me across my face. The slap did not hurt. It simply threw me completely aback. Calvin laughed. I was then embarrassed. Kim had hit me many times in the past. She was always more like a terrorizing big sister than a parent figure. I could always run and tell Mama to protect me from her terror.

"Tray, if I catch your ass down on Eager sellin' reefer, I'm gonna whip your ass." Kim was extremely serious. Therefore, I lifted myself from the second-hand couch that Kim had purchased to furnish our living room and feigned like I was going to another room of the house. I went through the dining room, directly through the kitchen, and out the back door. Before I cleared the yard, Kim was at the door yelling for me to get my ass back in the house. But I was beyond listening to her. Squirt and I had worked our way up to getting three to four pounds of weed at a time. I was not going to throw away what I had put together simply because Kim decided she wanted to play house.

I half-ran the fifteen or so blocks from our new house down to Eager Street. Squirt and Black were on the corner selling our weed.

"What's up boss?" Black had begun addressing me as "boss" ever since I recruited him to aid Squirt and me in our marijuana business.

"Yeah, nigga, what's up?" Squirt wanted to know, too. "You look like sumthin' heavy is on your mind."

I guess the program Kim was trying to put me under was troubling me in an obvious way. "Look man, if Kim come down here lookin' for me, tell her y'all ain't seen me."

Squirt and Black did not ask me any more questions. I suspect they knew something very personal and emotionally hurtful was going on inside me. I told Black and Squirt that I was going around to Tina's house to avoid Kim and her punk-ass boyfriend. I knew that one or both of them would come looking for me. I didn't want any drama. I needed to go somewhere to lay undergound to clear my thoughts about this new set-up being imposed upon me. I had been without strict supervision my entire life; now here comes Kim with this bullshit.

I proceeded to Tina's house, which was right up from our spot, on Durham and Eager streets. I cut through the alley because I did not want anyone to see me go in there. I had been using Tina's house to stash my weed for several weeks. Also, she was my personal freak, and it was most satisfying.

Tina was a grown woman. She was in her mid-to-late twenties with a small child of her own. My being twelve years old was not a problem for her. I was able to put anywhere from $100 to $200 in her pocket every day. Not many welfare recipients with a low sense of morality would pass up an opportunity to have sex with a handsome kid and pocket a pretty penny, too.

I accepted the fact that Tina was expensive, but Squirt and I split the expense. We were using her house as a stash spot. Therefore, we were expected to pay her a wage. Two hundred dollars was an outrageous wage. We were only holding our weed there. We were not running in and out and tipping off the neighbors that we were operating from her house. Tina got the extra money because she was giving me sex, and her sister Sharon, who also lived there, was bestowing sexual favors upon Squirt. We needed the house and the sex was there. So we paid generously.

We were gullible when it came to girls or women. Squirt and I would pay five dollar tricks fifty dollars for sex. We were young. I was twelve and Squirt was two years older. Our hormones were raging out of control, and our business prevented us from pursuing a steady girlfriend. Selling weed the way we were selling it was a twenty-four-hour-a-day job and we did it seven days a week during the summer of 1980. We had to bring Black on board to help us run our business because we hardly had time to rest, eat, and bathe. We were utterly engrossed in our illegal narcotics business and robbed of our childhood.

I must admit, at the time, I did not feel like I was being robbed. I kept a pocket full of money. I was being sexually fulfilled by Tina, a chocolate statuesque, very black queen. Sexually, Tina was totally uninhibited. She taught me things that later sexual partners would salute me for learning.

It was at Tina's house where Squirt and I generally hung out. We came and went from Tina's house in the most clandestine manner possible. We kept the major portion of our entire marijuana inventory there. A stick-up boy could easily follow one of us into the house and rob us for everything. When Squirt and I came to Tina's house or left from there, we strictly observed the rules of "hide and go seek." We were involved solely in the sale of weed, the drug of choice for the innocent. We did not attract the attention of stick-up-boys and narcotic police. Squirt, Black, and I were simply three young ghetto kids doing our ghetto summer jobs. However, one could never be too careful in the 'hood. The biggest threat to our enterprise was my beloved Aunt Kim wanting to play house.

When I came into Tina's house through the back door and saw her sitting at the kitchen table, my mood instantly improved. Tina was a very feminine woman, and feminine qualities have always served as an emotional elixir for me.

"Why you got the back door open?" I gently asked, suppressing my irritation. "Anybody could've just walked up in here."

"The door was not open," Tina was being facetious. "It just wasn't locked."

"Don't be stupid," I snapped. "You know what the fuck I mean."

"Don't be so mean, baby." She soothingly said, rising up from the table, coming to me. "What got you so upset?"

Before I could answer, she had embraced me and kissed me. I returned her kiss, but I was not going to let her change the subject so easily. "Why you leave the door unlock?"

"I saw you comin' up the alley." She was probably lying. But who was I that she could not lie to? Women like Tina traveled through life by lying, stealing, manipulating, and using their body. I understood that. I was not reared to be naïve and innocent. I never believed in the Toothfairy or Santa Claus. Moreover, I knew that people told lies. Some for very good reasons and others for no reason at all. Tina had just told me a lie; I sensed it. Therefore, it was only befitting that I tell her one in return.

"Tina, I ain't trying to be found by nobody," I begun laying the foundation for my lie. "Niggas been worrying me all day 'bout dumb shit."

I paused for effect. No great liar completes a lie without taking an early assessment to see the impact of his words.

"Squirt and Black know where I'm at," it was okay to complete the lie. Her eyes suggested that she be lied to; the truth would have only encouraged her to ask annoying questions. "Once they knock down the rest of the weed, everybody can get their cut and we can re-back up."

"Okay," I knew the suggestion of paying her money would make her agreeable. "You wanna lay down and rest or eat something first?"

I mumbled that I was all right, and headed up stairs to Tina's beautifully decorated and comfortable bedroom to rest on her suitable-for-a-king bed. I hoped she would not follow me. I needed some time alone to assess my situation. I loved my Aunt Kim. But I did not want her to be my mother. I had no mother or father. I figured it must have been meant for me to live freely—without restricting parents molding and shaping me into what they wanted me to be.

I saw Eggy Scott's bank roll, I saw Kenny's fancy cars and fancy women. I had heard the fabulous stories about Frank Matthew and Little Melvin. I saw how well crime paid; I was determined to mold and shape myself. I had been ignored for most of my life. Now, Kim decides she wants me to be a part of her happy home. Fuck that! I had been fed well, sheltered well, and clothed well. Every now and again, someone stepped in to teach me a moral lesson. But for the most part, I navigated my own way through life. I learned that it was never what you did that got you into trouble, it was how you did it. I learned that it is much more beneficial to an individual to be charming and lovable than not to be.

My great-grandmother, Grandma, used to say, "You catch more flies with honey than with vinegar." I have been a charming person, if nothing else, my entire life. Plus, I am a thinker. Daddy used to say, "Boy, think 'fore you act." I hoped Tina would leave me alone to let me think. I knew that I could not avoid Kim forever. I would have to confront her sooner or later. She was going to be angry, I was certain. I had run from her, but she was not my mother. Her plans for my life contradicted mine. If she had consulted me, we may have been able to work something out. As it was, she had hooked up with Calvin and decided to be my authoritarian parent.

I know that you cannot wait until a child is twelve, and then decide you are going to be his proper parent. If someone does that, there is bound to be conflict and rebellion. Kim and I had a lot of obstacles to overcome. Unfortunately, we never overcame them. Kim died from a heroin overdose before I was able to impress upon her that I loved her and appreciated what she desperately tried to do for me. I know her love for me was genuine. However, it was expressed through impatience, fear, and anger. I responded to her love and care in similar fashion. It was a miracle Kim and I did not kill each other—or did we?

A Cry For Me

Chapter 12

Tina left me alone. She told me that she was going to run some errands and visit some friends. Her son, Tyree, was staying with his father. I did not have to worry about being disturbed by him. Sharon was out in the streets somewhere. I had the house to myself. I could have the silence necessary to sort out my dilemma. Do I stay with Kim and follow her program or do I avoid her my entire life?

I knew that I could not avoid Kim my entire life. It was idiotic to even think that I could. It was even more idiotic for Kim to think that she could make me submit to her parental authority overnight. She had to have known that the street life had already captured me. Perhaps even won my soul. I had no idea what I wanted from life; all I knew was what I didn't want. I did not want to leave Eager Street, and I did not want Kim telling me what to do, or not to do. I did not want to live under the same roof as Calvin. He was my competitor. His weed shop on Washington Street was jumping. His bags contained a greater quantity and quality of marijuana than mine. Hell, it was because of Calvin that I had to keep my shop open well into the wee hours. I often had to wait until he sold out of his inventory or closed his business for the day in order to sell my weed.

Out of all the tall dark handsome men in the world, Kim had to choose this nigga as a boyfriend. It was as if some cosmic joke was being played on me. I had not been to church or prayed since my great-grand parents' death four or five years prior. Therefore, God was manipulating the laws of the universe to upset my life. That's the only explanation for Kim's abrupt behavior.

During the school session, I attended regularly. I had done all right in school. I had passed to the seventh grade. When school start up in September, I planned on being there. I was finished with elementary school; I was looking forward to my first year of junior high. I wanted to attend Hampstead where all my homeys went.

Kim was ruining that, too. She had taken it upon herself to enroll me into Clifton Park. It was the high school in the district where we moved. I asked her, "Why can't we just keep usin' Mama's address?"

"Because we ain't," she had replied. "I ain't gonna be sendin' you to school to hang out with yo' friends."

My academic fate was sealed. I had to attend school with them up the hill niggas. I would be on foreign soil. All my friends from 101 Elmer A. Henderson Elementary School went to Hampstead or Herring Run Junior High. Black, Squirt. Wayne, Kirk, and Greg were already attending Hampstead. They were a year or two ahead of me. I had been looking forward to joining my niggas up at the school. I had concentrated on my studies. I had been very diligent with my home and class assignments so that I would be promoted to the next grade level. I had maintained good behavior; I was not taking any chances. I wanted to go to Hampstead.

I pleaded with Kim, "I wanna go to Hampstead.

"You goin' to Clifton."

"I'm gonna ask Mama can I go to Hampstead."

"Mama don't have custody of you, I do," Kim said. "You will go to school where I say."

It was a dictatorship. The only way to be liberated was to rebel. I had to make myself unwanted by Kim. I had to be such a problem for her that she would send me back to Mama, where I was certain to be ignored.

My thoughts were running wild. I was there in Tina's bed plotting and scheming, trying to come up with a way to escape Kim's dictatorship until I dozed off to sleep. I was awakened by Tina's panic. "Tray, your Aunt Kim saw me 'round the corner," she was nervous. "She told me to tell you 'get your ass home.'"

"You ain't tell her where I was?" I had to know.

"No," Tina responded as if my question was stupid. "Why would I do that?"

The question did not require a response. "How mad was she?"

"Boy, Kim is mad as shit!" Tina was laughing as she described Kim's emotional state. But she was very concerned about the matter. "What's goin' on?"

"Nothin'."

"Don't give me no, 'nothin' shit," Tina was demanding an explanation. "Your aunt was hollerin' at me. Tellin' me that if I keep messin' with you, she gonna send me to jail—after she whips my ass."

Tina was in it now. I felt compelled to explain the situation to her. She might provide me with some clarity. "Kim want to start treatin' me like I'm some baby or somethin'. She want me to stop sellin' weed, come home by eleven o'clock. All kinds of dumb shit." I had a sympathetic ear and I was going to make my case. "I don't need nobody tryin' to be my mother."

Tina obviously agreed. She pulled me close to her and kissed me tenderly on the mouth. She told me that everything would be okay. "Worry about Kim tomorrow." She pushed me flat onto the bed and began to kiss me on my lips and neck while she undressed me. In moments, Tina and I were both disrobed and locked into a passionate embrace. We made love, which simply meant I kissed her and held her after sexual intercourse. I was not in love with Tina. She was not in love with me. I was a financial benefit to her, and she permitted me to bask in her feminine delicacies whenever I desired. Fair exchange ain't no robbery. I rarely, if ever, made love to women. I generally used them and ducked them afterward.

After intercourse, I felt no need or desire to hold a sexual partner in my arms to share intimacy. I learned early in life that emotional attachments are complicated and ultimately end in heartbreak and hardship. I had desperately tried to attach myself emotionally to my mother; she rejected me. It hurt like hell. I was not going to do that loving somebody stuff again. Women could not be trusted with my heart. I trusted my mother with it, and she broke it. I was determined not to ever let another woman hurt me via rejection.

I was profoundly afraid to be connected to a woman beyond anything sexual and superficial. I thoroughly enjoyed the satisfying comfort of women, but I did not trust them. Now Tina was trying her best to comfort me. She was kissing my body in places that had never been kissed before. She brought me to a complete state of relaxation and peace of mind. I remember I ejaculated several times that night. At that point in my life, no women had brought me as much sexual pleasure as Tina. I had only had about five or six sexual partners, but Tina stood head and shoulders above them all. Now, years later, only one or two other women have brought me better satisfaction.

Tina fucked me into a deep sleep. When I awoke, it was to Kim standing in Tina's bedroom swinging an electronic extension cord at our naked bodies. She was yelling at Tina, "Bitch didn't I tell you I was gonna whip your ass?"

Tina was reaching for the covers to shield herself from Kim's vicious attack. I was left exposed and likely looking pathetic. I leaped from the bed and cowered in the nearest corner, looking around for my clothes.

Tina had begun to fight back in vain, "Bitch you crazy."

The two women exchanged blows until Calvin appeared along with my cousin Terrance to separate them. In the confusion, I managed to find some of my clothing to cover myself. Kim and Tina shouted obscenities at each other and exchanged punches until Calvin pulled Kim from the bedroom. Kim and Tina shouted at each other through the closed door. "Bitch I ain't finished with you," Kim's angry voice was coming through the door. "I told you to leave my nephew alone."

"Well, bitch, I didn't," Tina shot back.

"Tray," Kim's anger was coming toward me. "Get your clothes on and get your ass out here 'fore I come back in there."

"I'm comin'," I mumbled like a defeated punk. "Fuck you Terrance," I shot at Terrance, who remained in the room to get a full look at Tina's naked body and a heartfelt laugh at my embarrassing situation.

Tina was too enraged, I suspect, to be embarrassed. She simply wanted to know how Kim, Terrance, and Calvin had gotten into her house. She presented the question to Terrance. He told her that Sharon, her sister, had allowed them in.

"Sharon," Tina bellowed. "Why you let these crazy mothafuckas in my house?" Sharon materialized; she came through the bedroom door as Tina and I got hurriedly and suitably dressed. "I ain't know," Sharon was trying desperately to withhold her laughter. "They just knocked on the door asking for you. When I open it, the big girl ran in and up the steps."

I decided I had better leave with Kim without protest. If I said anything at that point, I would have received further embarrassment. Tina was humiliated, and I did not want to compound the situation.

Kim was still holding the extension chord in her hand when I came from the bedroom. She pulled me by the ear with one hand and slapped me hard in the back of my head with her other one. "Get your ass in the car!" She instructed. "Calvin, hold him so he won't run."

"I ain't running no more," I was being firm. "We gonna get to the bottom of this 'cause you ain't my mother."

Kim told me that it didn't matter. She told Tina that if she caught her around me again, she was going to administer her a severe ass whipping. Kim went on to tell her that if I had contracted any venereal disease from her nasty ass, the police would be called and charges would be filed. Aunt Kim let Tina know that I was only twelve years old; she had no business letting me stay in her house all times of night. Kim concluded by telling Tina, "You ought to be ashamed of yo'self. You no good bitch."

Calvin's sky blue Chrysler was parked directly in front of Tina's house. He ushered me to the rear seat of the car and closed the door. He performed his duty as a security guard admirably. But if I wanted to flee, I could've. It would have been easy for me to punch Calvin in the face and run. But I was not going to run anymore. Kim and I were going to get to the bottom of this. I was profoundly embarrassed. It was about eight or nine o'clock in the morning. A lot of folks were out sitting on their steps and sweeping their fronts. I had been shamed in public, and I hated the feeling. Everyone seemed to find some kind of humor in this situation except for Kim, Tina, and me. Calvin, Sharon, Terrance, and everyone I saw in my peripheral vision were laughing.

When Kim got into the car and we pulled away from the scene of my utter humiliation, I was pleased. We drove in silence for quite some time. Kim was truly distraught. She was calling upon the Lord, Jesus, to grant her strength. Tears were coming from her eyes and she finally admitted to me, "Tray, I love you but I don't know what to do."

I had no response. This was the first time I ever saw Kim cry, and it was over me. She knew that I needed a parent figure in my life, and she was not equipped to be it. I had already experienced too much; I was already captured by the street life. I could not be subjected to parental authority. But for Kim's sake, I was going to try. Her tears convinced me that I should "play house" with her and Calvin. We just had to negotiate some terms. For instance, the summer was not over and an eleven o'clock curfew was going to be a problem. We might be able to work out the other matters, but we would definitely have to extend the hours of my curfew, if there was to be a curfew at all.

Busted

Chapter 13

The summer of 1980 was coming to an end, and life at 1800 N. Durham Street was pretty good. Kim and I had agreed to a midnight curfew. If there was a special party or if I was staying over at a friend's house, all I had to do was seek her approval, let her know where I was going to be. Kim told me that I could no longer sell weed or shoplift to earn money. I told Kim that I was sitting on a lot of David's weed. I told her once I sold the rest of what I had, I would not get anymore. There was no compromising on that issue. Kim told me, "Give that nigga back his shit today."

I protested, "Kim, that nigga ain't no joke; he ain't gonna go for me takin' his shit...." Kim slapped me across my lip before I could finish my sentence.

"You better watch your mouth 'fore you lose your teeth!"

I really didn't intend on employing any expletive, but it slipped out. "Kim, that nigga ain't no joke. He want his money for his product."

"You scared of David?" She was challenging my masculinity. "'Cause I'll take that shit around there and give it back to that punk-ass nigga."

I was silent. I could offer a response. Everyone knew that David was a punk. Calvin was one, too. But I didn't want to make the comparison. Calvin was proving to be a great provider to our little family.

"He ain't have no business givin' you no drugs anyway," Kim continued. "Who he think he is?"

"Okay," I was going to lie. "I'll give him his stuff back."

I had just copped three pounds of weed. I stood to make at least a thousand dollars; I was not going to pass up that golden opportunity. Kim could have cried until her eyes fell out, and she could have slapped me around until her hand turned blue and purple, I was going to get my cut of the profit from the sale of the weed. Besides, I had to consider Squirt and Black. They had a cut in the latest deal I had brokered with David. I could not disappoint my dogs. I was simply going to be discrete in selling the weed.

Kim seldom came down on Eager Street once we moved on Durham. She stayed up the hill, where we lived. The homemaker's role suited her nicely. She had decorated our home to be comfortable, prepared hot delicious meals everyday, and provided me with an environment that was almost normal. Almost, for Calvin was selling a lot of drugs. I thought he was only distributing marijuana, but he was selling heroin, too. He was keeping company with Boxie, a major player moving dope out of Flag House Project. Our house guests were some fascinating characters. Calvin was popular, and he employed many dealers in his operation. I knew the possibility was great that someone would tell Kim that I was still selling weed. But I didn't really care. Calvin was not going to be the only shot caller at 1800 N. Durham Street. I was going to handle my own affairs—even if I had to be secretive.

Calvin and I had begun to grow close. He knew I was still doing my thing. He had caught me selling a bag of weed to this young lady, Leslie, he was fucking. We made a pact, I told him that I would not tell my Aunt Kim he was cheating on her with Leslie if he did not tell her I was selling weed. Calvin had reservations about that deal. He was concerned that I may bring drugs into the house where we both laid our heads each night. I told Calvin that I had recently brokered a deal with David. I had close to three pounds of weed to get rid of, and once I finished selling what Squirt, Black, and I had left, I was going to be out of the business. I told him that I tried to express that to Kim, but she wouldn't have it. I told Calvin that if I pulled out right then, I would probably have a conflict with David, Squirt, and Black. He understood my dilemma, and told me that I had one week to tie up my loose ends. If there was a problem about money, he would make up the difference. Calvin went on to tell me that he loved Kim and that he wanted her to be happy. She was very afraid for me out there in the streets selling narcotics. Kim's fear for me was interfering with her happiness, so I had to stop selling drugs. Moreover, Calvin needed to know, "Why you wanna be out here sellin' this shit?" He let me know that he was going to take care of me. I was his family.

I told Calvin I was not impressed with his sentiments. I was capable of taking care of myself. But for the sake of peace, I was going to follow the program.

Fate had always had a peculiar way of dealing with me. I was down on Eager Street getting rid of the last of the weed when four or five narcotics police jumped out of their unmarked car and threw Squirt and me on the wall for a search and seizure. "Mr. Jones... Mr. Wilson, step over here." The narcotics police I knew as Peanut was holding me by my arms guiding me toward the wall of a store building on the corner of Durham and Eager Streets. "You little fuckers been selling quite a bit of marijuana on this corner. Where's y'all buddy?"

Totally flabbergasted, I asked, "Man what's this shit 'bout?"

"Yeah," Squirt joined in. "Why y'all crackers messin' with us?"

Peanut and another plainclothes detective searched Squirt and me. They went through our pockets and asked us stupid questions.

"Where the drugs?"

"Where the guns?"

"Where the money?"

Squirt and I stood next to each other with our arms raised high above our head, facing the wall with our hands pressed flat against the wall. The police were searching the area around us looking for illegal drugs and guns. Several people in the neighborhood began to gather around to see what was happening. A crowd formed in the late afternoon hours as the Baltimore City Narcotics Unit searched Squirt and me. It was very hot and humid, and I was nervous. I was sweating profusely and knew intuitively that this was more than just a routine frisk by the cops. These "knockers" came directly to Squirt and me, and they had specifically asked about Black. The best thing to do was to exercise my "right to remain silent" and pray that Squirt was smart enough to do likewise.

My arms were beginning to ache, but I was versed enough in this process to know to keep my arms up and not appear distraught. Play it tough and be cool. If I revealed any weakness, the police would come in for the kill and do everything they could to reduce me to a snitch, an informant. I had to let it be known from the beginning that I was not going to be a snitch. I was strong enough to carry my own weight. I knew the code, and it was time that I demonstrated it to the Baltimore City Police.

"Turn around and look at me," Peanut was granting me relief. "Y'all might as well talk, 'cause the ugly gold tooth son-of-bitch is telling us everything."

Squirt shot me quick nervous glance. He was talking about David, our connect. Something serious was afoot, Squirt and I realized that instantly.

"What do that gotta do with me?" Squirt was standing like a strong soldier.

I had already made up my mind that I was not going to utter another word until I was in the presence of my lawyer, or Aunt Kim. One of the strictest rules of the "code" is: Don't say shit to the police until you have a lawyer present. And even then, tell your lawyer before you say it to the police. "Be cool, man," I wanted Squirt to obey the strict rule of the code. "Let's wait 'til we get a lawyer."

"Look at the little dummies tryin' be smart," one of the white police officers said. "Call the wagon and let's get outta here."

"Where y'all takin' my son," Ms. Lawcy, Squirt's mother, was making her way through the crowd toward us. "What did he do?"

I felt a rush of comfort at seeing Ms. Lawcy. These white police were not going to frighten her. She would definitely get answers before she permitted them to cart her son off to jail.

Ms. Lawcy walked directly over to Squirt and me as if she was going to shield us from the threatening white police officers. "Why are y'all messin' with my boys?" I was included in the defense this time, and I was grateful.

"We have observed these two dealing with a drug dealer, David, around the corner—then come here to this corner to sell marijuana they got from him." The cop known as Peanut offered us an explanation for our arrest. "We came down here and searched the area and found a large quantity of the stuff."

"Hell no!" I was being lied on.

"Fuck no," Squirt was just as shocked about the police's last remark. "Where y'all find some reefer?"

The police ignored Squirt's question and directed his attention to Ms. Lawcy, "Ma'am, come down to Eastern District and we will answer all your questions there."

It was settled; Squirt and I were going to jail. How long we would be there was unknown. We had been detained by various store security officers for shoplifting until our respective parents came to retrieve us, but this was the very first time either Squirt or I were taken all the way to a police station.

Kim was going to be mad at me, I was certain. Whether or not she was going to leave me in jail was a matter I had doubts about. I had promised Kim only days prior that I was going to give David his reefer back. I assured her that I was going to stop dealing. Now, here I was on my way to the police station, under arrest for selling weed. Damn, fate had a way of dealing with me.

When the paddy wagon arrived to take Squirt and me to the police station, I was enraged. I had laid a perfect lie down. I was going to sell the rest of the weed I had, and get out of the business. All I needed was another two or three days, and I would have been out of the drug business. The police are forever messing up someone's get-rich-quick plans. I hated them. When they finally handcuffed me and put Squirt and me into the back of the wagon, I knew that I was not going to let the police get the upper hand on me. They had just told Ms. Lawcy a blatant lie. They did not find any weed where Squirt and I were. Our stuff was in Tina's house, and they did not go there. I was completely baffled about the large quantity of marijuana that was allegedly found.

"Squirt, you have some weed out there somewhere?" Squirt and I were finally alone in the back of the paddy wagon on our way to the police station.

"Fuck no," Squirt was being honest. "Them bitches gettin' ready to frame us."

Squirt and I decided to keep our mouth shut. If the police were going to frame us, there wasn't much we could do. It was the reality of our world. The police accused, and we denied. Sometimes they told the truth and sometimes they lied. Whichever side told the most persuasive tale would prevail in the court of law. Truth hardly ever mattered. I guess that's why so much credence is given to the adage, "The truth is what you make it." It's a legal concept.

David and the rest of his crew were at the police station by the time we got there. As we dismounted from the paddy wagon, I heard David hollering at us from one of the windows, "Hold strong, young bloods."

"No doubt, nigga," I felt brave. My nerves were settled. "Be cool."

Squirt remained silent, but I could detect from his body language that he felt a surge of confidence. David's voice was reassuring.

The police took us into a very small and cramped room with one small table and three plastic folding chairs. The room was dim, very poorly lit. The walls were gray or dirty white. The room reeked of tobacco and sweat. There were no windows and the only apparent ventilation was a noisy fan in the corner. "Sit down," a large white uniformed police officer ordered Squirt and me to take one of the chairs. "Somebody will be in here to talk to you."

We asked the police to take the handcuffs off of us, but he refused. He told us to get used to wearing handcuffs. He asked us our names, ages, and phone numbers. The questions were harmless enough, so we answered them truthfully. He left Squirt and me alone in the room, "I'm going to call your parents."

We waited alone in the room wondering where all this was leading. We were, without a doubt, in trouble. However, we were not going to torture ourselves about what we had no control over. We were victims of fate and products of our environment. Whatever happened, we had to meet it head on. Squirt and I did not yet know that we were capable of creating out of our world whatever we wished. Environment and fate could only have as much effect on us as we permit.

When Detective Moore, the first black officer I had seen up to that point, entered the room where Squirt and I were being held, my heart was already hardened. The police had long since murdered my father, and here they are poised to lie on me about some drugs that did not belong to me. I was not going to cooperate in my arrest or the arrest of anyone else. I was not going to be pleasant.

"Arlando," Detective Moore began, "where you get your reefer from?"

"Your mama," was my ugly retort.

I got a threatening look from the detective, but he left me alone and directed the same question to Squirt. Squirt told him that he got his reefer from the same place I got mine. Detective Moore asked us both a few more meaningless questions about David, but we insisted that we didn't know him.

Detective Moore told us that not only did they observe our countless dealings with David over the summer, they heard him speak to us as we arrived at the police station. I informed the officer that he was mistaken. I reminded the officer that I was only twelve and I was afraid. I wanted to see my grandmother or Aunt Kim. Squirt followed my lead. He said the exact same thing as I. The only exception was Squirt said that he was fourteen.

In obvious frustration and anger, Detective Moore knocked the table that was between us to the floor and slung the chair he was sitting in crashing into the wall.

"I'm tired of y'all shit," he grabbed me by the collar of my shirt and snatched me to my feet. "You answer my questions or I'm gonna kick your ass."

I was too angry to be afraid. I had on a brand new Polo shirt, and this son-of-a-bitch was ruining it. Besides, Detective Moore had a very strong odor coming from his mouth, and he was too close to my face.

"Did you fart, or is that your breath?"

My question enraged the detective. He threw me down to the floor in frustration and stormed from the room.

She Protects Her Young

Chapter 14

Kim was at the police station within the hour. I could detect her anger and nervousness being placed in this situation, but she maintained a dignified composure. She came into the little cramped room where Squirt and I had been sitting and sat down next to me. I sensed at that moment that Kim would do whatever she could to get me out of the clutches of the law. Good or bad, right or wrong, Kim was my ally. She would loyally stand at my side until the day she died.

Now, my Aunt Kim had a very pretty face. Her dimpled cheeks and radiant smile always had a way of soothing me. "What's goin' on Kim?" I was no longer afraid. I was prepared to face whatever was to come. However, I still wanted to go home. There was no marijuana found on me, or around me. I could see no reason why I should remain in police custody.

The smile and dimples were on display, "Your bad ass scared now, huh?"

If that dimpled smile had not been there, I might have been afraid—a little. "Nope," I was being honest. "I just wanna know what's goin' on."

"Me too," Squirt put in. "Where's my mother?"

"She's still out there talkin' to the lady from Juvenile Services," Kim informed. "I already talked to her. Now we gotta wait to see if she gonna let you go home."

"Kim, I ain't have no weed." I wanted Kim to know that I was about to be framed. I told her that the police had told Ms. Lawcy that they found a large quantity of marijuana, but it didn't have a thing to do with me. I wanted her to believe that I had honored my promise to her and that I gave David the weed back.

"Just shut the fuck up." Kim was determined to deal with that issue later, at home. That is, if I was released to her custody. Kim told Squirt and me that the lady from Juvenile Service would probably let us go home in our parents' custody. No drugs were actually discovered on or around Squirt and me. However, the narcotics unit was saying that they had had us under surveillance for the past seven days, and they knew we were dealing marijuana for David. Kim told the woman from Juvenile Services that the police were liars. Her child was not a drug dealer. Ms. Lawcy was presently in another room with the lady and narcotic detectives expressing the same point. The only difference was that Ms. Lawcy was not being as diplomatic as Kim had been. She was angrily and forcefully defending her son.

Kim and Ms. Lawcy obviously prevailed. Not long after Kim came into that dingy room, soothing me, Ms. Lawcy and the woman from Juvenile Services came to let Kim, Squirt, and me know that we were being released. However, we would have to appear in court before a juvenile master to determine our ultimate fate in the matter. A subpoena would be coming in the mail within the month. We were warned that if we were arrested for anything before then, we would be detained at the Maryland Training School for Boys until our court appearance. The only reason Squirt and I were being released was because this was our very first arrest. The charges were serious, but since nothing was found directly on us, we were going to get the benefit of the doubt.

Kim and Ms. Lawcy profusely thanked the elderly white woman from Juvenile Services for allowing Squirt and me to go home. Personally, I didn't think that I should have been arrested. No drugs or money were found on me. If I was guilty of anything, some evidence should have been provided. I should not have had to go through all this simply because some white police said they observed me doing something illegal. All niggas look alike to them, anyway. I was involved in criminal activity, but who is to say for certain I was not being accused of someone else's crime. I did not feel that the white woman from Juvenile Services deserved a "thank you" from me. She was doing her job. There was no evidence to support the charges against me. The corrupt bastards had no right throwing me against a wall and forcing me to hold my arms above my head until they ached. They were wrong to go through my pockets, handcuff me, and bring me to this ugly room in the basement of the police station. It was wrong for an officer to attempt to intimidate me and ultimately throw me to the floor. Why should I show gratitude? Moreover, I was going to be in trouble with Kim. Although the police did not have enough evidence to convince the woman from Juvenile Services to detain me in a penal facility, they had enough to prove to Kim that I had lied to her.

I Ain't Much, But I'm All I Got

Chapter 15

When Kim and I came home from the police station, she immediately tore into me. "You don't believe shit stink?" It was a question that did not warrant an answer. "Your ass goin' to Training School because you don't want to listen."

I knew from experience that I would fare better if I simply pretended to listen and not utter a word. Kim knew that she was right. If I attempted to prove her wrong, she would slap me, or worse, reach for an extension cord. I simply listened to everything she had to say, and wished that she would hurry up and complete her diatribe. I had a lot to think about and, possibly, to do. David and the whole crew had just been arrested. How much trouble was I really in? Moreover, I knew that Tina was a cruddy bitch. If I did not find her quickly, she would claim that she had to throw my weed away. Tina would claim that she panicked when she saw the police grab Squirt and me. I knew that she would do that because that is what I would do. I had every intention on telling David that I lost all the weed; the police got it. I threw it away when they ran down on me. I was going to tell him something. For one of the cruelest rules of the code is: if you get locked up holding another nigga's stuff, he doesn't get paid. When the police snatch up a crew, the boss loses all around the board. I guess that's why they say "it's lonely at the top."

"You ain't gonna take your ass out this house until school start," Kim was getting my attention. "And that ain't 'til September."

"Kim," I protested. "I ain't do nothin'. I stopped slingin' for dem niggas 'bout a week ago."

I had to convince her to let me go outside immediately. She had said I could not go outside for the rest of the summer. That was about three weeks away. Kim had to know that it was ridiculous to think that she could keep me in the house for three weeks. I imagine she was afraid for me. She had just picked me up from the police station. I had been accused of participating in a conspiracy to distribute narcotics. I would still be in police custody if I were not a minor child with an unblemished record. Kim was just trying to protect me.

The only reason I am probably still alive today is because others looked out for me—and prayed for me. I was too stupid to do either for myself. In any event, all I could think about was catching up with Tina so I could retrieve my narcotics and money. I had a pound of weed and twelve hundred dollars in cash at Tina's house.

I could not tell Kim about that. I needed Calvin to hurry up and bring his ass home. He would understand my crisis. Whether or not he would help me was another matter. Calvin had a way of keeping me confused. Sometimes he would act like a real nigga, and other times he would act like a sissy. It was hard to predict him. However things went, I was going down the hill to see Tina and find out what I could. I told Kim that I needed to know why I was arrested. Yes, I admitted, I was standing out there on the corner talking to Squirt and some other guys, but I was not selling reefer. Kim told me I was lying. She told me that she had heard from one of her friends that I was selling weed as recently as yesterday, the day before my arrest. Damn, which one of her friends told on me? It could have been any one of them. They all smoked weed, and I was not too discriminating about who I sold to. If he or she had the money to make a purchase, I would sell it. But that's how things were. No one was supposed to go back and say, "Kim, I bought some weed from your nephew."

I told Kim that whoever told her that he bought weed from me was lying. But it was all in vain. Kim told me that I was forbidden to leave the house until school began in September. I mumbled that she was out of her damn mind to think that I was going to stay in some house for three weeks. But she did not hear me. I was on my way to my bedroom when I mumbled the statement—out of her hearing range. When I got to my room and onto my bed, I was satisfied to be out of her presence. I did not want to hear any more threats about going to Training School. And I was certainly tired of hearing her go on and on about how she was the only one willing to take care of me.

It seemed like Kim rarely passed up an opportunity to let me know that she was making a significant sacrifice to be my legal guardian. I wanted to tell her that I was capable of taking care of myself. I did not need anyone or anything. Besides, I did not ask her to assume guardianship over me. I did not ask for anything or anyone. By the time Kim assumed guardianship over me, it was too late to mold me into some choirboy. I was beyond correction via petty punishments and whippings. Kim had to know that I was not going to stay in the house for the remaining three weeks of the summer. I wasn't even going to stay in the house for the remaining portion of the day. I had business to take care of. I needed clarity on the matter involving my arrest, and I needed to know whether David and the rest of the crew made it home. Above all, I had to find Tina to make sure she didn't mess up my stuff. I satisfied myself that I would wait until ten o'clock that night to sneak out to see Tina and check on David.

It was about eight o'clock and not quite nightfall. Kieshawn was outside in the neighborhood playing, and I had no idea where Yalanda was. Calvin, no doubt, was out in the street hustling. Kim and I were home. It was a Friday, and I was positive that Kim would step outdoors soon. If not, I would exit the house by the window. She would know I left. I would have to be extremely lucky to go unnoticed, but that was not going to happen. Kim was expecting me to escape punishment, and I was going to escape. It was a foregone conclusion.

It was Kim's parental duty to launch some kind of sanction against me, given the circumstances, and I had to feign acceptance because I loved her. In my heart, I did not fear the whippings. I did not even fear she would get tired of my constant disobedience and forfeit responsibility of me. I was seldom afraid of anything. I felt that whatever happened to me could not be worse than what had already happened.

Those who were responsible for rearing me had failed me. In my heart, at twelve years of age, I knew that I was all alone. I was not the primary objective in anyone's life. Kim had two children, and though her love for me was genuine, Kieshawn and Yalanda were her primary objective—before heroin addiction took over her life.

My grandmother loved me, too. But my Uncle Derrick, her youngest son, was her priority, next to alcohol, I suppose. I held no regrets for not being anyone's favorite child. I felt totally confident that I could spoil myself. I did not have to be anyone's favorite. All I needed was liberties. Let me run the streets without a curfew and I would clothe, feed, shelter, and love myself. I hated being at home. At home, I was generally ignored, or made to feel like a nuisance and a bother. Out on the corners with my friends, I felt acceptance.

I slept awhile and when I awoke, no one was in the house, and it was nearing ten o'clock. Almost five hours had passed since I was arrested and two hours since my release. Kim had instructed me not to leave the house under any circumstances, but I was not going to heed her instruction. I had damn near a thousand dollars worth of narcotics and over a thousand dollars in cash to retrieve. Kim would just have to be mad.

I brushed my teeth, washed my face, and left the house. I couldn't care less about Kim discovering me missing. Hell, I was not even certain I was coming back home. Kim had truly wounded me when she told me, "You ain't my child. I ain't gotta keep goin' through this shit with you." I did not understand, at that time, that she was simply frustrated. She probably did not mean any of what she said. She was a young black woman trying to rear a misguided boy into manhood. A lot of the things she did to me and said to me came from a sense of fear, frustration, and anger.

I walked the mile or so to Tina's house. I was not all that concerned about exercising discretion. I knocked on her front door, and it did not matter if someone saw me enter the house or not. I was checking on my wealth, and to hell with anybody who didn't understand. I was determined to be my own man; I couldn't permit Kim to regulate my life.

"Baby," Tina looked genuinely pleased to see me. "I thought y'all asses was gone." She laid the foundation for her scandalous lie as I stepped into the house and closed the door behind me.

But I was not about to get played—easily. "Well I'm here," I calmly stated. "I ain't nowhere but here."

"Tray, I thought they was gonna come in here. I threw the weed down the toilet."

There it was. She had complied with her nature and conformed to the laws of our game—beat a sucker every time you get the opportunity. The chance doesn't come too often.

I gave Tina a quizzical look to let her know that I was not fooled by her. But what could I do? She said that she flushed it down the toilet. I was going to tell David the same thing, or something similar.

"So the weed is gone."

"Yeap."

"Did you tell Squirt?"

"Yeah, he know," she walked in front of me as if to avoid my stare. "He upstairs with Sharon, now."

I went past Tina and up the stairs to Sharon's bedroom to see Squirt. I wanted to get his assessment of our day. I knew Squirt would know everything I needed to know. "Yo Yo," I called out before entering the bedroom. "What's happenin' baby-boy?"

"Shit real raggedy," Squirt stated in a matter-of-fact manner. "Ray-Ray and Monk out on bail, but they still holdin' David."

I wanted to know why David was still being held, but I knew that if Squirt had known he would have told me. I asked Squirt if he was okay, and he assured me that he was. He asked me how did I get out. He knew that Kim would have me on lock-down. I told him that I had simply left the house. "Fuck Kim, she don't tell me what to do."

At that, Sharon who had been silently covering her nakedness under the sheets, giggled loudly. "You better get out of here 'fore that crazy woman come back here lookin' for you with her extension cord."

Squirt and I laughed, then I snatched the sheet from Sharon. Damn, she was gorgeous. Squirt and I would have to discuss the possibility of sharing or switching sexual partners.

"Boy," she feigned anger, "stop playin' so damn much."

I ushered Squirt out of the room so that we could discuss the missing weed. "Squirt, you know these bitches beat us," I said the moment we were alone in the hall.

"Yeah," Squirt was being nonchalant. "I'm hip, but what can we do, kick their ass?" We both understood how ridiculous that would have been. We just had to get a pound's worth of sex, and be grateful that the $1,200 we had stashed in the house was undisturbed.

"Tina," I cheerfully called. "Come 'ere, boo." I headed to Tina's bedroom to get my initial payment for the missing weed. Squirt went back to Sharon's room.

• • •

Tina offered me a sexual treat like she had never before. She was extra sensual and more attentive to details. She kissed every part of my body, giving me the best head I ever had in my entire life. Future sexual partners would come close to affording me as much oral sex satisfaction as Tina had, but none bested her. She was totally uninhibited, and I had hoped that it was because I was special. It would tear at my self-esteem if word ever got back to me that Tina simply gave "good head." She didn't do anything for me that she didn't do for her other lovers.

Kim was going to kick my ass when I got home. I was absolutely sure about that. I even confessed that to Tina. I told her that Kim had ordered me to stay in the house until school started in about three weeks. I told Tina that the only reason I was defying Kim was because I had to be with her at least one more time. Of course, she knew I was lying. I came there to retrieve my weed and money.

It was a good thing Squirt and I elected not to tell Tina and Sharon about the money. We had long suspected that the sisters were using heroin and, therefore, could not be trusted. Squirt and I had discovered that our inventory of marijuana had been coming up short in the past. We had caught Tina and Sharon nodding on different occasions, but they would pretend to be sleepy. I recall seeing Tina nodding as if in a heroin-induced state, and I asked her, "What you done had?"

She told me that she had drunk alcohol and smoked marijuana. When I insisted that weed and liquor don't make anyone nod like she was nodding, she added that she was also tired from a lack of sleep. Sharon had offered similar excuses, but Squirt and I were not naïve. A lot of folks in our neighborhood were on heroin. If I could spot anything, I could spot a dope-fiend a mile away.

Tina and her sister were on heroin; that's why I had to hurry up and get to her about my narcotics. I knew in my heart that my weed was gone the minute Squirt and I were ushered away in handcuffs. My defying Kim's instruction and going to see Tina about the drugs was an exercise in futility and stupidity. Squirt would have retrieved our money and made certain that I received my share. I had to be a damn fool. Well, at least the head was great.

When I got home about two or three o'clock in the morning, Kim was sitting right there in the living room. She had positioned herself in the corner of the room where she was not immediately seen as I came through the door. I tried to close the door gently so as to not wake any one in the house that might be asleep. "Ain't no need in you tryin' to sneak your ass in here now," Kim was seething with anger. "You know I told you not to go out."

Kim's words froze me; I could not move. I simply stared at her shadow image rise from the couch and come toward me. I noticed the extension cord wrapped around her fist. I could not escape her fury. Kim was all over me, the extension chord was ripping into my flesh and the pain was wreaking havoc in my mind. I cried out and begged her to stop hitting me and let me explain why I had to leave the house. But it was to no avail. She whipped me until she got tired. And I swear, that woman did not tire easily or quickly.

"Now get upstairs and take a bath," Kim shouted at me after she was finished beating me. "And wash that funky bitch off you."

Without a moment of hesitation, I rushed to the bathroom. The noise of my whipping had awakened Kieshawn and Yalanda. They were crying along with me. I was thoroughly embarrassed and in considerable pain. I should have had enough sense to wear jeans or some other kind of long pants and shirt. I knew the ass-whipping was coming.

I ran water for a bath and decided that I was going to stay the hell away from Kim for the next few days, and do everything she instructed me to do. In a single day, I had gotta the worse ass whipping and the best blow job I had ever received in my entire life. I could not determine whether or not that day was a good one or a bad one.

I felt completely empty inside as I sat in the bathtub soaking my emotional and physical wounds. No one understood me, and I had no way of expressing to anyone that I felt absolutely alone in the world. I could not trust that anyone, other than myself, would take care of me. I did not want to be part of a family. It was too disappointing. Kim was being cruel to me. I did not want her love and attention. Why was she trying to insist that I be grateful to her for her affection, love, and parental supervision? I did not want it. I did not need anyone to care for me. I was perfectly capable of caring for myself. I had done okay for myself so far. Besides, the cosmos had prescribed that I navigate life alone. My loneliness was so profound, I thought that it was a natural part of existence.

I had intentionally set out to make myself unlovable, but Kim insisted on loving me. I rejected all her attempts to attach herself to me emotionally. She had Kieshawn and Yalanda. Mama had Derrick. I had no one, and I was content. I had soothed my own emotional hurts too many times to need assistance now.

Kim had won that round; I was going to comply with her wishes as long as they did not conflict with mine. For the time being, I was going to stay in the house and await my subpoena to appear in court before a juvenile master. I was going to accept my placement at Clifton Park Junior High. There was no avoiding school, although I had absolutely no use for academics. I could count from one to ten without difficulty, and the occupation I had chosen did not require education.

I have to admit, Kim set about making the perfect home. When I awoke in the late afternoon, she summoned me to the kitchen where she was preparing a meal. I can't recall what it was she was cooking, but I do recall it smelled good, and she gave me some. We sat at the kitchen table staring at each other in silence for what seemed like an eternity. Kieshawn was in the backyard playing some game with her playmates, and Yalanda was focused on some baby's toy in her high-chair. The mood was totally serene, distances away from the chaotic scene of that very same morning. The house was clean and smelling fresh. The atmosphere was so seductive that my anger toward Kim subsided... slightly.

"Tray," Kim was being gentle. "Do we gotta keep going through this shit?"

"No," I knew what she talking about. I also knew that she hated whipping me. She just did not know any other way to persuade me from the corner. She obviously could not reason with me on the matter. Her live-in boyfriend, Calvin, was selling more drugs than I ever had, and we were living quite decently because of if it. I grew up in a household under a grandfather who made a living from running numbers. I was surrounded by criminality. It was only reasonable that I would choose a lifestyle of crime. Besides, my father was a legendary "stick-up-boy." Folks around the neighborhood still spoke admiringly about his robbery capers.

"I'm gonna do right, Kim." She smiled lovingly at me.

"You don't have to stay in the house for the rest of the summer," Kim was offering a compromise. "Just don't go down the hill."

I had to accept that. Kim did not want me on Eager Street anymore. But the neighborhood we had moved to was just as crime-ridden. It would only be a matter of time, a day or two, before I discovered the underworld there. Hell, a lot of the jokers who lived around the eighteen hundred block of Durham often hung out "down the hill," in the 900 block of Durham. I was only about ten to twelve blocks away from my main stomping ground, and many of our new neighbors had patronized my weed shop.

I was in too deep. My entire moral constitution was built upon criminal codes of conduct, and my models for life were hustlers. I loved the "thug life," and for a long time, I thought it loved me. I was so disastrously wrong. The lifestyle I chose to live is incapable of producing and nurturing love. Everyone in the "thug life" gets used or uses. It is an unending cycle of use and abuse or get used and abused.

I did not know at twelve years of age that I had selected a lifestyle that would end in pure hardship and misery. My concept of life was that of a materialist. I wanted quick money—pockets full of it. I wanted fancy jewelry, cars, and an infamous image. I desired to be feared and revered.

My ascendancy to gangsterdom, a "thug-life-nigga," would have to wait. Kim wanted to be my parent, and she swung a mean whip. My skin was too damn tender to take that kind of abuse. Besides, life under Kim's and Calvin's parental supervision was not all that bad. Calvin had a host of boosters who brought him the latest fashions after they shoplifted from stores, so I stayed dressed in fashion. Calvin also had no problem with allowing me to wear his jewelry. His only concern was, "Don't let nobody take my shit from you."

I was hanging around my new neighborhood. I was not frequenting any areas where people got robbed. I started boxing again at Mack Lewis's Gym on Eager and Broadway. After training sessions ended, I went straight home, or close enough to home so as not to cause Kim to be concerned.

Kim thought I was plotting a scheme when I had asked her, "Can I go back to the gym?" I had quit boxing months prior. I had lost interest in the sport. The only reason I attended the gym in the first place was because Jab-Bo, one of my mother's boyfriends, had told me, "If you come in the gym, I'm gonna get my son to beat you up."

I rose to the challenge, and nearly everyday for a year, Vincent Pettaway, Jab-Bo's son, beat me up. I got tired of that kickin' Tray's ass" shit, so I left the gym. Pettaway tried to convince me to stay, but Squirt and the hustling game lured me into criminality.

I truly enjoyed the trips that Mr. Mack and Mr. Hatchet took me on to fight. We had a hell of a boxing team, most of our fighters won their matches. I had a five-wins-to-one-loss record before I left the gym—the first time.

"Tray," Kim was suspicious about my motive to return to the gym. "You just wanna get your ass back on Eager Street."

"No," I was being honest. "I just wanna box again."

Kim conceded and I started boxing again. Mr. Mack and Mr. Hatchet allowed me back into the gym without asking any questions. They had lost many children to the streets. They were sad when we left and rejoiced when we returned. Years into the future, when Mr. Mack would bring his fighters into the Penitentiary to stage exhibition fights with the Penitentiary's fighters, I would be grateful to him for not looking at me with shame and disappointment. He simply hugged me, inquired about my welfare, and passed no moral judgement. For that simple gesture of kindness and consideration, I will forever be grateful to him. Mr. Mack and Mr. Hatchet showed me

genuine concern, and they taught me how to fight. What more could I
have asked from two complete strangers? When Mr. Hatchet died, I truly
mourned his passing. I even offered a prayer for his kind soul.

The gym was truly my haven while I awaited my court subpoena and
the start of the school year. The physical exercise Mr. Hatchet took me
through was exhausting, and the camaraderie inside the gym was meaningful. I made it a priority to be in the gym each night, Monday through Friday, at 6 p.m. I always stayed there until eight o'clock. Sometimes, I stayed
until nine or ten. It depended upon what was happening.

Kim was quite pleased with me. My association with Squirt was dete-
riorating. I had absolutely no connections with anything negative. For the
last three weeks in the summer of 1980, I was a good kid. I did not sell any
drugs; I did not shoplift from any stores; I did not get any pussy. I came
damn close to being a choirboy.

By the time school started in September, I was in great physical condition. I was looking good and feeling good. Kim and Calvin had completed
my wardrobe with designer jeans of all sorts and every color of Lee pants
being marketed. Nike, Puma, and British Crates were the shoe-wear fashion,
and I had one or two pair of each. I definitely was not going to look like a
pauper in school. However, I had depleted my cash supply; my pockets were
empty. I could always ask Kim or Calvin for $5, or something like that, but
asking for money had always been too humbling an experience for me. The
clothes, food, and shelter came without me having to request them. Cash
was another matter entirely.

All the up the hill hustlers attended Clifton Park. Little Meaty, Fat
Dinky, and Little Timmy—and those cats were cool. But they were not my
dogs. Squirt, Ronald, Black, and Kirk were my dogs. I wanted to attend
school with them. I knew there was going to be conflict for me at Clifton
Park. I wanted to be with my dogs, but I was surrounded by cats. I was a
sharp dresser, fashioned in the latest designs. I was not shy around girls, and
I was in desperate need of some sexual satisfaction. I was not about to submit to the "Man, that's my girl" stuff. Where I came from, if you liked her
and she liked you, you "hit it." If some punk ass joker wanted to play the
jealous boyfriend role, whip his ass. I was from the dog pound, and I was
not going to allow them cats at Clifton Park to best me at anything. I didn't
care how cool they were. So, after one week at Clifton Park, the school's
administration acted as if they didn't want me to attend that raggedy school
anymore.

When Cats Scratch a Dog, He Bites

Chapter 16

Clifton Park Junior High School was an old three-story brownstone relic from the late nineteenth- or early twetieth-century. A simple glance at the structure would reveal that the school was not for rich kids. The ugly building was quite incongruent to the middle-class neighborhood it was situated in, sitting at the corner of 25th Street and Harford Road. The school building was likely an embarrassment to the city's officials. For that reason, probably, the structure sat back off the road, hidden. A train track was adjacent to the school, and most of us crossed the railroad tracks each morning on our way to school. The school's yard was huge, but it was never used for physical education purposes, or any other activities sponsored by the school. Inside the school building was worse. The lighting was extremely poor. It was always dim, and on cloudy days, without the sun's rays, it was outright dark. Some of the teachers brought their personal lamps from home for lighting.

I hated that school. It was truly depressing. It felt more like a penal institution than a place for learning. The rules were not strictly enforced—if there were any rules. One had to truly be bad to disturb the administration at Clifton Park. The girls visited the boys' bathrooms and the boys visited the girls'. We smoked weed and cigarettes in either lavatory. They were too filthy to do anything else in. I doubt that the school employed a maintenance crew to clean the building or make repairs. Aside from the main hallway, where the principal's office was located, the school looked disgraceful. Every other window was broken. The walls were covered with obscene graffiti; former students' names and addresses were scribbled on classroom doors and walls. The floors were scoffed and scraped. The school's building was woefully neglected. The Baltimore City school officials should have felt ashamed to allow a school such as Clifton Park to exist and operate in such condition.

The only good thing that Clifton Park offered me was the plethora of attractive girls and women who worked or attended there. There were two teachers at the school who I was simply in love with. One was a a Social Studies teacher and the other taught Science. I remember that the science teacher had the most gorgeous set of legs I ever laid eyes on. She was a tall very dark woman with ample everything: Ample round breast, ample round butt, and an ample smile. I routinely skipped my classes, but I rarely cut out of Science or Social Studies, and I never skipped them both on the same day. If I attended school on a particular day, I was certain to attend one or both of those classes. I seldom went to English, Math, or any of the other classes . There was a long hallway on the third floor, at the rear of the school, where we shot dice. Little Meaty had acquainted me with that gathering place my first day at the school. I lost my last ten dollars there, and I was determined to get it back. I only had the opportunity to attend one or two classes a day my first week at the school. Ms. Blum, the school's vice principal for the seventh grade, called me to her office one afternoon to tell me, "It would be nice if you went to some of your classes. You might actually learn something."

Ms. Blum wasn't being a disciplinarian, she was just offering me some friendly advice. I suppose Ms. Blum didn't want to offend me. She was an elderly white woman employed at an all-black inner-city school where teachers and other staff members were often assaulted by students and parents alike. Now that I look back , I understand why the school officials dealt with the student body at Clifton Park in a cavalier manner. They were afraid of us. Many of the students brought weapons to school, and were not afraid to use them. I learned just how prolific weapons were in the school one early afternoon when Little Timmy, Fat Dinky, some other cats, and myself assembled in the long hall to shoot some craps. Little Timmy told me that he was going to beat the game; therefore, I should wage my money on him. I had heard rumors that Little Timmy could cheat at dice. He loaded dice that could only land on certain numbers. I never knew how to cheat at craps, but I could spot a cheat, and since I was no lame ass nigga, I would bet on whomever was cheating. He was likely to win, and I always preferred winning to losing. On this particular day, I bet on Little Timmy at every roll of the dice. I won every time he won, and lost when he lost. Little Timmy was a pure gambler. I believe his father had passed the trade onto him. He knew when to win a round and when to lose a round, so as to not arouse suspicion.

I was not cheating, so I did not have to win some rounds and lose some rounds. My only fault was that I knew who was cheating, and I placed my bets on him. I was winning on almost every roll of the dice because I had picked up on Timmy's rhythm, when he would win and when he would lose. I bet my money so I would always win. This lame ass punk, Charles, accused me of cheating.

"Ah man, open your hands," Charles ordered me. "You gotta be cheatin' or sumthin'. How you just gonna keep winnin'?"

"Cause you niggas lame," I answered.

Charles was at least a full foot taller than I, and he weighed twenty or thirty pounds more. But he was not a fighter. I saw his punch well before he threw it. I connected to his jaw with a straight right cross. He stumbled backward, and just as I was about to unload on him with a barrage of punches, his friend, Moon, punched me in the back of my head. The blow was powerful; he was wearing brass knuckles. Charles gathered himself and attacked me with a barrage of punches of his own. I did not lose consciousness, but I definitely lost my footing. I went down to the hard concrete floor and Charles and Moon put one nasty ass whipping on me.

Little Timmy watched the entire incident without lending a hand to aid me. I was mad at that nigga, but I had no right to be. Moon and Charles were his homeys. If the shoe was on the other foot, and Squirt and Black were whipping his ass, I would not have aided him. Besides, a basic rule of the ghetto is "don't break up a fight." You either join in, take a side, or stay on the sideline and watch.

Them cats kicked my ass and robbed me of all my winnings. I had no choice other than to assemble my dogs and bring them up to the school with me—for the beef was on. Charles had flashed a small handgun in my face, and told me that he would fuck me up every day of my life if I even thought about some get-back shit. If the nigga had an ounce of sense, he would have known I would think of nothing else. I was a "down the hill" nigga. There was no way, under God's beautiful heaven, I was going to accept what he and Moon had done to me.

I left the school and went directly to Eager Street. It was close to the end of the school day, and I knew it would not be long before I spotted

Squirt, Black, Kirk, Wayne, Greg, and the rest of my dogs. Hell, for those punk ass cats, all I needed was one or two of my dogs.

"Man, what happened to you?" Black was the first one I saw. In fact, he spotted me first. My lips were swollen and the back of my head was cut. I had bruises all over my body, and I ached. But I was not severely hurt. My pride was hurt; a lot of the girls at the school had seen me get beaten and robbed. Things like that were not supposed to happen to "thug niggas." It was as if my card had gotten pulled, and I was revealed as being a coward or a punk.

I explained to Black what had happened. I told him, "Yo. I was 'bout to hook and jab this bitch-ass nigga to death. But his buddy snuck me from behind." I added to the story's end that Charles dared me to go get my sissy ass home-boys from down the hill.

I did not have to add that lie. Black was going to aid me in exacting revenge on Charles and Moon anyway. He was my dog, and it didn't matter what was said or not said. I got my ass whipped and, therefore, somebody else had to get his ass whipped in retaliation. It was how things went.

"Yo, lets get strapped and go find them niggas," Black wanted to get to the bottom of this shit immediately.

"Where you got the iron?" We had bought a .38 snub-nose pistol during the time of our marijuana business. After my early retirement, Squirt and Black had held on to it, continuing to hustle. In fact, they had moved up. Black and Squirt were selling heroin for Black's cousin, Greg.

"Round the stash house," Black answered my question as he led me toward Eager and Rutland and into a house located on the corner. We entered the house from the rear, which was the customary way to enter a stash house. "Yo, we got some big boy shit 'round this mother. Wait 'til I come back." He left me alone in the kitchen while he went into one of the front rooms of the house.

When he returned, he held a gun in each hand. The blue steel snub-nose .38 calibur pistol that belonged to Squirt, him, and me was in one hand. In the other, he held a blue steel, bulldog .357 magnum. He had a smile on his face that indicated pride and satisfaction. We were going to hurt some brothers, perhaps even kill them, and we felt no fear, regret, or remorse. We felt justified; they had violated us in beating me up.

"You know where they live?"

"No, but it won't be hard to find out."

"Where do we start?"

I told Black that Little Timmy should know where Charles and Moon lived. I knew that Timmy lived on Dallas Street and that he hung around on Federal Street. Black knew Timmy. Timmy was a gambler and quite popular; he always circled the community in search of a craps game. He was not known to be a tough guy. We had no doubt that he would tell us everything we wanted to know, or take the ass whipping that Moon and Charles were supposed to get.

We exited the house through the same door we entered. I had the 357 in my waistband covered over with a light sweat jacket, Black concealed the .38 in the deep pocket of his hooded sweat-shirt. We were not going to wait on anybody. We were more than capable of handling two faggot ass niggas who had to double jump me. Besides, we were in possession of some equalizers. Black and I were going to cause some mess. He was my dog, and I was his. Two dumb ass cats from "up the hill" were about to get bit.

• • •

Black told his cousin Greg that we had to go up the hill to take care of an important matter. He let him know that he might be awhile in returning. Greg sensed that Black and I were up to something vital, so he did not question Black about abandoning business. Perhaps, physically injuring another was more important than business. You can sell dope all day, any day. It is not too often that a legitimate reason arose to beat a nigga down. Moon and Charles were going to get a legitimate beat-down. But first, Black and I had to find them. The first leg of the mission was to locate Little Timmy. We went to his house on Dallas Street and was told by a lady, who appeared to be his mother, that he was not home. Black and I were not threatening and, therefore, the kind lady told us, "Timmy is around the corner somewhere shootin' them damn dice," she said. "If you find him, tell him I said, 'Get his butt home.'"

Black and I went around to Federal and Bethel Streets, and there Timmy was. He and a few other cats had a craps game in operation. It was a small nickel-and-dime affair, not anything that could not be broken up. "Where dem niggas live at?" I threateningly asked Timmy as I stepped in between the gamblers and grabbed him by the collar of his shirt and pulled him close enough to smell my breath.

The move shocked the small crowd of about three or four gamblers, but not enough to disrupt the flow of the neighborhood. They had all probably seen friends pulled over to be talked to with guns being banished in their faces. "Damn man," Timmy was not afraid. "You steppin' to me like I'm the one who done you wrong."

Black remained focused on the guys who were around Timmy and me to make certain that no one interfered with my interrogation. He held the .38 firmly in his grip with the hammer cocked and ready to be fired. He pointed the gun toward the ground so as not to offend anyone unnecessarily, but to convince everyone to be patient and mind his own damn business.

My gun was not drawn, but it was displayed in my waistband. "Motherfucker, I ain't tryin' to hear no dumb shit," my anger was apparent. "Where do dem bitches be at?" I violently pushed Timmy away from me and motioned toward the gun in my waistband.

Timmy was not afraid, or at least his eyes did not betray that feeling. "Yo, you ain't have to come at me like this. You my man. I don't fuck with Charles and that other coon-ass nigga."

"Yeah, cool," I didn't want to allow this moment to become too casual. "Where can I find dem niggas, now?"

"I don't know where them niggas live exactly. Moon live on Cliftview; they cross-the-track niggas." Timmy gave us the information we wanted and he resumed his craps game as if nothing out of the ordinary had occurred.

"Your mother said bring your ass home," I told Timmy as Black and I began to part.

"Check on Harford Road first," Timmy ignored the message from his mother. "Charles work in the store on the corner at Darley Avenue."

It was still quite early in the day, and our minds were set on destruction. It did not bother Black and me that we would have to walk another six blocks to exact vengeance. We went up to Harford Road and Cliftview. We circled the neighborhood awhile, and we approached every familiar face, asking him or her whether he or she knew Charles and Moon. We lucked out when I spotted Deniece, this pretty okay girl who was in my class at Clifton. We did not know each other well; it was just the first week of the new school year. But we had a good rapport, so when I saw her cross Harford Road, coming in our direction, I felt no need to bother with pleasantries and formalities. "Deniece, where can I find Moon or Charles?"

I am quite sure Deniece knew about the incident involving Charles, Moon, and me at school. If she did not, the cuts and bruises on my face were adequate enough to cause her to pause before giving me information that may result in someone getting hurt or even killed. Besides, the two that I was asking about were probably her childhood friends. They probably all grew up in the same community and attended elementary school together.

Deniece's hesitation was obvious, but when Black reached into his pocked and pulled out a ten dollar bill and offered it to her, she accepted it and said, "Moon down on the playground and Charles at work in the store."

She pointed us in the direction of the playground and the store where Charles worked. Black and I decided it would be best if we went to the playground and beat-up Moon first, then we would come back and beat-up Charles. We didn't want to go around to anyone's place of business and start any stuff. The police would likely be called before we had the chance to accomplish what we intended. We went around to Harford Heights to the playground where Deniece had informed us we would find Moon.

It did not take us long to get to the school yard playground. It was only about two blocks away. I spotted Moon almost instantly. He had quite distinct features. He had a short and stocky build. His skin complexion was very dark, and you could spot his wino pink lips a mile away.

Moon was playing a game of basketball with a group of men and teen-agers when Black and I approached the basketball court. He was so focused on his game, he did not see us enter onto the court. Black and I decided to sit down and rest a moment since the basketball court area was fenced in. There was only one way in and one way out. And we were sitting at that "way." Moon would not have been able to escape the court without having to confront Black and me first. There was no need for us to hurry. I was a little tired from all the walking, and I imagine Black was tired, too. The adrenaline had us going.

"Let's wait and see how that nigga look when he see me sittin' here," I whispered to Black.

After a moment's wait—five minutes or so—I walked onto the court and up to Moon and slapped him in the face with my .357. He had jumped me with his friend earlier; I did not feel like waiting until he finished his game. I concentrated my attention solely on getting my revenge. If another one of his friends, or anybody else for that matter, felt like interfering with my thirst for vengeance, Black would deal with that. He was my dog, and my confidence in him was complete.

The time would come when I would come to love Black and consider him the only brother I ever had. He would know that and return the love.

Everybody Loves a Winning Loser

Chapter 17

Black and I went around to his house to get me a change of clothes. I had beat Moon into a pulp; his blood had splashed all over me. I could not go home like that. Kim was already going to be angry with me for not coming directly home from school. It was nearing nine o'clock in the evening, and I had not returned home from school. My mind and heart were intent on vengeance. I wanted to hurt those who had hurt me. I was not familiar with the power of forgiveness, how enriching it is to the soul to forgive those who transgress against you.

After Charles and Moon jumped me, all I wanted to do was get some "get back." I exacted my vengeance on Moon. I was not sure whether or not he was dead. It really didn't matter. I was only concerned with the fact that I had beat him far worse than he and Charles had beat me. I also felt pride in the fact that I beat him down by myself. Black and I did not bank him like he and Charles had done me. Admittedly, I snuck up behind him while he was probably exhausted from playing basketball and slapped him extremely hard upon the head with a gun. But it was that nigga's fault to be caught "slippin'." That very same day, less than six hours prior, he and his friend beat me down with brass knuckles, then brandished a pistol in my face, and he was not prepared for retaliation. Moon was a dumb-ass nigga. I hoped that Charles would be just as foolish. He was the main culprit. He started this shit, and my anger toward him was greater than it was toward Moon. Moon had just aided his homeboy—prevented him from getting an ass whipping, fair and square. Moon, no doubt, was severely hurt. He was scarred for life, but he did live. He transgressed and "slipped" against me while I was still young. It was a good thing for him that I was not yet purely destructive and deadly. In other words, Moon was lucky. If had he jumped me a year or two later, he would have been killed.

He was not nearly as lucky as Charles. Black and I decided to get a change of clothes. Black knew how strict Kim was with me. She was not ready to allow me to be a man.

"Yo, I beat the shit out that coon-ass nigga," I was pleased with my accomplishment.

Black simply smiled as we proceeded to his house. I believe he was concerned about my appearance. Blood was splattered over my clothes, and I was totally disheveled. I beat the shit out of Moon. The first blow had knocked him out. When I kicked him in the face, as he laid there on the ground, he awoke. I then hit him a third time, again across the head with my .357. I overwhelmed him with a combination of blows with my pistol, feet, and fist. He went from unconscious to conscious to semi-conscious back to complete unconsciousness. None of the people around the basketball court interfered with me as I beat Moon down. However, it was likely that someone had called the police.

"Let's take the little streets and alleys 'til we get back down the hill." Black was always more calculating than I. He kept his focus, and was seldom distracted by irrelevancies. He was apparently not interested in my boasting. He wanted to get us safely home, out of the law's grasp.

I gratefully followed Black through the small streets and alley ways until we finally reached his house in the 800 block of Wolfe Street. No one, except for his youngest sister, Valanda, was there. We were able to go to his room and get me a change of clothes without anyone questioning my appearance.

"Nigga, Kim gonna whip your natural ass when you get home," Black was relaxed now. We were safely in his house. "You better stay strapped to keep her off you." We both laughed.

"Yo, you right." I was not looking forward to dealing with Kim. But she was not the most important matter before me. "You know I'm goin' up the school tomorrow."

"I'm with you, homey." We stood up from the bed and embraced each other in a brief but gentle way.

We left Black's house. He agreed to walk me half way up the hill, and he assured me that he, along with the rest of my dogs, would meet me at the corner of North Avenue and Wolfe Street in the morning. They would be attending Clifton Park Junior High with me the next day, and the next, if need be. We were going to get to the bottom of this "kicking Tray's ass shit" even if it required the entire school year.

We left both guns at Black's house. He knew that Kim would be all over me as soon as I got home. I would not have had time to sneak the gun in the house and stash it. Besides, we were confident that Charles or whoever he sought for help would not be bold enough to bother me anymore that day. But if things were not kosher when I got up the hill, I simply had to get back down the hill to my dogs. It wasn't hard to figure out. I was not vulnerable living where I lived. Charles and Moon were "cross-the-track niggas." They would likely seek vengeance against me once I came to school.

I had to deal with Kim; Charles was not relevant. I was supposed to come directly home from school. Kim had been adamant about that rule. The school day ends at 2:30 in the afternoon, and it was damn near ten o'clock in the evening, and I have not reported home yet. Damn, I could not think of a lie good enough to get out of this. I had just recently completed my punishment. Plus, I had bruises all over my head and face from the "beat down" I had received. My lips were swollen and my eyes were puffy. Kim would understand. I guess I could trust her with the truth.

Black and I parted company at Gay and Wolfe Streets, at the bridge. "See you in the mornin'," Black said to me as he turned and left.

I continued on, thinking about how I was going to confront Kim or how I would be confronted by her. I was satisfied that I was going to tell her most of the truth, as I perceived it to be. If she did not like it, I would leave. I was not going to accept another ass whipping that day.

Kim, Calvin, and Dollar Bill, Calvin's brother, were sitting in the living room lounging when I came through the door. "Boy, why didn't you bring your butt home?" Kim asked me as she came to me and folded me into her arms, close to her breast. "I was worried about you."

"I had to take care of somethin' real important," I answered.

"We heard some niggas dug in your ass up the school," Dollar Bill was not subtle. He was a down the hill nigga through and through. It was in his blood to be a thug. "What happened, Yo?" Bill was trying to pull me away from Kim's inspection.

"Hold up," Kim was determined to examine the amount of damage done to me. "That cut over your eye gonna leave a mark," she proclaimed.

"Good," Bill joked. "Little nigga too pretty anyway."

Calvin laughed and continued rolling marijuana cigarettes. Calvin was the quiet type; when he spoke, it was usually very brief. The nigga really liked me, though. I gave him much laughter. He had mad respect for me. Dollar Bill did, too. They understood that I was a "thug" in the making. Kim understood that as well. That's what she was trying to prevent. But I was not having it.

"What happened, Tray?" Kim asked.

"How y'all hear 'bout what happened up the school?" I was curious.

"Your little girlfriend came 'round here and told us," Calvin offered.

"My girlfriend?"

"Boy, what happened?" Kim was impatient.

"Fuck how we know. What happened?" Bill was anxious to know as well. From the look on Calvin's face, he was anxious to hear the story, too.

"Me and this dude name Timmy was walkin' down the hall," I begun my story. "And this boy Charles came up to me and said, 'You think you all that.' I told him, 'Naw, I know I'm all that.' Then he swung on me."

"And?" Kim was not buying my story.

"Let him finish," Calvin was prepared to hear the whole story without further interruption.

"I swung back, but his buddy, Moon, hit me in the back of my head with some brass knuckles." I paused to show them the knot on the back part of my head.

"Damn, I ain't see that," Kim came closer for further examination.

"They got me good," I continued. "So I went down the hill to get Black so I could have somebody watch my back while I fought them one at a time."

"You catch 'em, Yo?" Bill was excited.

"One of 'em," I answered. "The nigga Moon. He was up Harford Heights playin' ball when I ran down on him."

"That's what all those police was up the schoolyard for?" Kim was concerned.

"I don't know. I did what I had to do and left." I told Kim the truth on that account. I did not know if the police came up to the school because of the beat down I had applied to Moon. Black and I left before any police arrived. I told Kim that I went down to Black's house to change clothes because my clothes were messed up. Kim wanted to know why I didn't come home to change. I explained to her that I was mad, and I was afraid she wouldn't let me go back out to handle my affairs.

Kim asked whether or not I was hungry. I told her that I was, and when she left the room, Calvin and Dollar Bill wanted me to tell them the uncensored version. I did. I told them that Little Timmy was cheating in a craps game, but I was wrongly accused. I went on to tell them that I pistol whipped Moon, and I would not be surprised if the nigga was dead.

When Kim came back into the room, the conversation ceased. "Your food is on the table," she informed me. "Do you want me to go up the school with you tomorrow?"

"No," I adamantly stated as I went to the kitchen to eat my meal.

After I ate, I went into the living room to say "Good night" to everyone. Then I went up to take a bath and go to bed. I wanted to be well rested for tomorrow. The beef was on, and the cats from "up the hill" or "across the track" had started it. I did not make a distinction between "cross the tracks" niggas and "up the hill" niggas. They were one and the same to me. They were all cats, none of them were my dogs.

Black, Squirt, Wayne, and Kirk were my dogs. The next morning, just like Black had assured me, and I never doubted, they were all on the corner of Wolfe Street and North Avenue waiting for me. If they had come around to my house to get me, Kim would have known that something was afoot. As it was, she only suspected.

"Tray, are you gonna be all right?" Kim had asked me as I came down the stairs ready to head out the door for school.

"Yeah," I answered. "I told you last night, I'm cool." She kissed me on the cheek, I in turn, kissed Kieshawn on her cheek as she sat at the table finishing her breakfast, "Boy, get off me." Kieshawn feigned annoyance at my show of affection.

I rushed out the door, and met up with my dogs. We all greeted each other with hand shakes and brief embraces to demonstrate our mutual affection and allegiance. We proceeded to the school via the Wolfe Street route. A lot of morning commuters were out making their way to school or work. The traffic was thick and, therefore, it did not appear odd for Black, Squirt, Kirk, Wayne, and me to be walking together in a crowd. When we reached the railroad tracks that sat adjacent to the school, many Clifton Park students were there making their trek to school. We captured odd glances from the students, but it was not alarming. A lot of young teenagers who did not attend our school often came up to the school for various reasons. My dogs were simply coming up to the school to show that I had assistance in the event I got jumped again. Black was strapped, and so was Squirt. I wanted the .357 back, but Squirt was not about to part with it. He told me that he would do anything with it that needed to be done. Besides, I did not have my book bag. He could conceal it better than I could. I submitted, and Black and Squirt held onto the only guns we had.

I told my homeys that I was going to go into the school, and if we did not spot Charles by nine o'clock, they should leave and go to school themselves. It was not wise for them to hang around on school grounds with guns. They all protested, claiming that we would all fall together if need be. But I assured them that Charles was a weak ass nigga and that he did not constitute a real threat to me.

Little Timmy came up to us as we debated the matter. He told us that Charles was waving the "white flag." He heard about what I had done to Moon, and he was thoroughly afraid. Charles was "so damn scared, Timmy assured us, "He ain't comin' to school no more." Black and Squirt told Little Timmy in a belligerent manner that if I got jumped, he would answer for it. Little Timmy told them that it was no need to threaten him, he was on my side.

"Why wasn't you on his side yesterday, nigga?" Kirk shot at him.

"Yesterday was yesterday," Timmy matter-of-fact said.

Fat Kirk, Wayne, Squirt, and Black begrudgingly agreed to leave the school. They announced, practically in unison, that they would be back at the end of the school day, and if anything foul happened to me, they would burn the school down with everybody in it.

I was pleased to have my friends' support, but I could handle my own weight. All I needed was a burner, and I knew I would be safe. "Squirt, give me the .357. I'll give it back later."

Without hesitation, Squirt passed me his book bag with the gun inside. The school bell rung and Little Timmy and I headed for the school building and Wayne, Kirk, Black, and Squirt headed back toward the railroad track and off Clifton Park's grounds. "Y'all niggas gonna be late for school!" I shouted at them.

"Fuck you!" they shouted back.

Once I got into the school, I decided that it would not be a good idea to keep the gun on me, or in my locker. I had a premonition that I would be searched by school officials or the police. When I saw Michelle, a homely-looking girl who I felt had a crush on me, I asked her, with all the charm and persuasion I could muster, to allow me to put my book bag in her locker. She was aware of the battle I was involve in with Moon and Charles, but her obvious attraction to me compelled her to submit to my request. I put the gun into Michelle's locker and went to my homeroom class.

Little Timmy was already there, and he had a seat reserved for me next to him. "Man, you tore Moon ass up."

"What makes you think I did anything to that nigga?" I was not going to admit to anything.

"Man, why you and your boys keep treatin' me like I'm a sucker?" Timmy looked genuinely offended. But he didn't come to my aid when I was getting beat down, so I didn't owe him any consideration. Hell, I was doing him a favor by not whipping his ass for starting all this shit. "What's up with Moon?" I was interested in knowing.

"Man, that joker real messed up," he informed me. "Word is, he gonna have to get an operation on his head. He might got brain damage or somthin'."

"He shouldn't have fucked with me," I said. I felt no remorse. I felt absolutely justified.

The students who had seen my friends and me gathered around the school building earlier seemed to revere or revile us. It probably depended upon which side of the tracks they were from.

The teacher called the roll. By the time she got to my name, curiously enough, the school's security officer came through the door to retrieve me.

"Arlando Jones?" he asked while looking directly at me.

"Yeah," I felt butterflies forming in my stomach.

"I need to see you in the principal's office right now," he commanded.

I got up from my desk and followed this huge man, who later identified himself as Mr. Adams, to the main office. "Where are your books?" he asked me.

"I don't know," I was being honest. "I believe somebody stole them."

"No one stole your books," Mr. Adams said. "You left them in the hall yesterday—where you were fighting."

Mr. Adams had a false version of the truth. I was not fighting in school yesterday. I got my ass whipped by two guys who jumped me. "I wasn't fightin'." That was my story, and I was sticking to it.

"Listen to me you little bastard," he said to me as he turned around on his heel to grab me by my shirt collar. "This school year just started, and I ain't gonna take no shit from you."

My nerves were definitely on edge, but I was not afraid of this big, red-ass-nigga trying to intimidate me. "Nigga, if you don't take your hands off me, you gonna have a mothafuckin' nub there," I spoke as fiercely as I could.

I met the security officer's hard stare with courage. That's probably why he released me with gentleness, then ushered me, in front of him, toward the principal's office.

"Here's Arlando," Mr. Adams announced to the school's principal and the other personnel present in the office. "He's a tough guy, too."

"Arlando," the school's principal spoke in an authoritarian manner, "it has been reported that you were involved in a fight here, at the school yesterday."

The principal was a short, bland man with a balding head. "I just told Mr. Adams I wasn't in no fight, and he jacked me in my collar," I calmly said. "Now, I'm tellin' y'all, I was not in no fight."

"Well, I just called your mother, Kim Pittman, and she is on her way up here," the principal was dismissing my comment.

"Kim ain't my mother," I was angry and wanted everyone present to know I was angry. "She my aunt. My mother is dead."

"I am sorry," the principal apologized. "But nevertheless, she has been called, and we will have a discussion once she gets here."

I was then instructed to take a chair and wait until Kim arrived. The school officials felt that nothing could be accomplished by talking to me. I was familiar with the "code." I knew that I was not supposed to admit to anything. If the officials felt that I was guilty of some ill deed, it was their duty to prove it. I was not going to aid them. Past experience taught me that Kim would side with me. I was the victim of an assault. The school officials had no business getting involved, unless Charles or Moon got them involved. And it made no sense for them to do that; they initiated the fight.

When Kim arrived at the school, she was twisted. She was high as Fat Charles' ass. Wherever she copped her dope from that day, she had to be pleased. It was obvious to everyone in the principal's office that Kim was under the influence of something. Her speech was slurred, saliva was caked in the corner of her mouth, and she nodded and scratched herself. Kim had been snorting heroin. I knew it almost instantly.

The principal, if I recall properly, felt embarrassed for me, or at the situation. He stumbled over the typical greetings, and hurriedly ushered Kim, Mr. Adams, and me into the privacy of his office. Kim and I were directed to sit in the two chairs in front of the principal's desk, and he seated himself in his chair behind the desk. Mr. Adams stood at the side of the desk, facing Kim and me. He looked to the principal and the principal gave him a nod, indicating that he should start the discussion.

"Ms. Pittman, my name is Mr. Adams," he began. "I'm the school's security officer, and I have reason to believe that your son was involved in a fight here yesterday."

Mr. Adams paused for effect. We all remained silent, staring at him. Kim was struggling not to go into a nod.

"Although Arlando is scarred and bruised," Mr. Adams continued. "He denies that he was fighting."

"I ain't say I wasn't fightin'," I jumped in. "I said I wasn't fightin' in school."

"I found Arlando's books in the long hallway and it was reported to me by a reliable source that he had been fighting," Mr. Adams said. "I tried to locate Arlando, but I couldn't. He had left the school."

"Who's your reliable source?" Kim was on my side.

"It would not be prudent for me to divulge the name of my source," Mr. Adams said. "Suffice it to say, I trust my source."

"Good for you," Kim was being sarcastic. "I know about Arlando being in a fight yesterday. But it was not here."

Kim was high, no doubt. But she was very conscious of her surroundings. Moreover, she was not going to take sides against me with a school official, or any official for that matter. I had been jumped; I was the victim. Kim was not going to punish me for beatin' Moon down; she was going to do everything she could to make certain that I was not punished for it. From our perspective, I was right. The school had no interest in this matter. It was beyond its jurisdiction. It was a street matter.

The principal probably felt the same way. "Arlando, Ms. Pittman, we don't want whatever you're involved in to spill over and disrupt the activities of our school."

Kim and I nodded as if we cared about what the principal wanted.

He continued, "We were concerned that you were injured on school grounds. If that were the case, we would have to take action."

"That ain't the case," Kim was not intimidated. "Why did you call me up here?"

Mr. Adams and the principal were thrown aback by Kim's attitude. They both apologized for disturbing her unnecessarily. The principal did, however, tell Kim and me that I would be expelled from school if I was caught fighting in a situation related to the one under investigation. Kim took exception to the subtle threat and became belligerent. She asked, "Who in the fuck was he fightin'?"

The principal and Mr. Adams did not answer. Kim felt offended. "Y'all gonna threaten my child about expelling him, but y'all ain't talkin' 'bout expellin' nobody else. Was he fightin' his damn self?"

Mr. Adams and the principal did not want to have an ugly scene. They apologized once again and told me that I can go back to my class. Kim was not finished. She told me to go back to my class, and she assured me that she would see me once I got home from school. She kissed me on my forehead, and I retrieved my books and we parted.

When I got to my class, I learned from my fellow classmates that my locker and desk had been searched. I praised myself for being so wise as to get the gun off me. I was truly "street wise." The principal and other officials were not smart enough to catch me. I was convinced that I could outwit the world.

When the school day ended, Black, Wayne, Kirk, and Squirt were all waiting out front for me. I told them that I was cool. I told them that Charles was running scared and Moon was laid up in the hospital. I gave Squirt the gun and told him that I probably won't need it. I informed them about Kim's visit to the school and my promise to come home after school.

Black wanted to know what I intended to do about Charles. I told him that I was going to punish him as soon as we crossed paths. I was not going to admit that I was hoping that the whole affair was over. I had to maintain my façade. I told my dogs, "I'm gonna handle that nigga like I'm supposed to."

We parted, and I went home. Kim was still under the influence of heroin when I got there. Kieshawn and Yalanda were in the house playing. The music was on, the television was on, and the mood was quite festive. I decided to stay in the house and be a part of my family. Eventually, I decided to take Yalanda outside to sit on the front steps so that she could enjoy the fresh air with me. Kieshawn joined us, and we all sat there on the steps until some of Kieshawn's friends came up and they all played "double dutch" and teased each other.

This luxurious gray Cadillac, with silver rims and deep red leather interior, pulled up to the curb in front of our house and parked. Calvin climbed from the passenger side and this very large and very dark skinned man, who I knew as Fat Larry, climbed from the driver's side. It seemed as if all the activity occurring on the block stopped to watch Fat Larry and Calvin. Larry's fancy car and large bejeweled figure was quite a spectacle to behold. I was captivated by his presence, for I had always wanted to meet Fat Larry. He was one of the biggest drug-dealers in East Baltimore. He was running a twenty-four-hour-a-day narcotic operation on Eager Street and everyone I knew spoke of him with reverence.

He was a notorious, murdering drug-dealer. The niggas feared him and the women flocked to his bed. I wanted to be just like him. He stood well over six feet and weighed about two hundred and fifty pounds. He wore expensive jewelry and kept a pocket full of money. On the rare occasion when he appeared on Eager Street, and I saw him, I made it a point to come to him just to say, "Hello." I knew that in the ghetto a "hero ain't nothing but a sandwich," but I damn sure admired Fat Larry. He was the closest thing I had to a hero. I stood in awe that he was visiting my home. Calvin's standing, in my view, rose one thousand percent. He was an associate of Fat Larry.

"What's happenin' Fat Larry?" I completely ignored Calvin. I wanted to greet Fat Larry and be acknowledged by him, fuck Calvin!

"Hey there," he spoke to me and went into the house behind Calvin.

I was thoroughly impressed with Calvin. I knew he was hustling, and doing quite well for himself financially, but I had no idea he was "stompin' with the big dogs." I determined, in my heart and in my mind, that Calvin was going to let me into his business. I was tired of begging him or Kim for five or ten dollars every day, getting it sometimes and not getting it other times. I was a "thug nigga" from birth and a qualified hustler by practice. There was absolutely no need for my continued poverty. Besides, it was difficult for me to seduce the kind of young women and girls I was attracted to while broke. All my close friends, Squirt, Black, and Wayne were hustling. They had a cash flow; they were able to buy things and go places I was not simply because they possessed the ready cash.

Besides, Wayne was dating (or fucking, depending on how you looked at it), this girl named Annette who I really wanted for myself. I knew I could not have Annette because she only went with niggas who were hustling and had money to spend on her. I respected her position. My mother and aunts used to always say, "I ain't gonna fuck with no broke-ass nigga."

There was no doubt in my mind that Calvin was going to let me into his business. We had a good relationship, and I felt that he had to be tired of taking care of me, and me not earning my keep. All I had to do was convince him that he could trust me, and he needed my service. I knew that his dealers were stealing from him. I had overheard him complain to Kim a few times, "Niggas keep stealin' my shit." I wanted to interject that perhaps Kim was the culprit. She stayed high damn near every day—all day. In fact, Calvin and Kim were constantly arguing about her indulgence with heroin.

He had threatened her that he would leave her if she did not stop getting high. I doubt that Kim attributed any value to Calvin's threat because she kept using.

I would be good for Calvin. I was not using drugs. I smoked weed. Who didn't? But I was not on heroin or cocaine. I could be trusted, and that would make me an invaluable asset to him. If he was too dumb to see that, then fuck him. Fat Larry was in my home. I would make his acquaintance and make it possible for me to approach him for employment opportunities.

• • •

"Calvin, I'm tryin' to be down," I said to him as he came through the front door. "I'm tired of this broke shit."

"What you talkin' 'bout boy?'"

I had waited all day and night for Calvin to return home. It was in the wee hours, about three or four o'clock in the morning. I was tired and annoyed about waiting so long for Calvin to come home. I really did not want to play any silly games with him.

"I need to get some money, man," my annoyance had to be obvious. "I wanna be down with you."

"Kim ain't gonna have that shit," Calvin decided not to be silly after all. "You gone crazy or what?"

"Kim ain't gotta know nothing," I said. "What's between me and you is between me and you."

Calvin gave me a curious look and said, "We'll talk tomorrow." He went upstairs to the bathroom and then to bed.

I laid back down on the couch where I had been waiting all night for Calvin. The living room was just as comfortable as my room. I just needed to lay back and rest myself for school and analyze what had transpired between Calvin and me. I knew that he would not tell Kim that I had asked him to hire me into his illegal drug business. I was not concerned about that. I was concerned that Calvin would be too scared of Kim to hire me. It seemed like Kim just ran over him. He had told Kim to stop snorting heroin, and she ignored him. No "real nigga" would permit his "main girl" to use drugs. Plus, Kim was the dominant one in their relationship. She controlled the purse strings and never hesitated to admonish him about damn near anything. Dollar Bill, Calvin's younger brother, often jokingly referred to Calvin as a "petticoat." Well, I thought he was joking, but in time,

I learned that it was no joke. Kim dominated Calvin, just as all his other women did. The nigga just didn't have a backbone. I liked Calvin a lot, but he was a weak-ass nigga.

There came times when I was truly embarrassed to be associated with him. I suspect Calvin was truly afraid of physical confrontations. He would make any compromise imaginable to avoid conflict. He was a genuine milquetoast.

Calvin survived the game because he was likable, and he knew how to surround himself with thug niggas who handled his conflicts for him. His weak-ass partner, Fat Larry, was the same way.

I learned quite late that niggas like Calvin and Larry were able to project a notorious image because of the type of people they surrounded themselves with. They insulated themselves from direct conflict; otherwise, their true cowardly nature would show itself.

Calvin knew that I was a true thug at heart. It was not hard to convince him to deceive Kim and employ me. He needed me, and I wanted to work for him. The niggas he had in the stash house were robbing him blind. The money count and dope came up short almost every night.

"Tray, Tray," Kieshawn was shaking me awake. "Get up, boy 'fore my mother come downstairs."

Damn, I had overslept. I was usually the first one up in the house every morning. It was my duty to cook breakfast for Kieshawn before she left for school—a duty that I failed to perform most the time. Kieshawn loved to cook, but she was too young to operate the stove. Therefore, she and I had a simple agreement; she could cook her own damn breakfast meals when Kim was not around, as long as she didn't tell anyone that I allowed her to operate the stove.

I liked cooking myself, but Kieshawn reaped a far greater joy from cooking for the both of us than I. So I delegated the duty to her. She was my little sister, and I loved her. We argued and fought each other, but we had each other's back. It would tear at my heart when the "street life" began to rob her of her dignity, her self-respect, and her health.

"You owe me a dollar," Kieshawn announced. "I woke up before you."

"Girl, what you talkin' 'bout?"

"You said if I wake up before you, you would give me a dollar."

"Girl, get out my face."

"That's okay," she was dejected. "You just an ole liar."

"I'm gonna give you a damn dollar." I was a lot of things, but I was not a liar. My word has always had value.

I gathered myself and went upstairs to bathe and dress for school. When I came from the bathroom, Calvin was standing in my bedroom waiting for me.

"Come down the hill when you get outta school," he said to me, and then went into the bathroom.

All right! I was going to be back in the game. I was totally unaware of the pain stepping into the dope game would bring. I had sold weed, but marijuana did not bring in half the money that heroin brought in. Not only that, the prestige that came with selling dope was overwhelming. All the neighborhood girls wanted to fuck the dope-man. All I saw, at that time in my life, was the glamour of selling narcotics. The pain, frustration, overwhelming heartache, grief, and disaster that illegal narcotics wreak on lives and entire communities were alien to me.

My beloved Aunt Kim was becoming a dope-fiend right before my eyes, and yet, in my utter stupidity, I still desired to be a part of it. I knew that it was a disastrous life. I just did not know what disastrous truly meant. I was conditioned to be a "bad ass nigga" like my father and the other gangster type dudes who received all the accolades.

The most tragic thing about growing up in the ghetto is that criminality is glamorized. I was a very bright child; all the teachers said so at one time or another. I was also ruthless and courageous. I was not afraid of anything. I generally succeeded at all my endeavors. If I pursued a girl, I got her. If I desired a drug connection, I got it. If I wanted a piece of jewelry or a specific clothing item, I got it. Whatever I applied my focus to, I got.

I got dressed and supervised Kieshawn in cooking our breakfast. Then I ate and went to school. I was too excited about the prospect of working for my big shot uncle to dedicate any attention to Charles. If the nigga wanted some trouble I would give him all the trouble he could handle. I was not interested in doing anything other than getting the school day over, so that I could get to Eager Street to start my new job. I took it for granted that my pockets would be fat. I would have plenty of money.

I was so anxious about my new job that I left school early. I was not learning a damn thing. All that academic stuff was boring and did not apply to anything that interested me. I told Jermaine, the class's nerd, to get all my homework for me and do it, and I would look out for him later. I was popular at the school, and most certainly the most popular in my class. It was Jermaine's privilege and honor to do for me whatever I was gracious enough to permit him. I had to get to my new job. So I snuck out the side door and headed for Eager Street.

A House Too Haunted for a Ghost

Chapter 18

Eager Street was booming with activity when I got there to report to my very first dope-selling job. Folks were sitting on their front steps enjoying pleasant and innocent conversation with neighbors and family and friends. Everyone was taking in the fresh September air. The winos were on the corners of High Hats and Roses Bars drinking their wine and singing old Motown tunes. Drug addicts of all sorts were going up to respective dealers buying the narcotics of their choice. The uniformed police were making their occasional trips around the block harassing some folks and not harassing others. All in all, it was a typical day in the ghetto.

"Boody, you seen Calvin?" I asked. Boody was one of Calvin's runners, and I figured he would know Calvin's whereabouts.

"Naw, ain't nobody tell me it was my turn to watch him," Boody was being facetious. He had no reason to withhold information from me about Calvin's whereabouts. He knew that Calvin was my family and that it would be all right to let me know where he was.

"Man, I need to find Calvin," I knew that he had some clue as to where I could locate him. "It's real important."

"It ain't important to me."

"It could be," I said. "I might be your new boss, nigga."

"Yeah, you right," Boody laughed. "The nigga 'round here somewhere. Just lay; he'll show."

I stood out there on the corner talking to Boody about some bullshit while I waited for Calvin to appear. A few dope-fiends came up to us to cop drugs, and Boody simply directed them to the other runners in the crew. I was curious as to why Boody was not making any of the runs himself. "Why you sendin' work to everybody else?"

"When Larry and Calvin ain't here, I'm runnin' shit," he proudly replied.

"Calvin said he was gonna put me down," I informed Boody. "What you think I'm gonna be doin'?"

"How the fuck I know?" Boody was not a polite fellow. "You need to take your ass to school while you still young and leave this shit alone."

I was far from interested in Boddy's sage advice. I had been doing the nice little kid thing for the past several weeks and it had grown tedious. I was broke all the time while my friends kept a pocket full of money. I was reduced to begging Kim or Calvin for a few bucks every now and again. My financial situation had grown so despicable that it had ruined my sex life.

There was a host of girls at the school who liked me and would probably have sex with me, but I did not have enough funds to take them out to buy them things. I always felt inadequate and insecure without money. I had to have material things to feel confident. The dudes I hung out with all had a hustle going. It was imperative to have a cash flow. There were fancy clothes to be purchased, cars to be bought, and places to go. Moreover, there were "dime broads" to be fucked. If you did not hustle and make quick money, fun would be denied you.

I had been denied fun long enough. I was not about to consider anything Boody, or anyone else for that matter, had to say about me not hustling and getting some quick money. I told that to Boody, and he accepted my position.

Calvin showed up after only a few minutes. He motioned for me to walk with him so that we could talk in private. We strolled the block while he explained to me that ever since he merged his business with Fat Larry, he felt that he had been getting cheated out of his share of the profits. He told me that he needed me to sit in the stash house with Mustard and Bam to keep a count of all the dope and money. The only time I was to give anyone a bag of dope was when he gave me fifty dollars for it. I was warned not to trust Mustard or Bam. They were snakes and would likely try all kinds of things to convince me to leave the drugs unattended so that they could steal dope out of each bag.

I asked Calvin, "If you don't trust them niggas, why you got 'em in the stash house?"

"That's Larry's shit."

No more had to be said on the matter. Fat Larry was that nigga, he knew everything that needed to be known about selling dope. If he wanted Mustard and Bam to remain in the stash house despite their dishonesty and thievery, it was cool with me—and Calvin, too.

Calvin told me that I would be required to come directly to the stash house on Chapel Street everyday immediately after I got out of school. I would be entrusted with two hundred "fifties" every day. I was to make $100 a day. Just don't leave the drugs and money unattended. Mustard and Bam would act as my protection while I was in the stash house. Beacause they would have the guns.

I had to be really stupid. Calvin did not trust Mustard and Bam, yet he wanted me to sit in a house with them all day, while I held onto $10,000 worth of dope.

I graciously accepted my position. I was going to sit in a house with two armed, drug-crazed niggas for a hundred dollars a day. It seemed like a pretty good offer. I wanted to be out on the corner, to be recognized as a hustler. But I would shoot for that later. At the moment, I was needed for an important role. It was not too often that a young thug nigga gets his start in such a trusted position. By the time Calvin and I reached the stash house on Chapel Street, and entered through the back door, I felt that if I proved worthy, I would rise and be given the opportunity to make far more than a meager hundred bucks a day.

Calvin set me up in the stash house. He told Mustard and Bam that I would be holding. Neither man protested, and I was rendered confused. The way Calvin had explained things to me led me to believe that Mustard and Bam would not welcome my arrival. I felt that I was being called upon to take over things. Bam told Calvin, "It's about time y'all niggas found somebody else to sit in this trap."

Bam, apparently, had been pressing Calvin to get him out of stash house duty. "You and Mustard got this shit," Bam happily announced.

"Hold," Mustard protested. "How you get to roll first?"

Bam was an imposing man. He stood at least six-foot-five inches and wore well over two hundred and fifty pounds. He was muscular and spoke with an aggressively deep tone. Mustard, on the other hand, was short and skinny. He looked fairly healthy, but he did not look like he could rival Bam in a fist fight. Hell, I felt that I could whip Mustard's ass myself. He was at least twice my age, but his physical stature was not intimidating or threatening. His demeanor suggested that he was quite timid. I would dominate him in the stash house, I was sure.

Bam gave Mustard a hard stare and said, "Cause that's how it is."

Nothing else was said on the matter, Calvin retrieved a locked black box from the dresser drawer and sat it on the table before us. Bam reached into his pants pocket and handed Calvin the keys to the box. Calvin opened it and removed the contents. He counted one-hundred-and-sixty glassine bags of heroin. He told me that I was to receive $50 for every bag that left the house.

Calvin and Bam left Mustard and me there in the little cramped stash house. But before they left, they told Mustard to tell me how it all went. Calvin was anxious to get the hell out of the stash house. I was too awestruck to question why, but I soon learned. I learned it all quickly, and my rise and fall came just as quick.

Mustard told me that there were ten "runners" operating from our crew, and that they would come through the back door. We sold $50 bags of heroin, I was not to give anyone anything unless he gave me $50 for each bag. Mustard then showed me where the guns were. We had an assortment of small and large caliber pistols, about thirty in all. Any crew member could get a gun. If anyone in the crew asked for a gun, I was to go in the closest and give him one or two depending upon the circumstance.

I instantly fell in love with my new job. While Mustard thought that I was there to keep him company, my actual role was to watch his thieving ass. Calvin was my family, and when stuff got missing, it took food off my table. It did not really matter to me that Calvin had seemingly deceived me. From Bam and Mustard's reaction to my coming to the stash house, they were happy I was there. Calvin had given me the impression that I was coming to the house to take charge and that the guys in there would not like it. But Bam was grateful to have someone take his place.

It was never a dull moment in the house; activity was non-stop. The runners came back and forth to the house in a succession, and each one had an exciting story to tell each time he stopped in.

"Man, this dope-fiend bitch wanna suck my dick if I take her short money."

"Yo, Tiny just bat this nigga down for beatin' him out his shit."

"Man, the police just jumped out on 'em niggas down the block with Nut's shit."

It went on and on. Each comment creating its own conversation. By the time night fell, a couple of the runners had brought a freak broad around to the house to have sex. I was asked, "You tryin' to get your dick sucked or something man?" I declined. I assumed that it was a ploy to get me to take my eye off the box. Besides, the girl that was brought into the house, from what I saw, was an intravenous drug user. I was repulsed by such a woman. The tracks that ran up and down her body disgusted me, and I would not permit any female like that to get near me.

Mustard told me that the runners brought that kind of woman into the house all the time. He informed me, "When one 'em bitches is short on the loot, ten or fifteen dollars, they gotta suck a couple dicks or whatever to make up the difference."

I was not shocked by this disclosure. I had lived around this type of stuff my entire life. This was just my first direct contact with it. The only shocking thing to me was that so many individuals had access to the stash house. In the little time that I had been there, about $10,000 worth of dope had been sold, and the cash was still in the house.

"Yo, we ain't got nothin' but five bags left," I informed Mustard.

"Damn, why you wait so long to tell a nigga?" Mustard told me to hold the fort down until he came back, and he left.

As soon as Mustard exited the house, I went into the closet and selected a nickel plated, pearl-handled .38 caliber gun. It felt absolutely comforting.

When Mustard left me by myself in the house, I felt a little insecure and frightened. But as soon as I put that .38 in my hand, I felt secure. I felt overwhelmingly bold. After holding the gun in my hand for a moment or two, I put it away—in my waist band. From that moment on, I knew that I would take over the stash house. Calvin had told me that that would be my role. However, from the moment I stepped into the stash house, I was treated and spoken to as if I was a subordinate.

Mustard returned with Boody and Calvin. I was instructed to get the lock box that contained the money and drugs. We all counted the money and the remaining bags of dope. It was all accounted for. Calvin then ordered Boody to go somewhere and get more dope to re-supply me. It was close to midnight, and I was concerned about Kim. I did have a curfew, as Calvin was well aware.

"Calvin, how long you want me stay here?" I asked.

"Little nigga gotta curfew," Boody commented before leaving. "Better get yo' ass home for school in the mornin'."

Calvin and Mustard laughed, and I felt humiliated. I had to defend myself.

"Ain't got no curfew when I'm with Calvin," I said. "You can handle Kim for me, can't you?"

I put the burden on Calvin. I was having a lot of fun. I was connected to something very important, and I did not want the day to end. I had participated in the sale of nearly $10,000 worth of dope in less than eight hours. I found my niche in life, and I was not about to be hindered by any curfew.

"Yeah, I'll just say you was with me," Calvin was confident. "But I'm gonna take you home in another hour or so. "

Telling lies and manipulating the truth was a part of my culture. I sensed nothing wrong with lying to Kim, and it was apparent that Calvin felt the same. He was a drug-dealer; it was a part of the game. One simply did and said whatever he had to in order to carry out his plan. Calvin needed me to stay in the stash house for as long as possible to prevent the stealing. It did not matter to him that I had to go to school. Lying to his fiancée, my beloved Aunt Kim, was a moral issue that did not warrant the least consideration.

I had already learned, perhaps to my peril, that the "Golden Rules" taught in churches and at schools had no worth in my chosen field. In the game, you simply did and said whatever kept the money in your pockets. You associated with whomever would best serve your interest. No thoughts were committed to the future. Calvin had a lot of dope to sell. Fuck Kim's reaction to my staying out all day and night. Furthermore, fuck my education.

Without proper understanding and knowledge, I accepted the code, the rules, and regulations of the game. Well before I approached Calvin for employment, I knew many demands would be placed on my time. I had sold marijuana almost all summer. I knew there was no such thing as a part-time drug-dealer. Selling illegal narcotics was a full-time job. You are all the way in or all the way out.

"Calvin, check this out," I still had the .38 tucked safely away in my waist band. "I'm gonna be in this camp everyday for as long as it take to knock this stuff down. So you gonna have to keep Kim off my back."

"Man, I got you."

"You know how she is," I said.

Mustard was oblivious to what Calvin and I were talking about. He knew that Kim and Calvin were together in a serious relationship. Hell, everyone did. And it was no secret that I was Kim's child.

"Man, y'all work out that family shit later on," Mustard chimed in. "Where my money at for the day?"

"Damn, I forgot." Calvin said, and he reached into his jacket pocket, pulled out the stack of money we had counted, and gave Mustard $100. He put the money back into his pocket without giving me anything. I wanted to ask him about my salary, but I restrained myself. I assumed that if I exercised patience, I would be paid more than Mustard. After all, Calvin was my family.

Boody returned with two hundred fresh bags of heroin. We counted them, and then Calvin and he left Mustard and me alone to resume our duty well into the wee hours. By the time Calvin came to take me home to face Kim, it was nearing sun-rise. I had no doubt in my mind that I would not have to face Kim when I got home. She would be asleep or out herself.

We drove to the International House of Pancakes where we ate a hearty meal. On our way home, I asked Calvin about my pay. He told me that everything he had was mine. That as long as I kept a close eye on Mustard and all the rest of the niggas in the crew, we would have plenty of money. I appreciated his sentiments, but I still needed some money. He reached into his jacket pocket and pulled out the wad of cash that we had taken in for the entire day and said to me, "Take what you want."

He threw damn near $15,000 in my lap! I was hooked for life. I was certain that I was going to be a drug kingpin. No occupation appealed to me more. I did not care about the death and destruction that the trade wreaked on lives. I just wanted to be somebody, like David, like Fat Larry. They all wore fancy clothes, drove pretty cars, had plenty of good-looking women, and pocketed big money.

"Tray, we gonna tell Kim we hung out up my mother's house and fell asleep." Calvin had formed the lie, and we both knew that it would not be challenged.

I peeled two hundred bucks from the wad of cash and handed it back to Calvin. If I did not appear greedy, more would come, I was certain.

The Last Tear Was a Cry

Chapter 19

Kim was not home when Calvin and I got there. I was utterly surprised, but I suspect Calvin felt disrespected. It was truly inappropriate for Kim to stay out all night without letting anyone know where she would be. Moreover, it was thoughtless to leave Kieshawn and Yalanda in the house by themselves. Kieshawn was only eight and Yalanda was a toddler.

When Kim finally came home, at about noon that day, Calvin and she had a heated argument. He accused Kim of being so caught up in her drug usage that she did not care about anything or anyone. Kim accused him of being out with every girl in the neighborhood and not caring about her.

Calvin and Kim were so engrossed in their argument that Kim failed to notice that I had not gone to school. I had come home in the wee hours of the morning, and was still in bed. I simply held onto Yalanda to comfort her as she cried. The shouting between Calvin and Kim frightened her. Kieshawn was not there. She had woken up early in the morning, as usual, for school. She had tried to get me up for school, too. But I let her know in no uncertain terms to leave me alone. I was not going to school; Kieshawn did not push. She simply prepared herself for school and left Yalanda in bed with me. I distinctively recall Kieshawn saying to me, "Watch the baby." Then she left for school.

I was too naïve to understand that I would not have to explain to Kim why I stayed out all night ever again. For Calvin was absolutely right when he told Kim, "You so wrapped up in sniffin' that shit, you don't care 'bout shit."

Calvin stormed out of the house. He no longer wanted to argue with Kim about her drug usage, and Kim locked herself into their bedroom. I simply cared for Yalanda and watched some television until Kieshawn came home from school.

I was anxious to get down the hill to start my second day of work. It was apparent to me at that point that Kim was so consumed with issues over her and Calvin that I was unnoticed. And that was perfectly all right with me. I had interests of my own, and without interference, I could be the dope-dealer I wanted to be.

One thing was for certain, Kim was no longer going to interfere with my plans. Her drug addiction had become the center of her world, and I did not even see it coming. I knew that Kim was snorting heroin. I had seen her inhale the narcotic many times, but I had no idea that she would become just another dope-fiend. No different or better than the ones I degraded each day and sold narcotics to.

"Kieshawn, your mother still asleep," I said to her as soon as she entered the house. "You gotta watch Yalanda 'cause I gotta go out."

"I watched her all day yesterday," Kieshawn responded. "I ain't stayin' in watchin' her today too."

"Well, wake your mother up."

"You wake her up. I'm goin' outside to play."

Kieshawn had a true affection for money. A buck or two would shut her up and make her comply to damn near anything. "Here," I offered her a twenty dollar bill. "I'm goin' out. You watch Yalanda."

Kieshawn snatched the twenty out of my hand before I could change my mind, "Okay." I had never given her that much money before, and had I had a smaller bill, I would not have given her that much then. I simply wanted to get out of the house before Kim awoke. I did not want to risk not being able to report to work. Mustard may have already stolen too much shit. If I hurried to work, I could prevent him from stealing more.

I had not caught Mustard stealing anything. I did not even detect him trying to get me to take my eye off the lock box as Calvin said he would. But since Calvin said that he was a thief, I accepted that he was. The fact that Calvin left everything with him after he came to take me home escaped me.

I guess nothing in the narcotic trade made sense. It is a crazy lifestyle. Everyone involved, whether he be a user or a dealer, knows that the end result of the trade is jails, institutions, or death. The examples were abundant. Niggas like Peanut King, one of the biggest dope-dealers out of Baltimore, were in the Federal Penitentiary for life. Frank Matthew, Nick Bonds, and a multitude of other drug-dealing icons had already met their demise. Yeah, the end result was obvious. The devastation and hurt that the game wrought was all around me. Folks being put out of their homes because drug addictions prevented the rent from being paid. Children often going hungry because satisfying a drug habit was far more important than buying food. A house catching fire damn near everyday because some dope-fiend left underaged children in the house to fend for themselves.

The examples were everywhere, indeed. But the game was so alluring that it captivated everyone who got too close to it. My Aunt Kim and I both got too close to the game. It captivated us and devastated our lives in ways that we knew were possible. I guess our self-centered attitudes allowed us to go full speed ahead. Fuck the hurt, pain, and sheer devastation. I wanted to be a drug-dealer and she wanted to experience the euphoria of the narcotic as often as she could. Although Kim and I never agreed to support the other's negative choice, we tacitly did. We were partners in each other's destruction.

I reported to the stash house on Chapel Street and performed my duties well into the wee hours again. Calvin did not come home with me the second night, but there was no problem. Kim was not there to chastise me for staying out all day. Kieshawn was home with Yalanda alone—again. This became a routine. I would come home at about three or four o'clock in the morning to find Kieshawn and Yalanda home alone. Kim would come in at about noon or later, and go directly to bed. Calvin was hardly ever coming home. Therefore, Kieshawn and I had to run the house and care for Yalanda.

It was obvious to Kieshawn and me that something horrible was happening. We were not naïve children. We knew that Kim was on drugs. However, we did not speak about it. We simply accepted the fact that we would have to fend for ourselves, just like so many of our friends. Since I was the oldest, I would naturally take charge. I was just fortunate that Kieshawn was precocious. It made my job a lot easier. Also, Mama, my grandmother, came by the house often to collect Yalanda or to simply stay around until Kim showed. I was not really an issue; I was thirteen, practically a grown man in ghetto years. I was running the streets, hustling with Calvin—earning my keep.

Kim came out of her drug stupor every now and again to tell me to go to school, and I would go, sometimes. I always liked going up to the school to show off my new clothes and jewelry. After I had been working with Calvin and Fat Larry for about two weeks, I had accumulated quite a few trinkets. Kim was hardly at home, and I was earning $200 or $300 a night. I was spending more time at the stash house and less time at school. I shared the money I was earning generously with Kim and Kieshawn. Calvin had left Kim; however, he still came around from time to time to help out with the bills. Kim was not managing anything. Mama often came to our house to cook. Kieshawn cared for Yalanda. Sometimes, Kim would give her a reprieve by caring for Yalanda herself. I even watched Yalanda some. But my primary function was to earn enough money to pay our bills. The money Kim received from welfare went directly to the drugs.

I cannot be certain if Kim's decision to be a dope-fiend was sudden or gradual. I just know that within a month of my going to work for Calvin and Fat Larry, Kim was an outright dope-fiend. Totally self-centered and interested in nothing but her "blast."

I made sure Kieshawn went to school. I felt that it was the right thing to do. Besides, she really enjoyed going. I showed up at school occasionally. I never stayed the entire day, but I did make an appearance. Most of my time was spent in the stash house on Chapel Street maintaining an accurate count of the money and drugs. I had become so self-centered, like Kim, that I often neglected Kieshawn and Yalanda myself. On days when the narcotic trade was busy, I would stay out all night. I was not missed at home, and if things got too hectic for Kieshawn, she could always call Mama or Ms. Rose, her paternal grandmother.

I recall coming home one morning, in the wee hours, and Kim was laying down on the front room couch waiting for me. She was high on heroin, I could easily detect it. "Tray, where the hell you been?" Kim asked.

"Why?"

"This shit gotta stop," Kim broke into tears. "Calvin was driving me crazy. I had to get outta here. But I am back now."

"Well I hope so, 'cause I'm tired of takin' care of Yalanda by myself, and I know Kie is, too."

"I'm just so tired, Tray," Kim was truly grieving. "I don't know what to do."

Kim was in genuine emotional pain. She was reaching out to me. But I was too immature to be emotionally available to her. I dismissed her tears and comments as products of a-induced stupor.

Kim was twenty-two years old and responsible for three children, one of which was not biologically her own. She was an uneducated high school drop out. On top of that, she had a drug habit. Her relationship with Calvin ended with a lot of hurtful words, and she did not have anyone to turn to. She reached out to me, and I ignored her.

Kim had simply become another dope-fiend. We shared the same home and blood—and she had cared for me and nurtured me when my own mother would not. She gave me all that she had in love, food, and shelter. She protected me from the justice system and loneliness. It was painful to see her submit herself to heroin addiction. I suspect it was equally painful for her to see me give my life to criminality. We each foresaw the other's future, but our respective deficiencies prevented us from aiding the other in a way that would prevent so much pain, suffering, and hardship.

"Kim, I'll holla at you when I get up," I headed for my bedroom. "You high right now."

"Yeah, I'm high," Kim admitted as she went deeply into a heroin-induced nod.

I no longer feared Kim's reaction to my curfew violations or any other transgression. I was grown. Legally, Kim was my guardian, she was my beloved aunt, and I loved her dearly, but I knew that I could not save her and I definitely did not want to be saved. I wanted to move up in my chosen occupation. I had dedicated well over a month to the stash house. It was time that I make-my-bones and get acquainted with Fat Larry, the big fat boss, and move up.

Shoot 'em Up Bang

Chapter 20

"Yo, why Larry don't never come 'round here?" I asked Mustard.

"Cause he ain't got to." Mustard and I had started getting close. He always answered my questions as best he could. I suppose it made him feel somewhat important to be able to educate me in matters pertaining to our organization. "Calvin and Boody do everything. Larry just sit on his fat ass and count money."

That sounded like a pretty good job to me. I admired Fat Larry; I saw him occasionally. He knew that I was working the stash house, and apparently had no objection. I had determined in my mind that I was going to make his acquaintance. I was grateful to Calvin for employing me. But after working the stash house for a month and a half, I had grown tired of it. Besides, now that Kim was not overwhelming me with her restrictions, I could freely hang out on the corners where the excitement was, and where my chance to prove my value to the crew would improve.

Kim had said that she would stop using drugs and start staying home more, but she hadn't. Well, she did start staying home more, but she just started bringing her dope-fiend friends home with her. It was truly a mess. Our home did not become a "shootin' gallery," a place where drug addicts come to inject their narcotics. However, it was no longer a warm and comfortable place. There were new people coming to our house almost every day, and it was not uncommon for a guest to use my bedroom or Kieshawn's bedroom to have sex.

I knew it was useless to confront Kim on the matter of our home becoming a "flop house" and no longer safe for Kieshawn and Yalanda. Being self-centered is a symptom of drug addiction. All Kim cared about was her blast. All that talk about keeping home safe, preparing a good meal for the children, and monitoring the curfew shit was dead—a thing of the past. I could do whatever I wanted, as long as I did not interfere with Kim's blast. I finally had the freedom to destroy my life.

I had been reporting to the stash house by nine o'clock in the morning each day for the past week. I promised myself each day that the next day I would go to school, but something more exciting and interesting would prevent me from keeping that promise. Calvin was relying on me more and more. There were days when no one could be in the stash house other than me. Mustard had a family, a daughter and a wife. He had to leave the house for long periods of time to attend to personal family matters. And aside from Mustard, I was the only one who could be trusted with all the drugs and money. That's what I was told. I later learned that not too many people would be willing to sit in the stash house. It was the most dangerous position in the drug operation. If the "stick-up" boys came to rob the crew, the first place they would come is to the stash house. If the police were going to bust up our operation, they would come to the stash house first. In other words, the man managing the stash house was the most vulnerable. He was the primary target for the enemies of the crew. Also, he was the most restricted. The dealers out on the corners had the benefit of mobility and view. They could see what was coming and run from it. The man "holding" was stuck in the house holding the bags.

"Mustard, hold shit down," I had been in the stash house all day, ever since about nine o'clock that morning and it was nearing nine o'clock in the evening. "I need a break."

"Yo, don't be long," Mustard said. "I gotta be home by twelve."

How odd, just a little over a month ago I was the one who was concerned about getting home by midnight. Now, I sought to avoid home as much as possible. I felt far more comfortable in the stash house with its single bed in the front bedroom and a plain couch and dinner table in the kitchen than I did at home. The plethora of guns gave me far more security than the parade of dope-fiends invading our home—at Kim's invitation.

I needed some fresh air. I was restless and wanted to go out on the strip to see if I could catch up with Fat Larry. I wanted to tell him that I was tired of working the stash house and let him know that I would be more valuable out on the strip, running. I was going to tell Larry that I had asked Calvin to take me out of the stash house, but he continued to tell me that no one other than me could be trusted to hold the stash.

I knew that was bullshit; any dummy could be found to sit in a stash house. I felt confident that if I appealed to the great Fat Larry myself, he would elevate me. Calvin was okay; I truly liked him. He just could not appreciate my talents, or he felt that he owed Kim not to put me on the corner. Whatever Calvin was thinking or feeling, he would not let me leave the stash house. He consistently paid me well each night. He even paid most of the monthly bills at our house, though he and Kim were no longer romantically attached.

I went to the closet in the middle room and pulled out the .38 caliber, nickel-plated, pearl-handled handgun I had grown to like. I checked it to make sure it was loaded. It was, so I tucked it into my waistband, put on the black puff-leather coat I had recently purchased from the Diplomat at Old Town Mall and headed out the back door. I wanted to see what was happening on the strip. It was Friday night, and it was likely I would have to manage the stash house all by myself. I had to see what freak-bitch I could pay, with heroin, to keep me company.

When I got to Eager Street, I did not see Fat Larry or any appealing women to solicit. So I walked up to Ashland Avenue and Wolfe Street where I met up with my cousin, Boobie. I asked Boobie what was he up to. He told me that since I had started working for Fat Larry, he didn't see me much anymore. He asked me to accompany him on his journey "for old time's sake."

Boobie was one of my favorite cousins. He was a few years older and was pretty good with the ladies. He had no hustling abilities that I recognized and was always low on cash. I assumed that he mentioned my employment with Fat Larry because he was going to beg me for some money. I was generous, by nature; I would give Boobie a few dollars if he asked. He would not request more than ten or twenty bucks. I could easily handle that. It would not cost me much to walk with Boobie. Besides, I wanted to see Robin, Boobie's sister. She was fine, but my family had no place for incest.

"Cool, I'll roll with you," I accepted Boobie's offer to accompany him. "I ain't seen Robin in a long time," I joked. "Think she'll give me a hit of ass?"

"Buy me a beer and lend me ten dollars, and I'll damn sure ask her," he was serious.

"Damn nigga, every time I see you it cost me," I peeled a ten dollar bill from my bank roll. "You ain't never pay me the other two ten dollars I loaned you."

"I thought you gave it to me big shot," Boobie innocently said. "Let's go get that beer. You want one?"

We stopped at the bar on the corner of Chapel and Ashland and got two Miller beers, at my expense. Boobie popped the top and drank from his bottle and I did likewise. We left the bar and headed down Ashland Avenue toward Robin's house at Ashland and Collington. When we got there, Robin was standing on her front steps, dressed in a pair of blue jeans, an oversized gray sweat shirt, and tennis shoes arguing with a group of about six men. The argument looked rather intense, so Boobie and I hurried to get close.

"Naw, bitch, you ain't just gonna take my money," this short, stocky-built and very dark complexioned man was saying to Robin. "I gave you $40."

"And I gave you twenty-eight grams of weed," Robin shouted back. "If you ain't satisfied, you just shit outta luck."

"Man, I know you ain't gonna just let this bitch take your scratch," someone from the crowd offered.

"Give me my money back, bitch," the stocky man hounded. "That shit wasn't nothing."

"Hold tight, partner," I said to the belligerent man as I walked up to the crowd. "This my family."

"I ain't your muthafuckin' partner," he said to me. "And my name is Mouse."

"Robin, what's goin' on?" Boobie asked his sister.

I felt that it was utterly wrong for Boobie to ask Robin that question. It suggested that the possibility existed that we would take sides against her. There was no such thing as being neutral in a drug dispute. You chose a side, and fought from there. I understood that. Robin understood and the nigga who told me that his name was Mouse understood that concept as well. Boobie was the only naïve person present, and it obviously annoyed Robin.

"None of your business," Robin let Boobie know she was not pleased with his question. "I can handle this."

"You ain't gotta handle it by yourself, Cuz," I was staring directly into the eyes of Mouse. "I'm with you."

Robin felt a boost of instant courage, "Fuck these whore ass niggas. If they don't like what I sold 'em they can kiss my ass."

Without warning, Mouse reached out and grabbed Robin. He pulled her from the steps to the ground. He slapped her hard across the face and instructed her to speak to him with respect. Robin swung at him wildly, but it was to no avail. Mouse was too strong to be affected by her blows. Boobie launched at Mouse in a clumsy effort to rescue his sister, but Mouse simply threw Robin in Boobie's path. The quick move baffled Boobie, and before he could fully recover, Mouse hit him on the chin with a thunderous punch. Boobie went to the ground hard, but he was not hurt. He leaped to his feet and ran up Collington Avenue toward Madison Street like a frightened hare. Robin and I looked at each other in utter embarrassment. Boobie was a coward, and his cowardice left us more vulnerable than we were originally. For Mouse and his buddies became even more hostile and threatening.

"Nigga, you next or what?" Mouse asked me.

"I guess I am," I calmly said as I pulled the .38 from my waistband. I pointed the gun toward Mouse's face, closed my eyes, and pulled the trigger.

I heard the explosion from the gun and heard the many shouts of shocked onlookers. Everything seemed to move in slow motion. Mouse fell to the ground with blood gushing from his neck. His friends backed away then came toward me. I raised the gun again, and fired it until it was empty. Almost in a daze, I ran in the same direction Boobie had run only moments before. I had no idea where I was going. I was afraid. I thought I had killed Mouse and his friends. I just ran. When I finally came to a stop to collect my thoughts, I was in a predominantly white neighborhood in South Baltimore. I fixed my clothing, tossed the gun down a sewage drain, and turned north. I figured Mustard would know what I should do. He had told me that he had killed a man before. There wasn't anything to it. According to Mustard and ghetto logic, the only way a man can get respect is to kill somebody. If you ain't a "bad ass nigga" ain't nobody going to respect you. And without respect, don't even think about making any good money.

Well, Fat Larry will definitely hear about my exploit, and respect me for it. I had just shot a block up and dropped a few niggas. I was a "bad ass nigga" in the making. Surely, a promotion would not be denied me.

I would have to endure my first period of incarceration before I got my promotion, of course. Everyone knew about the incident. The police were looking for me, Fat Larry was looking for me, and Kim and Calvin were looking for me.

"Yo, wait here," Mustard said to me as soon as I came through the door. "I'm gonna go get Larry. He wanna see you."

My options were limited. I really had nowhere to go. According to Mustard, the police were probably at my house, or would be there. My safest place at the moment was at the stash house. Besides, I was about to get an audience with Fat Larry—my hero.

Mustard left the house through the back door. He came back after only a few minutes to announce, "Larry is parked up on Washington and Madison. He waitin' on you."

I went to meet Larry. He was parked on the corner with the motor running. He motioned for me to get into his silver-gray Cadillac Coupe Deville, with the thick red leather interior. I got in and he pulled away from the curve. "What's happenin'?" he asked me.

"Nigga slapped my cousins 'round, then tried to slap me 'round."

"What you do with the iron?"

Larry had to know whether or not his future best employee was smart. "I threw it away. It won't ever be found."

"Calvin and Kim gonna be with you. If you get locked up my lawyer will represent you."

"Where we goin'?" I was curious. I appreciated riding in the luxurious car, and I thoroughly enjoyed being in Fat Larry's presence, getting his attention. It was especially satisfying that he was not disappointed in me for shooting someone. On the contrary, he seemed kind of pleased. The way he spoke to me hinted that he respected me.

"Look Jack, dem niggas, Mouse and 'em be tryin' that lean shit all the time," Larry apparently knew more about the trouble I was in than I did. "You pulled their card. You gonna be all right. I'm takin' you home to Kim and Calvin so y'all can handle this."

I had complete faith in Larry; I sensed that he had already fixed everything for me. Otherwise, he wouldn't dare suggest that I turn myself in to the pigs. The ghetto's code was clear: don't turn yourself in! Let the police catch you when they catch you—unless you got everything under control.

Twisted Guidance

Chapter 21

Larry and I drove around for about an hour just talking. He let me know that he had been aware of the good work I was doing in the house. He told me that I was the first person who worked in the stash house who he did not receive any complaints about. All the others who worked the stash house stole small portions of drugs from each bag. Larry expressed to me that it was truly frustrating to work with so many petty people. He was rather stoic about the entire matter, though. "Jack, this a rotten ass business. If you ain't as rotten as the rest of these niggas out here, you ain't gonna make it."

Larry was quite successful, so I imagined he was among the most rotten. He was telling me that betrayal and treachery were standard codes of conduct, and I was willing to place my entire life in his hand. He told me that Calvin was weak and ineffectual as his second in command. Larry said to me, "I need you at my right hand. You a soldier."

All I had to do was shoot someone to get the notice I had sought for so long. Those who demonstrated gentleness and a sense of forgiveness were considered weak and ineffectual. They were continuously robbed and cheated of monetary profits. They could not command the respect and admiration of anyone. Calvin was a good man. However, he was a terrible liability in the drug game. Larry let me know, in no uncertain terms, that I would be his next lieutenant. When I asked him about Calvin, he simply said, "Fuck that nigga." I told Larry that I thought Calvin was his partner.

Larry let me know that he didn't have any partner, and if he had any, he would be a strong soldier like me.

Larry dropped me off a couple blocks from my house. "Handle this bullshit," he instructed me as I exited the car. "I need you out here with me. You got heart."

It was about two o'clock in the morning when I got home. Kim and Calvin were sitting on the living room couch watching television and waiting for me. "Boy, what happened?" Kim excitedly asked. "The police been here lookin' for you. They say you shot somebody."

"I did," I didn't feel a need to lie. "They say whether or not he die?"

"No," Kim was truly relaxed. She obviously had her blast in her. "He ain't dead. But the police say the guy is in real bad shape. You shot him in the neck."

"Tray," Calvin was going to take control. "We already handled dem niggas that was standing 'round. Me and Larry talked to everybody. When the police come to scoop you, just say the nigga pulled a knife out and tried to rob you and your cousin."

That was close enough to the truth for me. Mouse had threatened me. He did not have a knife, but in my opinion his fist was just as deadly. I was justified in shooting Mouse, at least by ghetto standards. If I was not justified in shooting Mouse, Larry made it so. Mouse was only some nigga who brought me the acclaim I longed for. I did not care whether he lived or died. When I asked Kim whether the police had disclosed Mouse's status, I was asking because I wanted to know the depth of my troubles.

Larry had calmed me down. I was no longer nervous and frightened. I felt that everything would be all right; Mouse was no more than a trouble-maker whom no one liked. He was a known stick-up boy. Not one segment of the community sympathized with him. I, on the other hand, was an up and coming player. It would have been an awful tragedy to sacrifice my life for his.

When the police came to my house to arrest me for the "attempted murder" of Mouse, I was prepared to go. I had my story together. Per Calvin's and Larry's instruction, I was not to tell anyone other than my attorney what happened. It was decided that I would not tell the police anything. I would tell my attorney my story, and leave it up to him to tell the police.

The police were not cruel to me. They simply came to my house to apprehend me. There was a loud knock on the door. Calvin asked, "Who is it?"

"Baltimore City Police," was the answer.

I opened the door, three uniformed police officers were standing at the front of the house. A short chubby cop asked me, "Are you Arlando Jones?"

My instinct was to lie, but I denied it and responded truthfully, "Yeah, what's up?"

The two other police quickly moved in on me from either side, taking hold of my arms and placing them behind my back. The short chubby cop announced, "You are under arrest for the attempted murder of...."

I was ushered to the police cruiser, handcuffed, and placed into the back seat. A tall white policeman was standing at our front steps talking to Kim. He was telling her why I was being arrested and obviously answering all of her other questions. The short chubby officer got into the cruiser on the driver's side. He slid behind the wheel, and his partner, a tall muscular young white officer, got into the passenger side.

We pulled away from the curb with two other police patrol cars directly behind us. I sat in the back of the cruiser in utter silence with my hands cuffed behind me. I was not afraid. In fact, I felt rather exhilarated.

"You really put it to that fucker, didn't you?"

I can't recall which of the officers asked the question; however, I do recall having to fight back an urge to say, "Yeah, I burned his ass up." I simply ignored the comment and endured the drive to Eastern Police District in absolute silence. Larry had instructed me not to say a damn word to anyone except his attorney. I was going to obey his instruction to the very letter. The police would surely use anything I said against me. It would be foolish to tell them anything. Let them construct their case against me with the words of witnesses, not mine. Larry had told me that it was stupid to answer police questions without first talking to an attorney. The police were clear in their warning "...everything you say can and will be used against you in the court of law."

I was not going to participate in my own demise. Well, at least not consciously. The moment I decided to participated in the illegal narcotic trade I was participating in my very own death. I just did not understand it at the time. I simply wanted to be a big nigga on the block—instead of an inconsequential, unnoticed, frightened little boy. I wanted to stand out in the crowd and be recognized as popular and worthy of attention and affection—and love.

A Course at the Little Big House

Chapter 22

No one wanted to hear my version of the story once I reached Eastern Police District. I was ushered into a cramped, isolated bullpen for juvenile offenders and instructed to wait until someone from Juvenile Services' intake unit came to determine what was to happen to me. I sat around on the benches with two other juvenile offender. I did not speak to them. I simply wanted to get out of that damn bullpen. The stench of the place nauseated me. It seemed as if folks had pissed on the floor as opposed to the urinals and no one bothered to clean it up. I felt very uncomfortable on the wood bench. I was tired and wanted to sleep. However, I was not going to lie down on the bench as did the other two occupants of the bullpen. They appeared to be comfortable, as if lying down on benches in a police station was natural to them. They engaged in idle conversation as if not bothered by whatever offense to society they were accused of.

The other two boys seemed to be older than I, so, I assumed it would be best if I followed their example and not display my impatience. It would not serve my interest to start acting like a sissy, whining to the police to please call someone down here to talk to me. I sorely needed to hear from someone. I had shot a man, I was special. I deserved more attention than I was getting. Didn't they know that I was up and coming in the narcotic trade? The police were supposed to come to interrogate me, knock me about my head and punch me in order to coerce a confession. I was prepared to meet that sort of brutality and not utter a word. But that never happened. A woman from Juvenile Services came to the bullpen at about six o'clock that morning to inform me that I was going to the Maryland Training School for Boys, and that I would go before a Baltimore City Circuit Court Master first thing Monday morning. My Aunt Kim had already been informed, and she would appear in court with me. The other two boys were given their walking papers. I overheard the lady tell them that as soon as their respective parents came to the station to retrieve them, they would be released. They were petty criminals; they were being charged with unauthorized use of an automobile. I, on the other hand, had banged that gun. A strong message had to be sent to me.

Shortly after being told that I would be going to Training School, a tall, youthful looking white city policeman came to get me. He handcuffed me and escorted me to a police cruiser. I was ushered into the back seat, and the officer got into his place behind the wheel and drove off. I was extremely tired. I dozed off, and when I awoke we were driving along a long road in a suburban community. The beauty and solitude threw me completely aback. I had never seen so many trees and manicured grasslands. I was moving up in the world. I had been surrounded by the noise and bright lights of the inner city my entire life. My perception was that communities such as the one I was being taken into were reserved for the wealthy.

The barbed wire fences and security booth with a large sign hung prominently above it reading "Maryland Training School for Boys" were the only things that isolated its palatial grounds as a place for confinement. When we stopped at the fence, the police officer who was escorting me to my new home exited the vehicle, went up to the fence and spoke to whomever was inside the booth. After papers were exchanged, he came back to the cruiser and announced to me, "This is your new home, boy. They got room for you."

I offered an indifferent look toward the officer as a response. I was not going to say anything to anyone, except my attorney. I was not going to complain about any treatment. I was going to endure everything like a "strong soldier"—the kind of nigga Fat Larry respected.

The officer got back into the cruiser and drove a few hundred yards farther down the road to the administration building. We stopped at the building's front entrance, and the officer opened the door to release me from the confines of the back of the cruiser. I stretched my cramped legs and allowed myself to be taken into the building. The officer who brought me to Training School told the fat black woman seated behind the huge desk, "Got one killer for you, Janice."

"Yeah, I heard he was comin'," she said. "Where's his paperwork?"

The officer gave Janice the folder he was carrying and said, "He's all yours now. See you later." He removed the handcuffs from my wrists and left.

It was that simple. I remained standing where I was until Janice motioned this other guy who was standing behind the desk with her to take me to another bullpen.

The administration building was rather crowded. Folks were coming in and out at frequent intervals. I couldn't distinguish the staff members from the inmates. They all looked pretty much alike. Besides, I was still very tired. I had not had any sleep, except for the brief nap I took during the drive from the police station. I just wanted to rest. I was exhausted physically and mentally. The magnitude of my crime had completely eluded me. I was simply going through some kind of police-criminal-justice system ritual.

I felt overwhelming gratitude when I was taken to an empty bullpen in the isolation unit and left alone. There were no benches or bathroom facilities in the place. There was only a clean, bare concrete floor. I laid down in the corner, stretched out fully, and went fast to sleep. I was not bothered by being locked away in a barren room. I had heard everyone's opinion about my situation, and what I should do. I was following Larry's instructions to the letter. Now, I was alone with my own thoughts. Rather than face those thoughts, I went to sleep. I was afraid of them. I had shot a man, nearly killed him. The fear of going to prison was too overwhelming. I did not want to think about what would happen if I had to face Mouse or his friends again. In my heart, I was a frightened little boy. However, I was called upon to play the role of a "bad ass nigga," a role I was too young to assume. I was not intellectually or emotionally mature enough to make that decision. Others had made it for me, and since I wanted to please everyone, I filled the role.

A counselor finally came to the bullpen to get me. He seemed to be a kind old gentleman. He told me to follow him. He led me to a small office with a tiny desk and some small plastic hard-back chairs. Sitting behind the desk in the only cushioned chair in the office, he then motioned for me to sit down in one of the hard-back plastic chairs. I sat down, and the man asked me, "Why did you do it?"

I couldn't meet this man's kind stare. His question wasn't accusing or condemning. It was simply kind and gentle. I looked down toward the floor and said, "I don't know."

"I'm going to send you to Unit Four with Ms. Patterson. She's a nice lady," he said to me. "If you have any problems talk to her. If you can't talk to her, send for me. My name is Mr. Whitey."

I grinned; the name, Mr. Whitey, fit this man perfectly. He was pale white, with the whitest gray hair I had ever seen. Moreover, Mr. Whitey had some pure white false teeth in his mouth. He was definitely an old man, at least sixty-five, beyond the years of having his natural teeth.

Mr. Whitey asked my age, address, whom to contact in the event of an emergency, and some other easy questions. I answered them all, and he wrote my answers in a yellow folder.

"Arlando, you will be going to court on Monday," Mr. Whitey said. "When you come back, I may have to move you to a different housing unit."

Fat Larry did not say that I would have to stay at Training School. He gave me the impression that everything had been taken care of. All I had to do was answer to the charges. Mr. Whitey must be mistaken. I told him I would not be coming back after I went before a judge; my people had everything under control. This was a ghetto matter. The courts had no need to interfere. The rules of the code would be strictly adhered to in this matter. I shot a guy who deserved being shot. Mouse had already been trivialized. If he was important, the police would have asked me questions about him. If I remembered correctly, one of the cops had referred to Mouse as a "piece of shit."

Mr. Whitey left me alone in the office for a moment. He had to go get someone to escort me over to Housing Unit Four. When he returned, he was accompanied by a tall muscular black man dressed in a blue staff security uniform. Mr. Whitey ordered the man to take me to Unit Four. I got up from the chair and followed the security officer out of the door and out of the administration building, and into the parking lot where a blue staff van awaited. The security officer opened the van's back door and motioned for me to get inside. I got into the van, seated myself on the bench and waited patiently to be taken to Housing Unit Four. I took in the beautiful scenery, amazed at how picturesque this place of confinement looked. There were tall lovely trees everywhere, and the lawns were well kept. I saw flower beds and neatly painted cottages. The officer got into the van and drove about a hundred yards. He stopped in front of one of the well-painted cottages that I assumed was the home of a well-to-do staff member. I was shocked when the officer came to the back of the van to let me out. "This is Unit Four," the officer announced. "Your new home."

I thought to myself that Housing Unit Four looked better than any home I had ever lived in from the outside. I was anxious to see what the inside looked like.

Before I reached the top of the steps, the door swung open and I was ushered into the building. I found myself standing in the center of a locked cage rather than a living room that would have complemented the outside of the building. The place was far larger inside than the outside led me to believe. Outside the cage were rows of tables where children about my age sat playing cards, watching television, or simply talking. No one, other than the staff officers, seemed to notice my entrance. The various conversations and other activities that were going on when I stepped into the cottage continued. The staff member inside the cage told the security officer who escorted me that she had me, I was hers. I did not mind. This lady was fairly attractive and was very shapely. Her body was well-proportioned: nice round butt, ample breasts, and smooth brown skin. She appeared to be much older than I; I guessed her age to be around forty-five, but she was well-kept. If I were hers, I wasn't mad at nobody because of it. She looked far better than any of the girls and women I had had.

The security officer left, and the lady introduced herself to me, "My name is Ms. Patterson. I'm the unit manager."

I liked Ms. Patterson from the start. I did not care about her personality traits. I wanted Ms. Patterson sexually, and I am willing to wager any amount of money that the look of pure, unadulterated lust on my face told her just that.

Ms. Patterson informed me that I would be expected to follow whatever instructions the staff members gave. I was expected to treat everyone with respect, and if I wanted to play ping-pong or pool, I had to place my name on a list. A staff person would tell me when my time came to play. I would have to go to each meal, bedtime was at ten o'clock, and wake-up call was at seven in the morning. I was expected to make my bed every day and was responsible for my personal hygiene. I had to take off my personal clothes and wear state-issued clothing. I could not have any personal items whatsoever.

Ms. Patterson opened the cage we were in and took me to a back room. The noise from the various conversations, ping-pong, and pool games was overwhelming, but I was not effected by it. I was too busy trying to see if I recognized any of the inmates in the cottage. I saw a few familiar faces, but I didn't see anyone whom I actually knew. I followed Ms. Patterson through the crowd of boys to the back room. We came to a locked door at the rear of a long hallway, and she told me, "This is the darkroom, the place where you are to come every day to get a change of clothes."

It was very dark in the room, It was dim even after Ms. Patterson turned on the lights.

"Take off your clothes."

"What?" I was shocked by the order. "Take my clothes off?"

"That's what I said," she was enjoying the moment. "You ain't shy are you?"

"No, I ain't shy," I took off my top clothes. The pants, shirt, jacket, and shoes I was wearing. I left my underwear on. "You happy?"

"Not quite," Ms. Patterson was amusing herself at my expense. "Take off all your clothes. Come out your drawers, socks—all that shit."

Cool, Ms. Patterson curses. She was not some self-righteous Christian woman. "You gonna take yours off too?"

"Boy, take your damn drawers off!" She wasn't offended. I suspect I wasn't the first to ask her the very same question.

I complied; I took off my clothes and I stood before her completely naked. I felt extremely uncomfortable and embarrassed. My penis just hung there, limp, and I knew that my body was simply a child's body. Ms. Patterson could not possibly be attracted to me. I was far from physically endowed. "Can you hurry up and give me something to cover up with?"

"What size you wear?"

"Medium underwear, twenty-nine waist pants."

"You a small underwear," she said as she reached onto the shelf behind her and gathered me some underclothes. "Put these on."

I didn't want to debate underwear size. I just wanted some drawers to put on. So I took the underclothes offered me. "What you gonna do with my stuff?"

"It'll be locked away in here until you go to court," she answered. "Don't worry about it."

I was issued an outfit for the day. Ms. Patterson informed me that I would be given a change of clothes every day. I was taken out to the recreation area and told that I would find out how things went as the day progressed. "Just follow the program."

I could do that. I followed the program of the criminal element my entire life. It would not be difficult for me to fit into the Maryland Training School for Boys. All I had to do was hook up with someone from my 'hood and let him show me how things went. I had seen a few familiar faces when I first came through the door. Surely, someone would put my boots on, give me a thorough orientation. I had been told already that staff members don't run the joint. The bad ass niggas do.

• • •

I hooked up with Onion, a cat I was familiar with from the hustlers' circuit. We had never been formally introduced. But we had seen each other on many occasions. At the disco spots, downtown at Crazy John's, the shopping malls, and at various crap houses. All the places in Baltimore City that hustlers patronize.

Soon as I stepped into the crowded recreation room, Onion came up to me and said, "What's happenin', Yo?"

"You tell me, hustler."

"Tryin' stay out these lame-ass-niggas way," Onion was beginning to orientate me to Training School. "These lames be tryin' to pull up on hustlers, actin' like they cool. But some of these niggas be real bitches. Tellin' about everything a nigga do."

Experience had taught me that when you are on unfamiliar territory, you keep your mouth shut until you learn everything that's necessary to navigate your own way. It was apparent that Onion had been there longer than a day or two. He seemed very comfortable with his surroundings. The others seemed to notice me once he came up to me. We were catching curious glances. When I first came into the housing unit, no one stopped to notice me. Now that Onion had come up to talk to me, everyone was looking in our direction. It was obvious that Onion possessed some kind of celebrity status.

"Hang on my team," Onion told me. "I don't hang with none of these lames. I don't even speak to 'em."

A guy came up to ask Onion, "What's happenin'," but he ignored him. He gave the guy a nasty look that indicated that we were not to be bothered. I was surprised the guy walked away from us without cursing Onion out for his arrogance. I guess Onion was right when he said that there was a host of lames in the cottage with us. For only a lame would've allowed himself to be treated with such indifference without protest.

"See how dem suckers just come up to a nigga tryin' to get familiar?" Onion asked me.

"Yeah, for real," I casually offered.

"Just put these suckers on the pay-you-no-mind list and you'll be all right."

Onion went on to tell me that the best way to serve out my time in the housing unit was to stay out of everyone's affair. Mind my own business. He then asked me why was I there. I told him, "I had put that burner on a few niggas 'round the way."

Larry was clear when he told me not to tell any officials about what I had done. I could confess to a fellow hustler about my ghetto exploit. Besides, I had to let someone know that I wasn't locked up for something petty. I was an important nigga, not to be confused with any of the lames in the unit. Also, I needed to confess my crimes. Onion gave me the opportunity to do that without damning myself in the process. No one had given me the opportunity to confess my sins. I did what I did, and there was nothing to be said about it.

I couldn't tell Onion how afraid I was to have to face the possible consequences of my action. I couldn't have him qualify me as one of the lames in the unit. However, I could tell him that I did it, and that made me feel somewhat better. A great weight was on my shoulders, and I did not know how to lift it. Telling Onion that I shot a few guys served to boost my image and assuage my emotional pain and confusion.

"Yeah man," I was going to share as much about my crime with Onion as was ghetto permissible. "Suckers tried to rob me and my cousin, so I banged on 'em."

"How shit look for you?" Onion knew that it would have been inappropriate to ask the identity of the victims. They might have been his family or friends.

"I go to court Monday," I said. "Fat Larry said he got everything under control."

Onion was definitely impressed. I could detect his admiration. Mentioning Fat Larry's name did that. Fat Larry was some kind of an icon in East Baltimore. It was good for my image to be associated with him.

Onion had suggested that we go down to the gym to play ping-pong or shoot some pool. The gym was adjacent to the recreation room. All we had to do to reach our destination was walk about ten to fifteen feet and go directly down a single flight of steps. In the gym, there was a group of boys playing a game of basketball at a single basket attached to the wall at the end of the gym. A pool table and ping-pong table were at the opposite end, where Onion and I stood. There were two staff members in the gym monitoring about fifty of us delinquent boys. One of the staff members was playing a game of ping-pong, so he was not doing too much monitoring of us.

Onion walked up to one of the guys playing pool and asked him, "Let me have this game?"

The guy looked a little dejected, but he handed the pool stick over to Onion without protest. Onion made a few shots and missed a few, and the other guy did likewise. I stood by and watched. Eventually, the guy beat Onion, but Onion told him to forfeit his winners so that he and I could play. The guy gave me his pool stick. Onion started collecting the balls from their pockets, and I reached for the rack so that we could start a new game. Before we could start the game, Ms. Patterson yelled down from the top of the steps, "Michael and Arlando, it ain't y'all game. Get on the list if you want to play."

Onion protested; he told Ms. Patterson that no one else wanted to play. Therefore, it was only proper to let him play his homeboy. Ms. Patterson disregarded his protest and insisted that Onion and I put the pool sticks down and get on the list. She then ordered Mr. Waters, the staff personnel sitting in the only cushioned chair in the gym, to monitor the pool list. She did not say anything to the staff person playing ping-pong. I guess he was doing his job. He had a large number of inmates lined up ready to play him. He was beating everyone who challenged him. The youth inmates seemed to be enjoying themselves trying to put this man off the pin-pong table. They were trash-talking, and one after the next vowed to beat him the next game. I asked Onion who was the staff person beating everyone at ping-pong. He informed me that the man's name was Mr. Stippio. He told me that Mr. Stippio was cool, all he did the entire time he was there was play ping-pong, cards, and nap. Onion also said that he believed that Mr. Stippio was a closet homosexual. He felt that Mr. Stippio derived some kind of strange pleasure from watching the guys on the unit take showers.

I knew how to play ping-pong. I had learned the game from playing it at the recreation center around my neighborhood, and I wanted to play. I asked who was last. Some skinny, tall, freckled-face white kid told me that he was last. I was to play after him. Mr. Stippio told everyone that he would permit me to play the next game. He said that he had beaten everyone else, and he wanted some new meat. No one objected. So after he soundly defeated the kid he was playing, I was given the paddle and told to try my hand.

Mr. Stippio beat me just as soundly as he had beaten everyone else. However, he did assure me that I had potential. He said that he should have beaten me by a far greater margin than he did. I was new there; he felt that he should have skunked me.

I assured Mr. Stippio, like the others before me, that I would beat him the next time we played. Ms. Patterson announced from the top of the gym stairs that it was time for lunch. Everyone in the gym started leaving. I followed alongside Onion. We made our way to a large lavatory with two long rows of wash basins, about twenty to thirty in all. We all washed our hands and came back out to the recreational area. We were ordered to line up. One by one we went out the door in a single file. Mr. Waters and Mr. Stippio counted us. We were ushered onto a bus that had steel grills covering the windows. Once we were all on the bus, I heard someone yell, "Got seventy-one of 'em."

"That's what I got," someone else said.

Ms. Patterson was the last one onto the bus. She announced, "All clear; let's go eat."

Conversations erupted all over the bus. From the moment we all left the lavatory and began lining up around the recreation room wall, no one spoke a word. I had asked Onion what was going on once we started lining up, but he had quieted me quickly by holding his hand to his lip motioning for me to be silent. I held my question. Now that conversations were going on again, I felt it appropriate to ask, "What the fuck was that all about?"

"When they count us you gotta be quiet," Onion informed me. "They'll put a nigga in the hole 'bout that count shit."

I wanted to ask Onion what was the hole, but I felt I should know what it was, so I didn't ask. I just knew the hole wasn't a place I wanted to go. I sensed it was an awful place. Meanwhile, we were going to the cafeteria. Onion told me that I would see a lot of my homies over there. He told me that I could holler to them across the room, but I was not to have any physical contact with anyone outside of our housing unit. He told me that once I sit down, don't get up for anything. The consequence of a violation of the last rule in the cafeteria was spending the night in the hole. I had a plethora of questions to ask, but I felt that I would appear naïve if I posed them. I simply followed the program and did what everyone else did. All I had to do was endure this dumb shit for a single weekend, and I would go home first thing Monday. I had an esteemed position awaiting me upon my release. Larry had all but promised me that I would be his lieutenant.

We pulled up to the cafeteria's entrance, and Onion motioned me to be quiet again. We exited the bus in single file, and we were counted again. I held my tongue until we got into the cafeteria, "Yo, how many times we gotta do this shut-up shit?"

"Yo, I know this shit is a trip," Onion said. "I can't wait 'til I get on the committed side." I couldn't understand why Onion wanted to go to the committed side opposed to home. I had to ask, "Why you want to go over there?"

"Man, this my fourth dope charge," he answered. "I know the judge ain't gonna let me go home. I might as well go where it's better."

Onion went onto to inform me that once a juvenile is found to be a delinquent by the court, he is sent over to the committed side of the institution. There he is allowed to wear his own clothing, have a job assignment to earn money to purchase items from the commissary, and earn weekend trips home. More than anything, the committed guys get to attend parties with the hot-ass girls who were locked up at Montrose. I still was not impressed. I wanted to go home.

I heartily ate my meal and hollered my "What's ups" across the cafeteria to homies I had not seen in months. It was strange, I saw guys from my neighborhood I had not seen in ages. Some I had actually wondered about from time to time. Most I had not. After about a half-hour to fourty-five minutes, Ms. Patterson announced that lunch was over, and we lined up and went back onto the bus in single file, in silence, and counted. We got back to our housing unit cottage and the same was done. I had been counted four times, and I had only been in the housing unit a few hours. I felt that something very demeaning had happened to me.

By the time Monday came, I had been counted more times than I could count. I was also repulsed by the fact that I had to wear clothing that others had worn. When bedtime arrived, and I was to spend my first night at the Maryland Training School for Boys, I was utterly relieved. I was truly exhausted emotionally and physically.

I would be absolutely devastated when the judge didn't let me go home Monday. I had anxiously awakened that morning, got dressed in my very own clothes and headed off to court with about five others. I had told Onion the night before that I would not be returning. I had bragged that Fat Larry was handling my legal situation. I told Onion that Larry's fancy lawyer was going to represent me. I felt confident I would be released.

I got to court feeling upbeat and confident. I was informed that my Aunt Kim was there and that as soon as the juvenile master was ready for me, I would be called into the courtroom. I asked the security staff if I could see my Aunt Kim, but was told that I could not see her until I got into the courtroom. I sat down on a hard wooden bench and waited for my name to be called.

I grew impatient; I kept asking the staff members where was my Aunt Kim and when was someone going to call me. I was told time and time again to "sit down and shut the fuck up." I was a nuisance, but I didn't care. I wanted to see someone who could tell me about my situation. So far, I had not talked to anyone who was prepared to advocate for me. Hell, the only person I was able to tell that I was justified in shooting Mouse was Onion. I did not tell anyone the story that Larry and Calvin had devised for me. "Arlando Jones," some white man dressed in a suit and tie was looking for me. "Arlando Jones, come to the grill, please."

I stepped forward and announced that I was Arlando Jones, then I asked the man, "Who you?"

"My name is Mr. Roberts, I am from the Public Defenders' Office. I will be representing you in this matter."

I was truly confused. Where was Fat Larry's lawyer? This was the first time I had ever been before a judge, I was totally ignorant about the criminal justice process. However, I knew enough to know that I didn't want to be represented by anyone from the Public Defenders' Office. Word on the street was that the lawyers from the Public Defenders' Office were the most inept attorneys anywhere.

"You gonna represent me?" I asked incredulously.

"Yeah, I am," Mr. Roberts replied. "I have read your file. I have the police version of the story. Now, I need yours."

I told Mr. Roberts that Mouse had pulled a knife on my cousin and me in an attempt to rob us, and that is why I shot him. Mr. Roberts asked me where did I get the gun. I told him that I had bought the gun from a stranger for twenty bucks, and I carried it around for protection. Mr. Roberts took notes on a yellow legal pad, and made facial expressions as if he didn't believe a word I said. I didn't trust Mr. Roberts to protect my best interest, but I did not tell him that. I needed to see if he could get me home.

"Am I goin' home today?" I asked.

Mr. Roberts came very close to laughing in my face. "You can't possibly think that you're going home today. The victim is still in the hospital."

I was speechless. Mr. Robert's comment had knocked the wind out of me. I truly didn't relish spending another night locked in that pissy-ass cell at Training School. I did not want to be confined in a single cottage with seventy other boys sharing the same underwear and other clothing. I felt it very demeaning to shower with twenty to thirty others every night, and I absolutely hated being herded and counted all day everyday.

"I was protecting myself, Mr. Roberts," I cried. "I don't see why I can't go home."

Mr. Roberts explained to me that the master hearing my case had already determined that I would be remanded to Training School until my hearing to actually determine whether or not I was a "delinquent youth." Mr. Roberts told me that Kim and he had tried to convince the master to permit me to go home in Kim's custody, but it was to no avail. The pending drug charge I had from the summer was enough to convince the judge to hold me at Training School.

I didn't let Mr. Roberts know I was surprised that he would mention my narcotics charge. I had not heard anything about that charge since the lady from Juvenile Services told me I would receive a summons to appear in court for it. I had assumed that my case had gotten lost in the system since so much time had elapsed. Besides, David and all the rest of the dudes who got arrested with me were home and still selling drugs. Squirt was still hangin' out with David and his crew selling more weed than ever before. How could it be that that incident would play a role in keeping me detained? It just didn't seem fair. This public defender was just an incompetent attorney. If Fat Larry had honored his word and sent his lawyer to represent me, I would have been able to go home. I felt betrayed. I did not feel that I was responsible for my situation. The only fault I bore was that I should not have turned myself in to the law. I should have stayed at my grandmother's house or at the stash house until the matter blew over. Mouse was not a man of consequence. After a few days, the police probably would have forgotten all about the case. Fat Larry had given me bad advice, but he was still my nigga.

Mr. Roberts informed me that I would be called into the courtroom in a matter of minutes. The juvenile master would simply read the statement of facts and remand me to the Maryland Training School for Boys until my next court date. I would not get the opportunity to say anything. I asked Mr. Roberts whether I would be allowed to speak to Kim; he told me I would be allowed to sit with her in the courtroom.

Mr. Roberts told me that he had to leave; however, he would see me shortly. He exited the bullpen area, and I went back to sit on the bench. No more than ten minutes passed before the security officer came to the bullpen's grill to order me to come to the gate. I was wanted in court. The guard opened the gate and placed a handcuff on my wrist and the other cuff to his. It felt utterly discomforting to be shackled to a white man.

"How long we gonna be hooked up together?"

"Until we get to Master Goldstein's courtroom," was his curt reply.

We entered the courtroom, and true to his word, he took the handcuff from his wrist, and put it on my free wrist.

• • •

I sat down next to Kim. She put her arms around me to offer me a comfort I didn't realize I desperately needed. I asked her about the attorney Fat Larry was supposed to have secured for me. She told me that she had not heard from Larry. However, she did talk to Mr. Roberts, the public defender who would be representing me. She told me that she honestly felt that he would represent me diligently. Kim assured me that if Mr. Roberts failed to handle my case properly, she would find the money from somewhere to get me a good lawyer. Kim was always on my side, and despite any handicap she possessed, she would overcome it to provide me with whatever I needed. Her love for me was strong.

The bailiff called my name and ordered me to come up to the master's bench. I felt extremely nervous. Butterflies started forming in the pit of my stomach. I did not want to leave the protection and comfort of Kim's arms, but she urged me to get up and move forward. Just as she had done that time when I was afraid to fight this kid who had been bullying me, "Go handle your business, baby."

I stepped up and stood next to Mr. Roberts before the master. I really wanted to sit down, my nerves were wreaking havoc on my legs. They felt rubbery, as if they would betray me at any moment. It was a relief that I didn't have to speak. Mr. Roberts spoke for me. He said, "Your honor, per our agreement in chambers, we will submit that Arlando be remanded to the Maryland Training School for Boys until the date of his hearing."

I heard every word Mr. Roberts said, and I understood that I would be going back to Training School. However, I did not agree. I wanted to go home, and I so desperately wanted to express my desire. I just didn't have the courage to speak out. I was thoroughly intimidated by the process; the master sitting up high behind his bench in the black robe of justice, the prosecuting attorney sitting across from me impeccably dressed in a dark blue suit, and my attorney adorned likewise. I was out of my league. Aside from what Mr. Roberts said, I didn't comprehend anything else. The language was too sophisticated.

I look back, and it's hard to believe that I sat in a stash house, surrounded by armed drug-crazed addicts, unafraid, but was terrified by these three white people who were not armed. Mustard or Bam would have put a bullet in the back of my head at the least provocation, and I was not afraid of that situation. I could not comprehend this fear. I simply accepted it and endured the maligning.

"Arlando, I am going to order you to return to the Maryland Training School for Boys until such time as your hearing," Master Goldstein was speaking to me for the first time. "I'm going to set the date for that hearing for January 16th."

Damn, I was going to be locked up during the holidays. This was fucked up, but I could not summon the courage to tell these white folks that I should be allowed to go home. Besides, the prosecutor had said something about my not attending school. I had a pending drug charge, and that, from all appearances, I had little to no adult supervision whatsoever. I couldn't conceptualize an argument to counter the negative things she said about me, and it was obvious that Mr. Roberts couldn't, either. He just kept asserting that it would be improper to adjudicate the matter without having all the facts.

I was utterly relieved when the security officer came to escort me back to the bullpen. I was so overwhelmed by what had happened that I totally ignored Kim's warm kiss upon my cheek and gentle hug as I left the courtroom. I wanted to cry. I needed to cry. But I had to have absolute privacy to do that. I was an up and coming bad ass nigga. It would not have been proper to allow anyone to see me cry.

By the time I reached the bullpen, I was fully collected. My outward demeanor of indifference was in place. The only emotional sign I displayed was anger. I walked into the bullpen and announced, "Them bitches in there crazy," I was angry. "They sendin' me back out that mothafuckin' Training School."

I was not talking to anyone in particular. I simply needed to shout, and that is exactly what I did. I shouted, then I went to the bench in the rear of the bullpen and laid down. I now wanted to get back to Training School so I could let everyone know just how mad I was for having to be there.

• • •

"Why 'n the fuck I gotta take off all my clothes?" I asked Mr. Waters as I stood before him completely naked in the housing unit's darkroom.

"Cause you locked up and you do what you're told," he truthfully answered.

This was one insult too many to my fragile ego. "You faggy mothafucka, you don't run nuthin'."

"You give me your clothes," Mr. Waters said. "And watch your mouth."

Mr. Waters was a small man, no more than five and half feet tall and very thin. He resembled many of the winos from my neighborhood. He would be the most convenient person for me to express my rage. I accepted the clothes he gave me, and once I put them on, I looked him directly in the eye and said to him, "Bitch you don't tell me what to say outta my mouth."

Mr. Waters was not intimidated; he came toward me and grabbed me by my shirt collar and said, "Your ass goin' to isolation."

"I ain't goin' nowhere," I said as I pulled away from his grasp and threw a vicious straight right fist toward his head.

The punch landed squarely on Mr. Waters's chin; the impact knocked him to the floor. He looked up at me with pure rage and hatred. I responded in kind. I kicked him in the face before he could recover, and pounded him with an assortment of uncoordinated blows. I felt such relief pouring from me as Mr. Waters laid there totally unable to defend himself from my awesome attack.

Someone grabbed me from behind and locked my neck into a painful choke hold. I felt myself grasping for air, but none was forthcoming. I begun to grow light-headed, and then I saw Mr. Waters pick himself up and come toward me. I saw him draw back his fist, but the vice-like grip around my neck prevented me from defending myself. The first blow caught me in the mouth. I could taste the blood pouring in and a profound hatred permeating my soul.

I lost consciousness, and when I awoke I was lying on a concrete floor, in a very cold and dark cell in the isolation unit of the administration building. My entire body ached severely, and my lips and eye were swollen. I gathered consciousness and sat up on the bare mattress in the cell. I placed my head in my hand and cried for the very first time in my life. I was in excruciating emotional and physical pain. I wanted to die. I wanted to be with my mother and father—resting in peace. I couldn't cope with the turmoil and confusion in my life. Larry had betrayed me, Kim had sat there hopeless while those white folks said the most horribly imaginable things about me. I was condemned to spend time in confinement.

I was not thinking about what I had done to Mouse. I felt that I had been wronged more than I had wronged. Mouse and I were involved in the ghetto game, doing ghetto things. The criminal justice system had no right to punish me for doing the only thing I knew how to do. I never stepped outside my world to interfere with anyone, why were these white folks stepping into my world to interfere with me? It just didn't seem right.

I prayed and I cried, and I hurt. I sought relief by shifting my body around to various positions. I sought relief by asking God to give it to me. None came; I cursed God, my dismal life, and accepted my lonliness. I was by myself and convinced that it was solely my responsibility to find relief for myself. Kim and Mama were on my side, but they were addicted to drugs and alcohol, respectively. They were totally ineffectual and a great disappointment.

Eventually, the gray steel door that kept me contained in that tomb opened, and someone tossed me a brown paper bag containing food. I believe it was a cold bologna sandwich and cold green peas. I was famished; however, the bitterness I was feeling prevented me from eating a single bite. I tossed the bag of food toward the wall of the cell just as casually as it was tossed to me. I no longer felt a need to be loved or loving. I only wanted to survive. I didn't want to die after all. I wanted to get even with Mr. Waters, with whomever grabbed me from behind and choked the air from my lungs, and all the folks who failed to protect me from what I was facing.

I don't recall how much time passed before two security officers came to remove me from the isolation cell. But I do know that I had become just as cold inside my heart as the cell that contained me.

"You're going to the infirmary," one of the officers informed me. "Then we're taking you to see Mr. Whitey."

I was taken to the infirmary, which was located in the administration building, and cared for by a kind, mature-looking lady. She was gentle. She cleaned my wounds and placed ice on my face. She asked me how I felt. I told her that I was okay, and she assured me that I would live. At no time did she ask me how I got my wounds. She probably already knew. That would account for the gentleness and sympathy she showed me.

Once I had been treated for my wounds, the security officers took me to see Mr. Whitey.

"Sit down, son," Mr. Whitey instructed. "I can't have you 'round here striking my staff members."

Mr. Whitey was not harsh. His tone was matter-of-fact. "I don't condone violence or abuse to any of the children here. But you hit one of my staff. You got what you deserved."

"Fuck you, Mr. Whitey," I said. I truly did not care about being punished any further. I had endured all the suffering that could be bestowed upon any child, and it hadn't killed me. It simply hardened me and made me more aware of the reality of my life.

"You won't be going back to Unit Four," Mr. Whitey replied. "I'm sending you over to Two."

That hurt; I wanted to go back to Unit Four so that I could fuck Mr. Waters up, again—and beat up whoever it was that aided him in beating me up. I was not fazed by going to Unit Two for any other reason. I wanted revenge, and the switch to another housing unit would prevent that.

The Worst Place Is My Preferred Place

Chapter 23

The outside structure of Housing Unit Two was no different than Four. It was a single-story red brick building with a manicured lawn out front and perfect shrubs and trees bordering the perimeter. The inside of Unit Two was far different than Four, however. The noise was more intense. Upon entering, one would think that he had entered an insane asylum. Unlike Four, there were bars on all the windows to let you know that you were in a place for punishment. Moreover, the kids in Unit Two were much bigger, physically, than the kids in Unit Four. I also noticed that Housing Unit Two was not as brightly lit as Unit Four. It was rather dim and depressing, in fact.

A young man who introduced himself to me as Mr. Williams informed me that Mr. Gossie was the unit manager. He told me that I was simply to follow orders; do whatever I was told and I would not have any problems. My personal effects had already been sent over from Unit Four. I would receive a change of clothes each day, same as in Unit Four. The only differences between Unit Four and Unit Two were that in Unit Two we ate in the cottage as opposed to the cafeteria, and all our recreational privileges occurred in the cottage. We would not be permitted to attend the school's gymnasium like the children in other housing units. Hell, we would not even attend school; a teacher would have to come to the unit to instruct us.

Mr. Williams went on to inform me that Unit Two was truly okay. It was managed in a laissez-faire manner. If I wanted to play pool or ping-pong, just play. There were no lists to follow. Housing Unit Two was where men resided. I had to hold my own. If I had any problems, solve them the best way I knew how. Just try my best not to come to the attention of the staff. They were simply there to serve an eight-hour work shift, no more or no less.

I liked Mr. Williams. He spoke my language. He was not trying to instill his will and values upon a brother. He understood that I was a bad boy and I would likely do bad things. He opened the cage to the unit and left me to my own devices. It was obvious from the moment I stepped through the door of my new housing unit that I would not have any problems becoming acclimated. There were more familiar faces to me in Unit Two than there were in Four. My nigga, Heads, was there. As soon as I came through the door, he came up to the cage that contained us and told Mr. Williams, while I was receiving my lecture on the do's and don'ts of the unit, "Yo, that's my man, Will, he ain't gotta hear that shit."

"Be cool Heads," Mr. Williams said. "He comin' in. I gotta tell him somthin' first."

"Come on down to the gym after Will get finish bullshittin' you," Heads said to me as he walked off. "Greg down there."

I was cool with Unit Two instantly. Heads and Greg had a little weed, and they smoked it with me to celebrate our reunion. It had been six or seven months since we had last seen each other. We all lived in the same neighborhood, stood on the same corners, and ran from the same police. I can't assert that Heads and Greg were my friends, but they were definitely my homeboys, and in the joint, automatic allies.

Heads and Greg teased me about my bruised face. They told me that it looked like Mr. Waters jumped straight in my ass. I told them that I was beating Mr. Waters up, but someone grabbed me from behind and that's how he was able to get the better of me. But I didn't have to explain the incident. They had already heard about it; the grape-vine was alive at Training School. They told me that it was Mr. Stippio who had grabbed me from behind. Heads even told me that the reason I could not break Mr. Sippio's grip was because he was a homosexual, and homosexual males were unusually strong.

I was feeling the euphoric effects of the marijuana we had been smoking, so it was easy for me to accept what Heads was saying. Besides, the humorous manner in which he spoke eased the savagery I had been exposed to.

Within days, I was just as popular in Housing Unit Two as Heads and Greg. I attended school sessions whenever a teacher could be found to come to our cottage to instruct us, played ping-pong and pool, and bullied the less aggressive inmates on the unit just as my friends did. By the time my court date arrived, I had been in too many fights to count. I lost one or two, but won most.

I was never a supporter of bankin' a person. I would rather fight one on one, but I never protested when one of my homies jumped in to aid me beat someone up. I recall Christmas Eve, 1981. It was to be my very first Christmas away from home. I was very depressed. The unit was in a rather subdued mood. Christmas carols were being sung on the radio. A sad, poorly decorated tree occupied the corner of the recreation area, nothing good was on television. It was nearing ten o'clock, time to lock in our barren cells with half gallon milk cartons to piss in if we had to use the bathroom in the middle of the night. This little red motherfucka named Nike started fuckin' with me.

"Ah Tray, would you suck Santa Claus' dick if he said he can get you home tonight?" Nike asked me.

Now, Nike and I were on good terms with each other. We played cards, ping-pong, and shot pool together. Our relationship was congenial, but he was not my friend or homeboy. I felt insulted by his question. I was already depressed, and he insulted me. I expressed myself the best way I knew how.

"Whore, what make you think you can play with me any way you want to?" I was ready to fight. It did not matter to me that we were in the central hallway and all the staff members were present, preparing to lock us all in for the night.

"Nigga, I know you ain't just call me no whore."

"Bitch, what I call you then?"

Nike moved toward me, and I toward him. It was on. But I was unable to strike him before Heads hit him with a savage blow to the head. The punch knocked Nike to the ground and before he recovered, I was striking him with a myriad of blows. Someone attacked Heads in retaliation for what he had done to Nike, and Greg got into the fray. In moments, Housing Unit Two was the scene of a melee. It seemed as if each inmate was fighting someone. The staff members, about three or four in all, were desperately trying to break up the fights. But it was to no avail, too many fights were occurring at once. The security officers had to be called.

It took German Shepherds and batons upon our heads to end the melee. Once the fighting ended we were thrown into cells. Many of the inmates were hurt, bitten by the dogs or busted in the head by the batons. But it did not matter; the unit had to be secured. Order had to be restored. The injuries had to wait until some other time to be treated.

I laid in my cell that night experiencing a mixture of emotions. I was sad, lonely, and relieved all at the same time. I was not among the badly injured. I was grateful for that. I stopped pounding on Nike the moment I saw the security officers and dogs come through the door. I was among the first group hurried into a cell. The inmates who continued to engage in combat after the security officers arrived were the ones who sustained the greatest injuries. It may have been cowardly of me, but something inside of me compelled me to stop fighting once I saw the awesome force of the security team. I knew that I was no match for the batons, dogs, and shields that the officers wielded. I didn't see any guns, but I figured that they had them available. I simply gave Nike a last kick to his groin and went into an open cell.

I knew that tomorrow would be a busy day. The administration would want to know what had occurred. But that was not the case. Usually, our cells were opened at eight o'clock in the morning, but on the morning following the melee, the doors did not open. It became apparent at around noon that we would be locked in our cells all day, Christmas Day.

We were fed peanut-butter-and-jelly sandwiches in a brown paper bag and ignored by the staff who operated Unit Two. I heard many of the youths confined in the cells beg Mr. Williams and Mr. Gossie to let them out of the cell. They were saying that they were not involved in any of the fighting or that they didn't start it. I simply laid on the smelly bunk in the cell I was thrown into—isolated with my own confusing thoughts and emotions. I was not going to cry or beg the staff to let me out of that cell. There was a part of me that was pleased to be there, away from having to pretend to everyone that I was all right; that I was unaffected by being incarcerated. I did not feel like having to erect a nonchalant façade of indifference. I wanted to cry and be the confused and frightened child that I was. I was away from home for Christmas for the first time in my life. I was among older troubled teenagers. I was in an environment that was inherently cold. It was a good thing I was accustomed to such an environment; otherwise, I would have lost my mind.

By nightfall Christmas Day, it felt like someone had turned off the heat in the cottage. It was unbearably cold and dark in the unit. No one was speaking to anyone. Earlier during the day, others had been talking to each other from cell to cell. I had even spoken to Heads and Greg. I had called out to them to see how they were doing. I discovered that Heads had been bitten by a dog and that Greg had a busted head. Neither Greg nor Heads were in any shape to carry on a lengthy conversation. So, we concluded that it was best not to talk. Some folks would have to be labeled for starting the melee. I had no doubt that I would be named as an instigator or a leader. The inmates who could not tolerate being confined to a cell all day had already yelled, "Tray and Nike started this shit."

"No, it wasn't Nike, it was Heads."

"Yeah, Yo, it was dem niggas Tray, Heads, Nike, and Greg."

I heard the various voices. I had no doubt I would be taken to the administration building and placed in isolation for the maximum amount of time. I felt that I was destined to experience all the hardships that life could offer.

I did not want Heads to get involved in my fight. I felt confident I could beat Nike. But Heads was my homeboy, and if he felt a need to come to my aid, then I could not complain. I have to give Heads the benefit of the doubt. Nike was a full foot taller than I, and he weighed at least twenty to thirty pounds more than me. Heads didn't want to see me get beat up. He did not know that Nike couldn't beat me. Nike's heart was not as vicious as mine. I would have beaten him because of that. I was only thirteen, I had been abjectly neglected, beaten physically and emotionally, and taught nothing about kindness. I was hardened.

When the Soul Had Bars

Chapter 24

I was the first person brought from his cell, escorted to the administration building, and punished for taking part in the melee. Around noon, the day after Christmas, two white security officers came to my cell to get me. They both looked rather menacing, standing at least six-feet tall outside my cell door in their dark blue uniforms, carrying their batons at the ready. I felt the butterflies coming up in my stomach. I just knew I was going to get another ass whipping.

The security officers were known for their brutality. Every time they were called to break up a fight or to get an inmate, someone usually got hurt. The two officers that came for me were known for their excessive use of force. I could not beat them, I knew. Everyone was locked in his cell. I was isolated and would have to face these officers alone.

"Jones," the tallest of the two said to me, "step out the cell and keep your hands above your head."

I was not going to aggravate the situation unnecessarily. I was in enough trouble, so I complied without offering any comment. I did not even protest when one of the officers slung me against the wall with unnecessary brute force. I simply committed to myself that I would eventually kill him for whatever cruelty he subjected me to. Meanwhile, I would endure, in total humility, the extra pushes toward the door, the extra tightening of the handcuff around my wrist, and the kick in my ass as I was thrown into the back of the van that was used to transport me to the administration building. I did not say a word. I suffered in silence and allowed my heart to absorb all the hatred and thirst for vengeance that it could handle.

I did not relish being locked into that isolation cell again, but I was determined not to cry or voice a protest against anything that was to be done to me. I was not going to reveal any vulnerabilities. I nonchalantly accepted the single blanket, riddled with holes, given to me when we finally reached my isolation cell. I knew that the blanket would not keep me warm. It was not intended to. I just walked into the cell with an aura of dignity and courageousness.

I knew that I would suffer a physical and psychological torture in that cell. It was extremely cold and dark in there. The air conditioning ran all year long to make certain that it stayed cold, and the lights were covered to keep the area dim. There were no toilets or running water in the cells. You either pissed or took a shit on the floor or waited until someone felt like giving you a bathroom break, which were not frequently given.

The squalor in isolation was almost unbearable. I suspect that is why a juvenile was not supposed to spend more than eight hours in an isolation cell. But I often spent days there. My offenses were generally more extreme than those of other youths who were at Training School.

Mr. Dean, the superintendent at the facility, told me that he would eventually break my spirit with his isolation cells. I assured him that he wouldn't. The three days that I spent in isolation for assaulting and then being assaulted by Mr. Waters had hardened my heart and prepared me for every challenge that the criminal justice system would ever throw at me. The world was a cruel and miserable place. I understood that concept. Training School was teaching me that the sooner I embrace that as a reality, the less complicated my life would be.

I was swallowed by the cell's coldness, its misery, its emptiness. When the door finally opened, I was sitting on the floor in a fetal position in the far corner. I was hungry, cold, and completely dehumanized. I had pissed and shitted in the cell. I smelled awful and looked worse. The stink of the cell and the stink of life had attached itself to me, and it would be years before I could get it off.

"Come on son, Mr. Dean wants to see you," the voice was coming from the open door. "You have to take a shower and put on some clean clothes first."

"Good," I said. "I wanna see the mothafucka who had me locked in this bitch."

"Young man, please watch your language."

He said "please," therefore, I refrained from using further vituperations. Besides, this inconsequential man seemed nice; he was being polite. I permitted him to direct me to the shower, and I gratefully accepted the soap, shampoo, and clean clothes he offered. I took a shower under his watchful eye. I felt uncomfortable with him watching me so closely as I bathed. I had an instinctive notion that this middle-aged man was an old faggot.

I was taken to another administration building on the other side of the compound. This building was much smaller than the first administration building. It looked much older, but well maintained. Where the other building was constructed of sandstone, this one was constructed with red bricks. It was isolated, and I knew instantly that this building was where the important persons had their offices. Inside the place, the atmosphere was rather subdued, as if the personnel were concentrating on work-related matters. Type-writers were clicking away, about two or three women who appeared to be professional secretaries or receptionists were doing various tasks. The sound of classical musical was coming from some hidden place. I felt, and looked, odd standing in that professional atmosphere handcuffed and dressed in oversized state-issued clothing.

The security officer who was functioning as my escort announced to this elderly white woman that, "I got one here to see Mr. Dean."

"Oh yes, that must be Arlando," she replied. "He's waiting for him."

I didn't realize I was that important. The big boss was waiting for me. Well, here I am. The old lady led the way down a long hallway to a door that had a sign on it that read "Superintendent's Office."

I found myself standing on some very thick brown carpet in a huge office. The lady motioned for the security officer to keep me where I stood, while she went on into the inner office. She was gone for less then five seconds before I heard Mr. Dean's booming voice. "Bring his bad ass in here, now!"

I was ushered into Mr. Dean's luxurious office. It was quite fancy, brown panel lined the walls, there were thick leather chairs and a couch, end tables, diplomas on the wall, pretty lamps. I was shocked that an office of such grace belonged to a hillbilly.

Mr. Dean was a very large man. He stood at least seven or eight inches above six feet. He was dressed in a lumberjack shirt, state-issued blue jeans, and black work boots. His white skin was extremely pale and his teeth were covered with tobacco stains. This man was incongruent with his surroundings, but he ran Training School—there were no doubts about that. The brute commanded much respect.

"Take dem 'cuffs off him," Mr. Dean ordered. "He ain't so tough."

The officer took the handcuffs from my wrist, and Mr. Dean came from behind his desk and stood directly in front of me. He dwarfed me, and I imagined he positioned himself before me in the manner he did because he wanted to intimidate me.

"Ms. Daniels, Mr. Taylor that'll be all," Mr. Dean dismissed them. He wanted to have a private conversation with me. "I'll call for you when I am done, Taylor."

Ms. Daniels and Mr. Taylor exited the office, leaving Mr. Dean and me alone staring at each other.

"You like to fight?" Mr. Dean started. "Wanta fight me?"

I wanted to answer by punching him in the mouth for asking me that stupid-ass question, but I figured I would just get my ass whipped, again. I simply kept quiet and maintained my stare. I was determined not to allow this giant of a white man to intimidate me. I was not going to allow him to even think that he could. I had been beaten and subjected to all manner of inhumane treatment since I arrived at Training School. I was too embittered to be frightened by this hillbilly. I was enraged that he was even trying this shit with me. I had just endured three days of total hell in this man's isolation cell. I had missed my family terribly during the holiday season, and this son-of-bitch was trying to scare me. What more could be done to me?

"Son, I have seen a million just like you in the thirty years I've been doing this," Mr. Dean changed his approach. "You're going to go to prison for the rest of your life or somebody is gonna kill you. One thing is certain, I ain't gonna waste no time on you. I'm gonna break you."

My stare or some other look I gave Mr. Dean convinced him that it was useless to try to scare me. So he simply spoke his piece and returned to his seat totally exasperated. He did not offer me a chair, and I understood intuitively that it would have been inappropriate for me to just sit down. I just stood there, in front of Mr. Dean's desk and locked my eyes on his while he sat there. I hated this man, and I did not care that my look would betray my emotion.

Five or ten minutes passed before Mr. Dean spoke again. When he did, all he did was condemn me. He let me know that he thought I was a coward because I had shot a man. He told me that I was scum because I was a drug dealer, and he warned me that if I assaulted another one of his staff members, he would personally whip my ass. I made it a point not to say anything. There was nothing to be said. Mr. Dean was convinced that I was going to end up dead or in prison. He knew that I despised him, and

I knew he despised me. If I had spoken a word, I would have antagonized the situation, and I could not possibly benefit by antagonizing Mr. Dean. He was the boss; everyone at Training School knew that. He was a crazy-ass hillbilly whom no one fooled with. I was not going to challenge him.

The only thing Mr. Dean said that I was pleased to hear was that he was sending me back to Housing Unit Two. I had served an adequate amount of time in isolation. It was now time for the other fellows who had participated in the melee to serve their punishment.

Mr. Taylor was summoned to retrieve me. He took me back to Unit Two. Once there, Head, Greg, Nike, and two other guys were taken out of the unit. I assumed they were being taken to the administration building to serve their time in isolation, but otherwise the unit was back to normal. We sat around playing pool, watching television, and engaging in conversation. It was all good.

Mr. Gossie, the unit manager, called me into his office and asked me whether or not the conflict between Nike and me was over. I assured him that I was not angry with Nike. I let Mr. Gossie know that if Nike didn't start any shit, there wouldn't be any. My comments apparently satisfied Mr. Gossie, so he dismissed me. He permitted me to leave his office and go back to the recreation area to hang out with my buddies.

Everyone was curious about my conversation with Mr. Gossie and my overall experience at the administration building. Everyone expressed his shock at my being maintained in isolation for three days. It was very unusual for anyone to be locked away in an isolation cell for such a long period of time. I was considered to be amazingly strong to endure such a hardship. I felt a peculiar pride. I was a strong soldier; not many could endure what I had endured and remain stable.

My less-than-humble opinion of myself was reinforced when I saw Heads, Greg, Nike, and the other guys come back into the unit minutes before bedtime. I was required to spend three days in isolation, and they only had to spend the usual eight hours there. I did not begrudge them. Inside, I felt that I deserved all the unfair treatment I received. The hood's creed was "you get what your hand calls for." I also heard that "God would not place a burden on my shoulder greater than I could bear." I was a strong soldier by all accounts. It was such a tragedy that others would misuse me and manipulate my strength for their benefit—and my demise.

Arlando "Tray" Jones

Freed and Not Redeemable

Chapter 25

My last two weeks at Training School went rather smoothly. I spent a few eight-hour stints in isolation for minor offenses, such as disrespect toward a staff member and a fight or two, but nothing significant. I got a little bigger from doing push-ups, eating, and sleeping properly. But above all, I became more convinced that my lifestyle choice was not so bad after all. Life was cold because all the people in it were cold. I came across a kind and gentle soul every now and then, but the world was dominated by folks out to serve their own selfish interests. It was up to me to serve mine. I had no natural allies. I was not the number one priority in anyone's life. The entire time I suffered in those isolation cells, no one was there to protect me, to tell Mr. Dean that he was mistreating me. I had no one on whom I could depend, and I accepted that. I had to be prepared to look out for myself.

In January of 1982, I went before Master Goldstein. He knew that any further punishment of me would be in vain. Mouse had come to court, as he was subpoenaed, and testified that I was not the one who shot him. The state's attorney told the juvenile master that I did, indeed, shoot Mouse. The state contended that Mouse was adhering to some street code: to not identify his assailant.

Master Goldstein told the state that if Mouse said I did not shoot him, he was inclined to believe him. I was feeling quite pleased at how things were going. I felt confident I was going home. Master Goldstein was talking good. Then he dropped the bomb on me.

"The court finds Arlando Jones delinquent," Master Goldstein ruled. "Records indicate that this young man is involved with illegal drug activity. He isn't attending school regularly, and if he did not shoot this man here, it's only a matter of time before he shoots someone."

Mr. Roberts, the public defender assigned to represent me, spoke on my behalf. He told the master that my grandmother, Ms. Leola Pittman, would take a more active role in my development. He explained to Master Goldstein that he had interviewed my family members, and they had all agreed that I had been running wild. My Aunt Kim was too young to rear me alone. Mr. Roberts entreated the master to permit me to go home to my grandmother. He advised the master that I would do much better.

I was damn impressed with Mr. Roberts; he told the court about my not having any parents and that I had endured many hardships. He went on to say that I had a loving family who were willing to take me home and provide me with more guidance and nurturing than any juvenile facility could. The state's attorney opposed Mr. Robert's position. She told the court, Master Goldstein, that I was a potential menace to society, and that my family's situation was in such disarray, I would receive no structure or guidance whatsoever if I was released from Training School.

Master Goldstein ruled that I was to go to a group home. He ruled that I was going to be maintained under a court-controlled commitment. I was to be assigned a probation officer—a wonderful man, I learned—by the name of Mr. Lawrence. Meanwhile, I would have to go back to Training School for a day or two until arrangements could be made to place me in a group home. Mr. Roberts told me to just be cool. I would be home in no time at all. But I wanted to go home that day.

"Man, fuck that. Why can't I go home today?" I had been locked up for about a month and a half. I had missed the Christmas and New Year Holidays. "The man said I ain't shoot him."

"Arlando," Mr. Roberts was speaking to me in a hushed tone, "you will be in a group home in a day or two."

I did not understand what a group home was, exactly. However, I did sense that it was not as bad as Training School. "What the fuck is a group home?" I kept my voice low so that no one aside from Mr. Roberts could hear me.

Mr. Roberts informed me that a group home was simply a state-operated house in a community. I would be required to stay there until the court felt that I could go home to my grandmother's house. I voiced some alarm about being locked up, but Mr. Roberts assured me that I would be allowed to go and come pretty much as I pleased while I was at the group home. He told me that there would be a curfew in place and my school attendance would likely be monitored. But it was a hell of a lot better than Training School.

"Is there a problem, Mr. Roberts?" Master Goldstein asked.

"I'm sorry your Honor," Mr. Roberts apologized for disturbing the court. "My client didn't understand your ruling, and I was explaining it to him."

"Well, my ruling is final. You can take your client to the rear of the court and explain it to him and his family."

I got up from the defense table with my attorney and joined my Aunt Kim and grandmother in the rear of the courtroom. After Kim and Mama hugged and kissed me and told me how much they missed me, Mr. Roberts explained the details of the court's ruling to us. I was going to be appointed a probation officer who would take me to the group home. I would have to stay there until it was decided I could come home permanently. My commitment was a court-controlled one. Therefore, decisions pertaining to me would be based upon the probation officer's reports. I would learn the rules of the group home once I got there. Mr. Roberts only knew that, in all likelihood, I would be able to come home daily and arrangements would be made to ensure that I got to and from school. How quickly I got home depended upon my family and me. Mr. Roberts simply encouraged us to develop a good relationship with whomever was assigned to me as a probation officer.

Mr. Roberts wished my family and me well and exited the courtroom. The security officer came over to us to tell me that he would allow me an additional fifteen minutes to visit with my grandmother and aunt. I was truly thankful to him for that. I had missed Kim and Mama. I had secretly hoped that they would visit me while I was at Training School. I felt truly alone and lonely on visiting days. I would see all the other kids on my unit go to their visits on Sundays to be with their family, and I would envy them.

I had not seen these two women, my two mothers, in about seven weeks. I had missed them. I wanted to ask them why didn't they come to visit me but I felt that would be a sign of weakness. I could not whine over missed visits. It would have contradicted everything I had determined myself to be: bad ass nigga gangster.

I sat there with Mama and Kim, and we engaged in idle talk. I told them that I had handled my own weight at Training School. I told them about my getting jumped by Mr. Waters and Mr. Stippio, the times I spent in isolation, the melee, everything. I explained it as if it was trivial. I let Mama and Kim know that the state had thrown its best at me, and I was still determined to do wrong. Mama just told me, "A hard head make a soft ass."

Kim told me that Calvin was locked up. She told me that the feds had him on an old bank robbery charge, and that it was likely he would do time. She also told me that Squirt was locked up. He had stolen a car and robbed someone. He was being charged as an adult and was at the Baltimore City Jail.

I recall asking Kim, "Dag, you got any good news?"

"Terrance done blew up outta nowhere," she answered. "He gettin' all the money 'round the way."

I was surprised to hear that my cousin Terrance was getting money. When I left, Terrance had been working a regular job at a shoe store and only hustling a little on the side. I would have to see for myself that Terrance was getting all the money around the 'hood. Kim might have been exaggerating. "Terrance ain't gettin' it like Larry is he?"

"Boy, please," Kim said, "Larry ain't shit. T.I. is the man."

Mama seemed to have been ignoring Kim and me while we conversed. I thought she was too involved with watching the other court procedures to know what Kim and I were talking about, but she knew exactly what we were talking about. She chimed in, "Yeah boy, that Terrance done got himself rich."

The security officer came to get me after the fifteen minutes had expired. Mama and Kim thanked him for awarding us the additional time to visit. I felt that I should have been given more time to visit. Mouse had told the court that I didn't shoot him; I should have been going home, not back to Training School and then to some group home. A gangster's life is a tough one; sometimes we get what we are supposed to get, but most times we just get what we get.

I was in fairly good spirits by the time I got back to Training School. I joked around with Greg and Heads. I assured them both that I would give them a meaningful job once they came home. I even hung out with Nike; he and I had made up and were the best of friends. Nike and I started sharing notes on how to treat women. We shared similar views on romantic relationships. For example I used to tell Nike that the only women who could be trusted were mothers and grandmothers. Nike used to say, "Don't trust none 'em bitches." He didn't exclude any female.

I really enjoyed talking to Nike about women. He had style, with fine wavy hair and a muscular abdomen. He had a lot women. The thing that brought him great popularity was that he had this older woman coming up to Training School to visit him each week. She feigned to be his mother; that was the only way she could get in. No one could visit us except parents or legal guardians. Nike and this woman, who everyone said was fine, used to sneak away to have sex. A lot of rumors were going around about female staff members having sexual relationships with some of the juvenile residents, but Nike was the only confirmed plumber in the spot. It was, indeed, my honor and privilege to hear everything he had to say about women. It was great that his opinions about women did not deviate far from mine. In one rap session that Nike and I shared, he told me that, "Relationships happen for one of three purposes; a reason, a season, or a lifetime."

"It's the work of a lame ass nigga to sweat it when a bitch wanna roll, or hurt because a relationship end. 'Cause all relationships are gonna fulfill their purpose." Enjoy them while they last.

Nike certainly knew women. His impressive collection of phone numbers, nude photographs of various females from around the 'hood, flow of mail, and phone calls testified to that. I once asked Nike, "You ever gonna be a pimp?"

His reply was, "Naw, being a gigolo keeps me too busy to pimp."

Naming that place "The Maryland Training School for Boys" was definitely no mistake. By the time Mr. Lawrence came to get me, three days after my court hearing, I had learned more about women, drug connections, gambling, pan-handling, and all other types of criminal activity than I had learned anywhere. I even felt more confident about my fighting skills. The Maryland Training School for Boys trained me for the 'hood and the state's penitentiary.

A Homecoming Fit for a King
Chapter 26

When Mr. Lawrence and I pulled up to the Boys' Group Home, I was amazed at its location. I had passed the facility at least a thousand times on my way to and from Mondawmin Mall. I used to wonder what the two odd-looking houses that sat atop the hill were.

The two houses located at 907 and 909 Druid Hill Lake Drive stood out from the rest of the neighborhood. While the other buildings on the block were three-story, square-shaped apartment buildings, 907 and 909 were two story, circular houses. Hidden by two large trees, with huge windows, the houses were similar to green houses.

It was obvious that wealthy folks once occupied the houses. High ceilings and long spiral stairs that led onto landings that used to be gorgeous. Each room in the houses was large and spacious. The floors were made of beautiful sandalwood, and the glossy sheen revealed that they were frequently buffed. I was rather impressed with my new home. I did not want to stay too long, but it was okay for the moment. It was not far from my 'hood and I was familiar with the neighborhood. I had hung out around the Whitelock section before. I knew quite a few people around there.

I was relaxed when Mr. Lawrence took me to the facility's only office to have me processed into the home.

"Johnny," Mr. Lawrence said to this tall, balding, middle-aged black man seated behind the desk. "This is Arlando Jones; we talked about him earlier."

"Yeah," he stood up, shook my hand, then Mr. Lawrence's hand, and confirmed to me that he was, indeed, the tallest brother I had ever seen in my life. "How y'all doin'?"

Mr. Lawrence answered that he was doing well; I just nodded my head, indicating that I, too, was well.

"My name is Mr. Driver," he was speaking to me. "I'm the director here."

Mr. Driver's demeanor told me that he was all right. He was not some self-rightous, hard-ass bureaucrat. He was a brother that I would be able to work with. I was also impressed with his casual dress. He was decked out in designer jeans and a neat pull-over sweater. No stiff suit and tie, like Mr. Lawrence was wearing.

"Look," Mr. Lawrence said. "I got a busy schedule today. I gotta go, Johnny. He's all yours."

Mr. Lawrence left, and I was turned over to Mr. Driver's control. He invited me to take a seat. He left the office, leaving me there alone. I settled into an oversized leather chair and awaited his return. I had a distinct feeling that I would be okay under the control of Mr. Driver at the Boys' Group Home. All the guys at Training School told me that the group home was "sweet as shit." One dude even argued that the group home was better than home.

Of course, I would never accept that any level of incarceration is better than home, but I was going to give the group home a try. I had no intention of running away, and I could have easily done so. There were no locks on the doors or bars on the windows. It was obvious I could go and come as I pleased.

Mr. Driver came back into the office holding papers. He told me that the rules and regulations of the group home were printed on them. He told me that he would like for me to read them. Afterward, I was to sign the bottom of the last page, to signify that I had received a copy of the rules.

I could not read, and I suspect Mr. Driver knew that. Therefore, he explained to me the essentials. Mr. Driver told me, "We are pretty loose 'round here. I, personally, don't like seeing my young black brothers stuck up at Training School or nowhere else locked up. You respect me and what I gotta do, and I'm gonna look out for you as best I can. Be in here by eleven o'clock on weekdays, and no later than twelve-thirty on weekends. Keep your room and clothes clean. Go to school when we get you in school, and we can work with you from there."

I signed my name on the paper and handed it to Mr. Driver. I told him that I understood all the rules and would obey them.

"You ain't gonna follow all the rules," Mr. Driver said. "You'll probably break most of 'em. But if you respect me and do right by me, I'll do right by you."

That was simple enough. Mr. Driver was a likable man; it would be easy to respect him. But first, I had to find out about an important matter. "When can I go out?"

"Usually, I require new residents to stay in the house for a fourteen-day probation period," he replied. "But that won't be needed in this case."

I knew Mr. Driver was a good man and that we would have a fantastic relationship. He told me that he was going to allow me a one day pass to go home to get some clothes. I had to be back in by eleven o'clock. First, he wanted to settle me into my room and introduce me to my roommates. It was not yet noon, and most of the residents were in school. I would have plenty of time to hang out. I also had to decide what school I wanted to attend. It was more convenient to the state and to Mr. Driver to enroll me into Francis M. Wood Junior High School. It was closer, and most of the children at the group home attended there.

I wanted to attend Hampstead; most of my dogs still went there. Besides, it would be harder for the staff members at the group home to monitor me if I attended a school on the other side of town. I figured out that complicated scheme in the brief discussion I had with Mr. Driver. He advised me to talk to my Aunt Kim and grandmother about enrolling in school as quickly as possible. If the state had to enroll me in school, it might suggest to the court that my family had little involvement with me. The greater participation my aunt and grandmother had in my life, the easier it would be to get released from my court-controlled commitment. Mr. Driver urged me to let my family know all of that. He was emphatic about my not being able to leave the group home until I started school. I had to make it a priority to get in one. He did not care which school I enrolled in, just as long as I enrolled in one.

I was taken over to 909 house, which was identical to 907 house. Mr. Driver introduced me to this young white woman, Ms. Toni. He told me that she was one of six staff. She was a house parent and was to be treated with respect. Ms. Toni told Mr. Driver that he didn't have to speak on her behalf. She jokingly told Mr. Driver and me, "I can handle him. If he acts up, I'll just beat his little ass and send him home."

"When I first got in Training School," I said in response to Ms. Toni's comment, "a lady name Ms. Patterson made me get naked right in front of her. I ain't gotta do that here, do I?"

Mr. Driver laughed and said that once Ms. Toni showed me to my room, introduced me to my roommates and the others in the house, I was to come back over to his office. He wanted to make arrangements for me to go home on a "home visit pass." There were only two other residents in the house aside from me. Tony Jackson, who was to be one of my roommates, and this guy named Warren Davis. They were in the house because they had been suspended from school. Ms. Toni called them downstairs to the desk. She introduced us all, then instructed Tony and Warren to show me where I would sleep.

Tony, Warren, and I hit it off instantly. They told me what I suspected, that Mr. Driver was "cool as a mothafucka." The only reason they could not go out was because they had just been suspended the day prior. Warren was confident that if Ms. Toni was not working that particular day, they would've been able to go out. Tony was certain that if he truly had somewhere to go, he would be allowed out. I learned from talking with Tony and Warren that each house held fifteen boys. At present, the house we lived in had thirteen residents. Most of the niggas in 909 house were real niggas. The suckers lived in 907. I told Warren and Tony that they could hip me to what I needed to know later. I was anxious to get home on my pass. I had to pick up some clothes and straighten out some important matters with my family. They understood. Besides, we didn't really know each other. It was a major violation of ghetto etiquette to act like life-long buddies when just meeting someone.

I went back to Mr. Driver's office. He was there sitting at his desk talking to someone on the phone. He motioned for me to sit down in a chair opposite him, concluded his phone conversation, and retrieved a folder from his desk draw. It was my personal file. He explained to me that he had to contact my parents before he issued a pass for my home visit. I understood and only hoped that my Aunt Kim or grandmother could be reached. It had been nearly two months since I had been home, and I didn't want anything to interfere.

Mr. Driver looked at my personal file, collected my grandmother's phone number, and dialed it. It seemed like an eternity passed before I could detect that someone was on the other end of the line. I heard him say, "Ms. Pittman, I'm sending Arlando home on a pass. It'll be your responsibility to make certain that he's back here by eleven o'clock."

I was not sure which Ms. Pittman he was speaking to, my Aunt Kim or my grandmother. It didn't matter; I was going home. Mr. Driver hung up the phone and began writing on some official-looking paper. He handed it to me and informed me that it was my "home visiting pass." He instructed me to go directly home, pick up some clothing, and discuss with my aunt what school I would be attending. He emphasized that the sooner I was placed in school, the sooner I could receive daily passes to go home. If everything worked out well, I could go home and stay all weekend.

Mr. Driver gave me $5. He told me that the group home awarded its residents a $5 allowance each week on Fridays. I had to perform whatever chore I was assigned to ensure that I received my allowance. He was advancing me the $5 because he knew I didn't have any carfare to get home. I wanted to tell him that I had a $50 check in my pocket. When I was arrested, I had $50 on me, and when I was released from Training School earlier that morning, it was returned to me in the form of a check. I kept that information to myself. I was not about to pass up the $5. The state owed me something—considering all the hell I had been put through.

Mr. Driver asked me whether or not I knew my way home from where I was located. I assured him that I knew the neighborhood. Obviously satisfied, he dismissed me by advising me that the quickest route to my grandmother's house was to walk down Eutaw Street to North Avenue and catch the #13 bus. He told me that it would drop me off on Wolfe Street, on my grandmother's block. (My grandmother had moved from Madison Street to Wolfe Street while I was incarcerated.) I was grateful for his advice. I knew how to get to North Avenue, but I did not know what bus to take. I exited the group home, and was thoroughly pleased to finally be outside under no one's custody. I really felt free. It didn't bother me that the thin Big Ben state-issued coat was not significant enough to keep me warm from the brisk January cold. The euphoria brought on from feeling free kept me warm enough. I was so overcome with the excitement of being outside alone, I half skipped and half jogged to the bus stop. I didn't feel in the least self-conscious about being dressed in a state-issued outfit. Not many people were out in the community. It was barely afternoon. Most folks were probably still at work or in school., plus it was too cold outside for folks to stand around and engage in idle chatter. The few people that I saw were focused on reaching their intended destination. No one had time to assess my outfit to see that I had just been released from a penal facility. I was not recognized for being a criminal until I got on the bus.

Once I reached the bus stop on North Avenue, others directed me to the bus that would get me to Wolfe Street. The bus I needed was there within minutes. I had not bothered to get exact change for the fare. I simply put a whole dollar in the box. The driver gave me a strange stare, and the people on the bus looked at me in a curious manner. I then began to feel very self-conscious about my dress. Everyone on the bus knew that I had recently been released from the Maryland Training School for Boys. It was literally printed across my back.

After placing my fare in the box, I bowed my head in shame and went to the back of the bus to sit. I positioned myself where I would not be in anyone's peripheral view. The only way the other passengers could see me would be if they turned completely around. I was at the extreme rear of the bus, looking out the window, staring at everything I could and not wanting anyone to stare at me. I was not ready to be seen. The façade I wanted had not been erected, yet.

When the bus finally reached my destination, my 'hood, I got off. I stood on the corner of Wolfe Street and Ashland Avenue and inhaled a fresh breath of air. I felt that I was home at last. I walked the additional few yards to my grandmother's house. Before I could knock on the door, it flew open and I found myself in my beloved Aunt Kim's arms. Home at last. She was genuinely pleased to see me. Her tight embrace proved it. Thank God almighty, home at last.

My grandmother, step-grandfather (Daddy-Pain), and cousin Terrance were all there to warmly welcome me. They told me that they missed me, and Mama promised to prepare my favorite meal. She said to me, "Boy, I started gettin' your chittlings ready as soon as they told me you was comin' home."

I told Kim that she had to enroll me in school as soon as possible so that I could come home every day. I informed her that I preferred to attend Hampstead, the school I had always wanted to attend. No problem; she said that she would start the process the very next day. It was early in the week. Kim felt that she would have me enrolled before the week ended.

I asked where my things were. I was locked up when Kim moved back to Mama's house. I had no idea where my things were, or even if I had anything left. Prior to going away, I had amassed quite an impressive wardrobe. I had a few leather coats and a plethora of jeans, shirts, and tennis shoes. All my ill-gotten gain went toward clothes.

"Your stuff 'round here somewhere," Kim said. "We had to move and a lot of stuff got lost."

I didn't like the sound of that. Kim was still getting high. She looked as if her dependence on drugs had increased since I left. My clothes were gone. I was not there to protect my belongings, so they were gone. What a man can't defend, he doesn't have a right to. That's a natural law.

Terrance chimed in to save me, "Nigga, don't worry 'bout that outdated shit you had. I got you."

"You should." I was grateful. "I hear you a millionaire, nigga."

"Naw," his face broke into a broad grin, "I'm just close as a mothafucka."

Terrance truly looked "ghetto rich." He was a handsome man. He was short and a little on the chubby side, but he had muscles. He was even athletic in an odd sort of way. He maintained a well-groomed mustache and beard, and his brown skin was as smooth as a baby's. The thick gold chain and diamond-studded medallion around his neck and the multiple karat diamond ring on his finger highlighted his natural beauty. He looked prosperous.

"T.I., I need some clothes today," I used Terrance's nickname. "What I got on my back is all I got, and I gotta be back by eleven."

"Small thing, hustler, be cool."

A mysterious bottle of alcohol appeared and Mama, Daddy-Pain, and Kim started drinking. Terrance and I went off into another room. He gave me an update on everything that had happened during my absence. He informed me that Kim was still getting high. He suspected that she was injecting heroin as opposed to snorting it. She had gotten evicted from the house on Durham Street, and in all likelihood, she sold my clothes or passed them down to Kieshawn. Terrance also told me that Fat Larry was semi-retired from the narcotics trade. He retailed fruits and vegetables from his truck; occasionally he bought cocaine from Terrance at a wholesale price to distribute. But he was no longer the big nigga on the block; Terrance had that esteemed distinction.

Terrance and I had always been close. Prior to my going away, he would come to me to get money or advise about where to buy the cheapest wholesale marijuana. He did not know a lot about the illegal narcotic trade. Terrance was a basketball player. While I was learning how to gather the wealth, ghetto style, Terrance was tightening up his jump shot. He was naïve in matters relating to selling dope. I was his initial guide and teacher. It was only proper that I be offered an instant partnership.

Terrance had a connection whereby he was given a half kilogram of cocaine on consignment while he purchased the other half. He had three dealers working the package for him down on Eager Street. But now that I was home, things would be modified. An expansion had to be made to the business to make room for me, but first, I had to go shopping. I was going to be a partner in a prestigious firm. My wardrobe had to complement my position. The state gear I was sporting just wouldn't do.

Terrance and I let Kim and Mama know that we were going shopping to pick me up a few outfits. I promised Mama that I would be back in time to enjoy the repast she prepared for me.

I had a lot of things to do in such a brief period of time. I had to locate Annette to satisfy those urges that incarceration brings; and I had to make sure Kim did not get too drunk or high on heroin to start the process of getting me enrolled in school. I had much to do.

Terrance and I went to the strip on Eager Street. His crew, Wayne, Kirk, and Kevin were out there on the corner selling his product—cocaine. I knew everyone, and everyone knew me. We had all grown up together; we were childhood friends. I had a close bond with Wayne and Kirk, and it showed by the way they embraced me and expressed their excitement at seeing me. They all asked me how I was doing and entreated me to tell them about my experience at Training School. I told them that I had handled my business. I represented myself in a manner that would make them all very proud. I described some of the fights I had had been involved in, modifying the details so as to put me in the most favorable light.

"Yo, dem west-side niggas and D.C. niggas tryin' to run shit," I recall saying. "But me and the homies wasn't havin' none of that shit."

"Yeah, nigga," Kirk was encouraging my lies. "I see you put on some muscles. You been workin' out or what?"

"I got some push-ups in."

"You look strong," Wayne commented. "You better go get some pussy 'fore you hurt yourself."

We all laughed about that. Wayne had a point. Therefore, I reminded Terrance about my time schedule. I told him that I wanted to go get me some clothes and catch up with Annette. I knew that Annette was Wayne's first love, and he hated the fact that I was sexually involved with her. But I was not mature enough to be sensitive toward another man's broken heart. At the moment, my only concern was the cold weather. I was impressed with how much coke Terrance's crew was selling, and I was confident I would make a positive contribution to the crew. But my current focus was to get to the mall or the downtown shopping stores to collect my gear. I expressed my impatience to Terrance. He went over to the phone booth and made a telephone call. Meanwhile, I stood out there on the corner with Kirk and the others while they sold their coke to the multitude of addicts who came up to them to cop.

"Wayne," Terrance said as he came back over to where we gathered. "Go get me two gees. I'm gonna take this nigga shoppin' so he can stop whinnin'."

Wayne went to get the money and Terrance told me that we had to wait until our cousin, Charles, arrived. He was Terrance's driver. I asked whether or not it would take forever for him to come. I was assured that he would be there within fifteen minutes. I was cold, so I went over to the corner store, purchased me a hot chocolate, a snack, and played a video game. I was not going to brave the cold any further. Besides, I wanted to see Mr. Lee, the Chinese proprietor of the store. He and I had always had an excellent rapport. We used to talk shit to each other from time to time. Hell, Mr. Lee talked shit to all the hustlers who operated their illegal business outside his store. He knew that we represented at least 50 percent of his business. We, the hustlers, also protected Mr. Lee from the stickup boys.

I did not get a chance to speak to Mr. Lee. Terrance poked his head through the store's entrance no sooner than I started playing the video game, and yelled, "Come on man, Charles here."

"Damn man," I said. "You ain't gonna let me get my game in."

"You better bring that ass on! The way you been sweatin' me 'bout you needin' some clothes."

Terrance had a point, and I was not about to argue. I could do without playing the video game. I could not do without a new wardrobe. I would see Mr. Lee later. I followed Terrance toward Charles' '82 gray Thunderbird. Before I could get into the car, Charles leaped out the driver's side and wrapped his arms around me in a warm embrace. He was pleased to see me. We were family. Terrance seemed to be impatient; he instructed us to put an end to all that love stuff and get into the car.

Charles was in love with cocaine, and Terrance was his benefactor. I needed to benefit from Terrance's generosity, too. We complied to his instruction without further ado.

"Let's hit Mondawmin first," Terrance said as he adjusted himself in the front seat next to Charles, "I'm gonna hook you up with my man."

Terrance definitely hooked me up with his man. He had a friend who worked at Foot Locker who outfitted me in the latest sportswear. Terrance purchased damn near every sweat suit and tennis shoe the guy picked out for me. Then we went downtown to Gages where he bought me some designer blue jeans, slacks, winter sweaters, and a pretty full-length puff leather coat. There was barely enough room in the car's trunk and back seat where I sat to put all the purchases.

We were driving toward my grandmother's house after our shopping spree when Terrance said to me, "Nigga, I just spent over two gees on your ass, you better be worth it."

"If I wasn't worth it, you wouldn't kick me out."

"T.I. know your worth, Cuz," Charles put in. "He definitely couldn't stop talkin' 'bout, 'I be glad when Tray come home.'"

"Wayne and 'em gonna be mad at you. They know you gonna take over shit. 'Cause Terrance don't like bein' out there. The knockers hot on his ass."

Charles was our cousin, but we were not going to discuss any specifics in his presence as to what my role was going to be in Terrance's drug operation. It was apparent that I was going to be Terrance's right hand long before I came home. Everyone seemed to know that except me. I had only found out earlier that day. If Terrance wasn't so prosperous, or if I had any greater prospects, I would have been offended.

"Tray, you ain't gonna take all this shit to the group home, is you?" Terrance wanted to know.

I had not thought about that. It did not seem like a smart thing to take all my new clothes to the group home. "I'm gonna leave most my shit at Mama's," I answered.

Charles laughed aloud and Terrance tried in vain to restrain his laughter. I was curious as to what was so damn funny. I asked, "What y'all find so mothafuckin' funny?"

"Kim down on the strip sellin' your shit," Charles said.

I didn't like the suggestion that was being made about my Aunt Kim. I felt that I could trust her. She had cared for me and loved me when no one else could or would. I was going to leave my clothes at Mama's house. If my things came up missing, I didn't deserve them.

It was close to seven o'clock in the evening. I was racing the clock. I told Terrance and Charles that I would like to get to Mama's house to take a bath, put some uptown clothes on, eat something decent, and go find Annette before I went back to the group home. Charles eventually pulled up in front of my grandmother's house, and we all went inside.

There was plenty of chittlings, collard greens, potato salad, and corn bread for Terrance, Charles, and me. Kieshawn was there waiting for me. She was so overjoyed at seeing me that she could not stop crying. She put a hundred kisses upon my cheek and face. I had to wrestle myself away from her in order to eat and take a bath. Yalanda still wasn't home. I would have to wait until the next day to see her. Kim had left, too. Mama and Daddy-Pain were there, however. Mama told me that had I not come back home, she would have hunted me down and killed me. She put a lot of effort into cooking for me. I sensed that she was rather disappointed that I had not spent more time at home, but she understood. When she saw all the clothes Terrance had purchased for me, she voiced her gratitude. She thanked Terrance for looking out for me. Terrance told Mama that it wasn't necessary to thank him for looking out for his family. But Mama insisted that it was only appropriate that she tell him thanks.

Mama and Daddy-Pain had been drinking. They were not totally intoxicated, but Mama's thinking and attitude were definitely influenced by the alcohol. Terrance simply agreed to everything she said by saying, "Okay, Aunt Ola." Charles did likewise.

I finally got away to take my bath. Then I chose my brand new dark blue Adidas sweat suit, Herman Survivor boots, and puff leather coat to wear. It was quite stylish at the time. I selected five different outfits to take with me to the group home, and I put my other clothing items in Mama's bedroom closet. Daddy-Pain assured me that he would keep my belongings under lock and key. That was all right with me. I had already lost one wardrobe. I trusted Kim, but I understood the nature of drug addiction. A dope-fiend would steal from wherever and whomever to get that fix. I couldn't risk having my clothes stolen. I didn't know how great my income was going to be.

I borrowed a suitcase from Daddy-Pain, and with Mama's aid, I packed it with enough things to hold me over for a week. Thanks to her, I packed soap and other cosmetic items; the group home only had inferior state-issued cosmetics. I was truly happy she helped me pack. I didn't know anything about packing a suitcase to stay away from home.

At about nine o'clock I left my grandmother's house to go to Annette's house. I had reached her on the phone and she promised to be at home awaiting my arrival. Her mother was at work and her brothers were running the streets. She had the entire house to herself. I told Annette that my time was limited. I explained to her in the least ambiguous terms possible that I wanted some pussy, and I only had about an hour.

Annette only lived about six or seven blocks away from my grandmother. I didn't have time to waste. I asked Charles to drive me there. Before Charles could answer my request, Terrance told me that Charles would take me there, then meet me back at Mama's house at ten-thirty to take me to the group home. Terrance insisted that I not return late. He expressed that it was important that I get relief from my court-controlled commitment as quickly as possible. We had some major hangin' out to do. The group home would be an annoyance, to say the least.

I asked Terrance, "Will you be here when I get back?"

"I don't know. Why?"

"I need one more favor," I said, "I got a $50 check, I need the cash for fare. I ain't got no money."

"Shit, I ain't got much neither." Terrance reached into his pocket and gave me the last of the money he had in his possession. I didn't bother to count it. I just gratefully accepted it, and placed it into my pocket.

"Come on, Charles," I excitedly said. "I gotta go buff some ass 'fore that eleven o'clock thing."

A Role for the Bread

Chapter 27

I made it back to the group home on time. Charles was at my grandmother's house waiting for me just as Terrance had instructed him. Kim was also there; I had the opportunity to remind her to start the process of getting me enrolled into school. She agreed by assuring me that she would get up early the next morning and go up to Hampstead. I was feeling so great after spending the past hour or so with Annette, I was prepared to believe anything. Nothing could disappoint me. Annette had caressed every portion of my body. She was good; she completely satisfied my sexual appetite.

"Hi ya doin', Mr. Jones?" Mr. Small was the night shift house parent. He was a very pleasant middle-aged white man. I came to appreciate his integrity and warm sense-of-humor.

"I'm okay," I replied. "And you?"

"You the new guy, right?"

I answered affirmatively. He wanted to know whether or not I had been assigned a room. I told him that I had. I told Mr. Small that I was given a pass to go home to pick up some clothes. He told me that was obvious; he noticed the suitcase I was carrying.

"I ain't gotta check your suitcase, do I?" Mr. Small asked.

"Naw, I ain't got nothing but my clothes in here."

"Man, leave that man alone," Tony Jackson came into the room and directed his comment to Mr. Small. "We gonna put him down with what he need to know."

"Mind your fuckin' business, Jackson," Mr. Small told Tony.

"He in the room with me," Tony was not going to give up. "Mr. Driver told me to show him around when he got back from his pass."

"Well, show him around!"

Tony and I went upstairs to our room. He introduced me to our other roommate, a guy named Mike. He also showed me where I should place my clothes. He told me that I should purchase a lock as soon as possible because a lot of stealing occurred at the group home. Since my things were new, and I was new at the group home, it was likely that someone would try to steal from me. He cautioned me to keep a close watch on my belongings.

I sat around and conversed with Tony, Mike, Warren, and a few other guys at the group home. We got along fairly well. We had mutual friends, and we shared similar experiences from Training School. The guys seemed very impressed with my new clothes. I told them that my cousin took me shopping. I did not tell them I had a lot of other clothes as well. I made it seem as if I had brought all the clothes I had with me.

I shared the details of my romantic interlude with Annette. She was too good for me to keep it to myself. Warren accused me of lying about Annette's attractiveness. I told Warren and the others, "I don't fuck with nothing but dimes."

"Yo, you probably got a bunch of buns like the rest of these niggas."

Tony came to my aid, "Nigga, you the only one be fuckin' bitches we don't even know what to feed."

We went back and forth all night. Eventually, we all agreed to bring our respective girlfriends to the group home for a visit the next day. Visitors were permitted each day from 4 p.m. until 11 p.m. Whoever failed to bring a girl in for show-and-tell was a liar and would be held to the worst ridicule imaginable.

Around three or four o'clock in the morning, Mr. Small came up to order us to our respective rooms. It was time to turn the lights out. I was very tired—exhausted actually. I fell asleep as soon as I hit the bed. The beds were much more comfortable there than the bunks at Training School. It was also warm. I guess the state was attempting to introduce us delinquent youth offenders back into society in the most humane manner possible.

It has been over twenty years since I was at the Boys' Group Home, and I still recall the fresh winter breeze that came off the reservoir. It was so refreshing; I would go to the window each morning when I awoke just to inhale the fresh air. Under other circumstances, I might have appreciated it far more.

"Breakfast, breakfast," various voices yelled. "Come and get your breakfast."

Mike and Tony, my roommates, were up before me. It was mandatory that everyone come to breakfast at six o'clock each weekday morning. It did not matter whether you were enrolled in school. We ate breakfast and then received our assignment for the day at the seven o'clock meeting.

I can not recall exactly what our meal was my first full day at the group home, but I do recall gathering in the dining room with the thirty or so residents eating a wholesome meal. I also recall getting assigned to washing the dishes. I was mad about that. Mr. Driver informed me that the newest arrivals generally had to wash the dishes after the breakfast meal. I had to sweep and mop the kitchen and dining room floors, too. He told me that once I got enrolled into school, someone else would likely get the menial tasks. For the moment, Tony and Warren would have to help. They were suspended from school. They didn't have anything else to do.

There were about five or six of us juvenile delinquents left in the house to clean up the place. We were supervised by three staff members, aside from Mr. Driver. Each time one of us offered a complaint about having to perform whatever menial task he was instructed to perform, he was told, "If you had your ass in school, you wouldn't be here to do it."

I worked my ass off. I swept and mopped floors, washed dishes, and wiped off table tops until about noon. The 909 house was clean, and I could finally take a break. Tony and Warren went up to their rooms to take a nap, I got on the phone to call home.

"Mama, is Kim home?" I asked my grandmother as soon as I heard her voice on the other end of the line.

"No," Mama said. "She went out to see 'bout getting you in school. Charles came and got her early this morning."

Mama could not have known how pleased I was to hear her confirm for me that Kim had kept her promise to get me in school. I could not bear too many more days of doing so many household chores. I told Mama that I had to perform all kinds of duties around the group home until I was placed in school. She agreed with me that it was not fair that I should have to keep that place clean; after all, it was not my home. Mama and I felt the state should hire people to do its work. It was beyond cruel to force her baby to work like a slave.

"You just hold on, baby," Mama advised me. "We gonna get you outta there."

I told my grandmother that I would call her later in the day. I hung up the phone and went over to 907 house to see Mr. Driver. I had to request permission to go to the store to purchase a lock so that I could secure my belongings.

"Mr. Driver, I have to buy a lock so I can lock my stuff up?" I sort of asked.

"I'm gonna give you another home pass at four o'clock," Mr. Driver said. "You can get what you need then."

I was thrown completely aback by that. I had prepared myself to be stuck in the group home until I was enrolled into school.

"Someone from Hampstead Hill Junior High School called me," Mr. Driver continued. "Your family and you must be serious about your progress."

"Yeah, we is."

"I told you, you do right by me and I'll look out for you. You did a good job with your chores around the house."

I went up to my room. Tony and Warren were there hanging out, so I joined them. We all sat around and talked and listened to music. Warren had a ghetto-blaster and a whole lot of Whodini, Run-DMC, and damn near all the other hip-hop jams of the time. I told them that I would be allowed to go out on another pass. I would bring Annette with me at eleven o'clock when I came back. I felt an abiding need to prove to them that Annette was an attractive girl. I especially wanted to prove it to Warren.

"Why I gotta wait 'til four o'clock to get outta here?" I asked.

"We gotta have a group meeting," Tony answered. "That start at four when everybody gets in from school. It only takes 'bout ten or fifteen minutes, unless some nigga start bitchin' and whinin' 'bout some dumb shit. Then it take longer. After the meeting everybody that can get out for the day get their pass."

It seemed like four o'clock took forever to come. But when it finally came, and we had our group meeting and Mr. Driver gave everyone his home visit pass for the day, I was okay. Warren and Tony were angry because they were denied home visit passes. They were told at the meeting that they would be on restriction for at least a week. Once Tony calmed, I offered him ten dollars to keep an eye on my belongings. He graciously accepted my offer. He assured me that nothing of mine would be stolen under his watch.

Terrance had been extremely generous to me. He had given me close to two hundred bucks to hold me over. Instead of catching a bus, I took a cab. I went directly to Eager Street. Wayne, Kirk, and Kevin were all out on the strip distributing Terrance's cocaine when I arrived. I asked them had they seen Terrance, but I was informed that he rarely made an appearance on the strip before sundown.

It was no mystery; I was going to work with Wayne and the others. Hell, I was going to be their immediate supervisor. I simply jumped into the flow with the others. I had Wayne show me where the stash house was located. He took me there and introduced me to the stash man, a guy named Ronnie. He really didn't have to introduce me to Ronnie; he only had to let Ronnie know I would be running, too. It was kind of an orientation session. I needed to see exactly what we were selling. It was explained to me that we were selling twenty and forty dollar capsules of cocaine, halfs and wholes. We didn't take any short money. Our product was so good that we didn't have to negotiate price. Hell, our product was of such superior quality, we didn't even accept coinage or one dollar bills. If someone wanted to purchase our coke, he or she had to bring us bills in denominations of no less than five.

A lot of folks thought that we were arrogant or egotistical for having such a policy, but that wasn't the case. One dollar bills and coinage were too bulky and difficult to manage.

Wayne had explained the concept to me. I cursed him out when he first instructed me not to take any coinage or one dollar bills.

"Nigga, I'm takin' all money," I had said to him. "We ain't so rich we turn bread down."

"Man, just don't take that raggedy money."

Wayne's tone was nasty, as if he was annoyed with explaining something quite obvious to a naïve child. I felt offended. I told him, "Motherfucka, we takin' all money that spends."

I made my statement loud enough and clear enough for Kirk and Kevin to hear. I was Terrance's lieutenant. I had to assert myself as the second-in-charge.

There was no further protest. I could sense Wayne's aggravation, but it didn't matter. He complied with my instructions and that's all that really mattered. Disputes over rank, power, and money were resolved via violence in our trade. Wayne, Kirk, and Kevin would not want to get into a power play with me. They would lose. Everyone knew that I was there to take over as Terrance's second-in-command. It made perfect sense to stay on my good side.

When Terrance came to the strip later that night, Wayne nearly broke his neck to run up to him to tell him that I had them accepting coinage and one dollar bills. Terrance told Wayne not to concern himself with it; I would have to count the money and account for everything, since I made the decision to change his program. Wayne took some kind of morbid satisfaction in that. I could not understand it then, but after two days of counting the accumulated one dollar bills and coinage and discovering three to four hundred bucks missing, I immediately went back to the "no coinage and one dollar bills" policy.

I told Terrance that I wanted to bring Black on board with us. Black was still hustling with his cousin Greg on Eager Street. They were selling heroin, but it did not look as if their operation was very lucrative. Terrance didn't offer any opposition.

I had spotted Black down on the strip once I got into the smooth flow of selling our product. He was standing on the corner of Rutland and Eager, about half a block away from where I was standing.

"Kirk, is that Black down there?" I asked.

Kirk looked toward the direction I was staring and answered, "Yeah, that's him."

I yelled at the top of my lungs, "Black! Black!"

He responded by coming toward me and I toward him. We embraced each other with mad love and affection. He asked, "When did you come home?"

I told him that I was not really home. I was in a group home. I told him about my time restriction, and that I was hopeful about getting into school soon. I told him that I had to put up a grand façade in order to get relief from my court-controlled commitment. I let him know that I was running Terrance's crew. I told him that it looked like Terrance was getting plenty of money.

"Nigga, don't I know it," Black said. "I tried to get with him soon as he busted out. But he act like he don't fuck with me or something."

"Yeah!" I exclaimed.

"Man, he got them soft-ass niggas down with him."

"Yo, we gonna do this together. Them niggas can't hustle like we can."

"How you gonna pull that off?"

"Give me a day or two and it's all gonna be 'bout me and you," I asserted.

Eleven o'clock was nearing. I made it around to see my grandmother and Kim. They were both in the house, and they both were angry with me for not coming home sooner. Kim's anger was easy to assuage. She knew I was on Eager Street working. Mama went to bed mad at me.

"Tray, just make it a point to get here early in the morning," Kim instructed me. "I have to take you to school tomorrow."

Yalanda was already in bed, but I went up to see her anyway. I had really missed her, and I didn't want another day to pass without seeing her.

"Hey baby," I said to my baby sister as I kissed her tenderly on the lips. "I missed you."

My touch woke Yalanda up. She was thrilled to see me. She wanted me to stay with her. It nearly broke my heart to tell her that I had to leave. The only comfort I could provide was to let her know I would see her the next day. I knew she wouldn't understand my situation. Therefore, I entreated her to go back to sleep. All she needed to know was that her big brother was home.

I went back down to Eager Street where business was booming. I told Terrance that I had to start heading back to the group home. I also told him that Kim was getting me into school the next day. Terrance already knew; he had been Kim's transportation that day. He was dedicated to getting me released from my court controlled-commitment. He felt that I was the only person he could fully trust. It was imperative that I become his full-time business partner.

"Charles is 'round the corner," Terrance said. "Tell him to take you back."

It was apparent that Charles was going to be my chauffeur, too. I went around the corner to Wolfe Street. Charles was exactly where Terrance said he would be.

"You ready cuz?" Charles said to me as soon as he saw me approach.

"Take me up to Annette's house first," I instructed as I got into the passenger's seat next to him. "I want to see if she'll drive with us to the group home. I want them niggas to know I fucked a dime bitch last night."

Terrance must have been paying Charles a generous salary. He had absolutely no problem driving me wherever I requested. He took me to Annette's house; she was home. I asked her to take the drive with me to the group home. She agreed. I let her know that Charles would bring her back, but I couldn't accompany them. I had to stay at the group home.

I permitted Annette to sit up front on the drive to the group home. I played with her hair and kissed her on the neck from the back seat. I told her that I loved her and that I was going to treat her like a princess. She believed every word. I was a bad boy, and bad boys tell mad lies. Everyone was supposed to have known that.

When we reached our destination, I told Annette that I needed her to walk me to the house. I wanted to introduce her to a friend of mine. She didn't want to get out of the car, but once I explained to her that my friend believed that my girlfriend was ugly, she agreed to show off her looks.

"Mr. Small, this is my girlfriend, Annette," I told Mr. Small as soon as he opened the door to allow my entrance. "I want to introduce her to Warren. Can she wait here 'til I get him?"

It was five or ten minutes before eleven, and we were permitted visitors in the house until eleven o'clock. I couldn't foresee any complication with my request. Mr. Small didn't, either.

He said, "You got five minutes."

I raced up the stairs to get Warren and Tony. They were in Warren's room listening to his radio, "Yo, I got my honey downstairs. Come on and meet her."

Mr. Small and Annette were engaged in conversation when we reached the front room, the living room, where we were allowed to entertain our guests.

"Nigga, here's my sweety," I announced. "Ain't she fine?"

Annette turned herself around in a graceful circle. She modeled her well-proportioned, perfectly symmetrical body and facial features, and I was convinced that all were thoroughly impressed by her beauty—even Mr. Small.

The moment culminated when Annette planted a sensuous kiss on my lips and said to me, "I'll see you tomorrow, boo."

Annette exited, and I watched her make her way to Charles. They pulled off once she got into the car. I bemoaned my miserable situation. I didn't want to be in a house full of dudes. I wanted to be with Annette or home with my family. Hell, I would have settled with being out there on Eager Street, on that cold-ass corner, hustling with my dogs. Anywhere would have been better than being locked up.

Tending to the Details

Chapter 28

I was admitted into Hampstead Junior High without any complications. The Vice Principal, Mr. Earls, was made aware that I had been incarcerated for the past two months and that my brush with criminality had prevented me from focusing on academics. My records from Clifton Park, my previous school, suggested that a two-watt light bulb was brighter than I was. Therefore, Mr. Earls wanted to keep me in the seventh grade—a year behind.

"I went to school while I was locked up," I told Mr. Earls. "You can put me in my right grade."

Kim was determined to be of no further aid to me as we sat in Mr. Earls' office. She obviously felt that once she got me enrolled into school, her work was done. The grade I was assigned to was between Mr. Earls and me, and I was determined not to permit him to place me in the seventh grade. I wasn't concerned with school enough to really care about the academic stuff, but I still wanted to be in my proper grade. It was a social matter; it was not relevant that I perform at the grade level. I didn't want to be thirteen and still in the seventh grade.

Mr. Earls said to me, "Your last school records tell me that you were not attending school. You missed more days than I can count, and your grades are ridiculous."

Mr. Earls didn't mince words with me, or anyone else, I learned. He is one of the most sincere and honest men I have ever known.

"Look Mr. Earls," I pleaded. "Let me try out in my right grade. I'll do right. If I don't do right, then put me back in the seventh."

"Okay," he stood up from behind his desk and extended his hand to me. "If that's your word, I'll accept it."

I accepted Mr. Earls' handshake. There was something about his demeanor that compelled me to want to honor this man who was taking my word. From the moment Kim and I had entered his office, Mr. Earls had treated us with dignity. He offered Kim coffee and served her with the kind of courtesy one usually reserves for his betrothed. He was a man who treated everyone with decency and respect, no matter his or her social station. He didn't exude the arrogance that many other school administrators did. I was going to do good in the eighth grade. I would do everything necessary to impress Mr. Earls, except study and attend every damn class.

"I'm gonna do real good in school, Mr. Earls," I promised. I didn't value my promises then, but I truly wanted to honor that one.

Time and circumstances would not allow me to honor my promise to Mr. Earls. I was being put in charge of a major drug operation. I was going to make more money than either of my parents ever made. I was going to be the big nigga on the block, so learning how to read, write, and do arithmetic simply could not get the attention from me it deserved.

"Okay, Arlando," Mr. Earls concluded our meeting. "I'll see you Monday. And Miss Pittman, hopefully I won't have to see you until graduation."

I will never forget that day. It was a Thursday. Kim and I left the school after our meeting with Mr. Earls and met Charles on the parking lot. He had picked Kim up early that morning, and the two of them had come to the group home to get me. Mr. Driver excused me from all my chores once Kim came there to let him know she was taking me to school to be enrolled. I was riding high. Annette had given me bragging rights the night before, and now I had the entire day to hang out. Had Mr. Earls made me start school that day, I probably would have been pissed off. Things were going good.

"Charles, take me up Terrance's house," I commanded. Once Kim and I got into the car. "I wanna see him before I go down the way."

"Mr. Driver said you ain't gotta come back 'til eleven tonight," Kim informed me. "He also told me that if I get you in school, and if I wanted, I could let you come home this weekend."

Kim was my heart, and she always knew how to play me. "How you with money, Kim?"

"I ain't got none."

I reached into my pocket and pulled out my bank roll. I counted off a hundred dollars and handed it to her. Terrance had looked out for me. I had done good my first day on the job. "I'm gonna have somethin' else for you later," I said to her. "I know you been having it hard, but I'm here for you now."

Charles turned the volume up on the radio. There was no need to mess up a great day with being overly emotional. We enjoyed Stevie Wonder's "Living In The City" as we drove Kim the short distance home to my grandmother's house. She got out of the car and kissed me tenderly on my cheek as she had done on many occasions to display her affection. Charles then took me to see Terrance. I was about to start my second day on the job. I needed to be thoroughly oriented. I also wanted to let Terrance know that I was bringing Black on board.

Terrance was lounging around the house when Charles and I got there. He was watching television, listening to music, and waiting for me. He wanted to impress me with the brand new furniture he had adorned his home with. He gave me a tour of the entire place. He wanted to let me know how important it was to take care of family members by staying home and keeping the money there.

"I could easily have my own house or apartment somewhere," Terrance had said. "But I rather stay here with Fatty Pooh, Frog, and the kids to help them out and be with the family."

Terrance gave Charles some cocaine and money and instructed him to leave us. He wanted to talk to me in private. Charles left the house, and Terrance and I went down into the basement. Terrance had converted it into a bedroom, living room, and office. Everything was down there. A king-size bed, a floor model television set, a couch, a desk, and a huge safe. The basement was tastefully decorated, the carpet extremely comfortable. It only made sense that I had to take my shoes off before entering.

"T.I. you been takin' down big loot," I said. "You must got a strong ass connect."

Terrance went over to the safe located in the far corner of the large basement. It was inconspicuously covered with a table cloth with a night lamp atop. He opened its door and pulled out several wads of cash and told me, "This is twenty-five thousand. It could be a hundred but I ain't got the kinda niggas 'round me I need. Plus, you know I ain't really with this dope and coke shit. I'm a weed man. I been thinkin' 'bout not gettin' no more coke and shit, and goin' back to the weed. This shit is too fast for me."

"T.I. we ain't just gonna throw this shit away," I insisted. "I can handle all this. I want some loot like you got there."

"You can run everything," Terrance said. "I'll keep the connect goin' with Milt. You just make sure I get a little cut and keep Wayne and 'em on. Plus, you know Wayne is fucked up 'bout you handlin' things."

"I don't know why; his soft ass can't."

"You might have some problems outta Larry's fat ass, too." Terrance warned me. "I've been givin' him some coke on consignment. And now that he built up his bank, he might wanna take over shit. You know how he is. He fucked Calvin all around."

I was sure I could have a workable relationship with Fat Larry; we spoke the same language and I admired him. Hell, I looked forward to talking shop with him. Meanwhile, I had to work out the details of more immediate issues.

"I'm gonna roll with Black instead of Wayne and Kirk," I was rearranging the operation. "They ain't corner niggas."

"I know, but they all I had."

"They can work the stash, and we'll pay them the same."

"I was givin' 'em five bills a week."

Terrance told me that he was getting a thousand grams of cocaine each time he copped from the connect. He paid for five hundred and was fronted the other five hundred grams. The connect insisted that it be that way. The only person Terrance was giving large quantities of weight to was Larry.

Terrance didn't trust Larry, but he had a tremendous amount of respect for him. My cousin, Terrance's brother, Suddar, was a very dear friend to Larry. When Larry came to Terrance to reveal that he was facing difficult financial times, Terrance was compelled to aid him. He gave Larry two hundred grams of cocaine on consignment. Larry had supported Suddar's legal campaign to stay out of the Maryland Penitentiary. Suddar had shot a man for Larry, but the fact that Larry aided him throughout his legal battle meant a lot to Terrance.

Fat Larry was intrinsically linked to Terrance, and Terrance didn't like it one damn bit. Terrance hated Larry. He begged me not to trust him. The only reasons Terrance dealt with Larry was because he needed him to move two or three hundred grams of coke each time he got resupplied and Suddar asked him to. Terrance accepted the fact that he was not into heavy dealing. He could move small quantities of drugs, in time, he could move an entire kilogram. But time was of the essence. The connect wanted a kilo sold within a week's period. Wayne, Kirk, and Kevin couldn't meet that demand.

They were not accomplished drug dealers. They were not willing to do all the things necessary to move a kilogram within a week.

I was willing to do whatever it took to move large quantities of drugs. Specifically, insist that all the competitors on my block take their product some place else. I understood that in order to move a kilogram of cocaine, I had to hold a monopoly on a specific area. Terrance appreciated that fact as well. He just wasn't willing to exert the necessary force to accomplish such a feat.

I was the man for that job. I should not have taken the job, of course. It was a job for a devil, not a son of God. Much suffering and misery would be the consequences of my accepting a role reserved for the devil. (I long to make amends to the community I brought so much pain and suffering to as a result of my decision to be the "big nigga on the block.")

In order for me to fulfill the role, law abiding citizens in my 'hood had to stay in their home and not go shopping for essentials or allow their children to come outside to play. I insisted that no other drug dealers operate their shop within a twelve block radius from where I operated mine. Rival drug dealers felt that I could not insist that they move their operation. We settled the disputes through the ends of gun barrels. Each day and night for about a month, I settled one territorial dispute after another. A number of black mothers and fathers curse the day I was born because I brought such grief to their lives. They awaited the arrival of their son just to discover that he would never come home again. He lost a dispute against Tray. Many children grew up hating my name because their grandparents told them to.

I take a minor comfort in knowing that I have never stepped outside my arena to harm any innocent person. I acknowledge that many innocent people got hurt, but it was not my intent to hurt them. It was simply unfortunate that they loved someone who would have a dispute with the likes of me. I couldn't petition the court or some law enforcement agency when I felt that someone was monopolizing my drug corner. Hell, I couldn't even complain to the police when I got robbed. All my disputes were settled in a deadly fashion. Why God allowed me to live and others to perish is beyond my comprehension. My grandmother and aunt stood prepared to bury me many times. God just took my hand and walked with me. He permitted me to live on. I sometimes feel that my being alive is my punishment. For spending a life-time in prison may very well be worse than death.

Executive Decisions

Chapter 29

Terrance and I made our way down to Eager Street. We found Wayne, Kirk, and Kevin moving the cocaine. The brisk January weather did not seem to be significant enough to keep the coke-heads away. Our crew had a line of about ten or fifteen people waiting to be served.

"Wayne, Kirk—I wanna holla at y'all after you serve 'dese niggas, okay?" I announced as Terrance and I approached the gathering. "I'm gonna go get Black."

Terrance remained with the crew and supervised the operation while I went in search of Black. It wasn't difficult to find him. He was a block away, on Rutland, trying to sell the inferior product he was dealing with his cousin, Greg.

"Hey, Black," I yelled from across the street when I spotted him leaning on a blue mailbox. "Come on, man. We got business to handle."

"What's up?"

"We ready to roll," I informed him as I came close enough to receive his embrace. "You said you gonna roll with me once I got shit straight with T.I."

Black's eyes lit up. His excitement at the prospect of working for a prosperous crew was apparent. However, he was a little doubtful.

"You sure man?" he asked. "I told you, T.I. act like he don't fuck with me."

"I got this thing now, and I need you with me," I was being sincere. There was no one else that I trusted more than Black. "We gettin' ready to tell Wayne and 'em they gonna work the stash while we run the shop. Terrance is waitin' on you now."

Black knew I wouldn't lie about something as important as that. He abandoned his position with Greg without leaving a notice and accompanied me up the block to where Terrance, Wayne, and Kirk were waiting for us. Kevin was away serving customers, but we didn't feel that he was essential to what we had to discuss. We decided to go to Wayne's house, a few hundred feet from where we stood, to discuss business.

The mood was light; we were all childhood friends. No one would leave feeling betrayed or embittered, I hoped.

"Tray," Kirk broke the silence as we headed toward Wayne's house. "You ain't gonna fire us, is you?"

"Yeah," Wayne answered. "That mothafucka gettin' ready to throw us away."

"You niggas know I ain't gonna do no fucked up shit like that," I defended my integrity. "I'm just gonna get y'all punk asses off the corner."

"I know you like that," Kirk was speaking to Wayne. "I know you gettin' tired of dem niggas slappin' you 'round takin' shit from you every other day."

"Nigga you the one," Wayne was offended. But he played it off. I suspect he didn't want to disrupt the good mood. He would pay Kirk back later for revealing his cowardice.

We entered Wayne's house and settled into seats around the living room. No preliminaries were used to start the meeting. Terrance simply handed the ball to me, "Go 'head Tray and say what you gotta say."

"Wayne, I want you and Kirk to work the stash. Me and Black will work the corner."

"What about Kevin?" Kirk genuinely cared.

"What about him?" Black retorted. "His faggy ass ain't got no business gettin' no money."

Black was more than my dog, he was my best friend. He had given me his allegiance long ago. He never teased me about my alcoholic mother or other embarrassing matters that many others had teased me about. He had sided with me in ghetto battles without hesitation when others had not. He was my beloved brother, if not by blood, then definitely in spirit. Whatever authority I had, he had. Where I go, he would go.

I had truly forgotten about Kevin, but I was not about to take a side opposite to Black. If he wanted to abandon Kevin, then Kevin was out. And it most certainly seemed as if Black wanted him out. However, Terrance had a sense of fairness.

"Naw, man," Terrance said. "Kevin have been with us from the start."

"Kevin is a pussy," I said. "We really don't need him."

Terrance was about to defend Kevin further, but he was interrupted by a thunderous knock at the back door. Wayne rushed to the rear of the house to see who was there. We all stood up, tense and anxious. Wayne came back into the living room accompanied by Kevin, who was bloodied and disheveled.

"Man, what the fuck happened to you?" we asked in unison.

"That mothafuckin' nigga Blackface and one his buddies jumped me and took some coke," Kevin blurted. "The same nigga that got you, Wayne."

Terrance was enraged, "I gotta put a stop to this shit!"

"Don't worry 'bout it, cuz," I comforted. "I got it."

"What he take?" Black inquired.

Kevin told us that he was only robbed of two capsules of cocaine. Blackface had convinced him to go get the product without producing the eighty dollars that it cost. Black and I used the incident to highlight to Terrance just how naïve his crew was to the nature of drug dealing.

We concluded our meeting by ordering Wayne, Kirk, and Kevin to stay in the house. Terrance then went around to the stash house to relieve Ronnie of his duties to our crew. We decided to move the stash to Wayne's house until other arrangements could be made. Meanwhile, I needed a gun to avenge the insult visited upon us. Blackface had strong-arm-robbed two of our dealers on two different occasions. That shit could not go unanswered.

"Where you keep the iron?" I asked Terrance once we left Wayne's house.

"Up my house."

I wanted to chastise Terrance for keeping the gun so far away from the action, but I thought better of it. Terrance was not a career drug dealer. He had serendipitously come into the position. He knew that, and that's exactly why everything was being turned over to me.

"I still got the .38 and .357," Black said. "I can get to 'em in a minute."

"Let's just keep 'em on hand," Terrance suggested. "That nigga is probably gone now. But he'll show up later. Let's run the shop for now."

That was a good idea. Terrance and I went to our corner where a large crowd had gathered to purchase our blazing cocaine. Black went to his previous stash house to retrieve the guns. When he returned, we worked the package. We sold a lot of cocaine; the clientele did not seem to notice the change in personnel. The product was still the best damn coke around.

At around ten o'clock, I told Terrance and Black that it was getting close to the time when I had to start making it back to the group home. I told them that I wanted to catch up with Fat Larry before I left. Black said that he could handle everything in my absence, but Terrance insisted upon bringing Wayne back out to the corner to help make runs. Black begrudgingly accepted it, and I went up to High-Hats Bar to see Fat Larry. I had seen him go in there only moments before I announced to Terrance and Black that I had to leave.

"Larry," I was truly excited about seeing my hero. "I need to rap with you."

"Boy, it's good to see you," Fat Larry said as he grabbed my hand to shake, embracing me almost simultaneously. "When you get out?"

"A couple days ago."

The noise in the bar was very loud. Larry and I stepped outside. We had to discuss some important matters, and although High-Hats Bar was a haven for drug dealers and other felons, it would not have been appropriate to shout to Larry the matters relating to our business.

"Man, it's really good to see you." I told Fat Larry. "How you been doin'?"

"I been so-so," Larry answered as we stood in the front of the bar bearing the brisk temperature of the January night.

"I heard," there was no need beating around the bush. "Terrance got me runnin' shit."

A profound silence fell between us, and Larry turned on his heels and began to walk up Wolfe Street. I followed. I could not detect whether or not he was offended by the announcement that I was his new boss. I could not read his mood; I was baffled. I moved away from the subject once I could no longer tolerate the silence. I didn't relish offending my hero.

"I gotta get back to the group home by eleven," I informed.

"Jack, this is the best news I done had all day," Larry was pleased. "T.I. is tough as nails. Plus, he in above his head."

I did not respond to that. I knew that Terrance was in above his head. But he was my family, and I was not going to speak ill of him to anyone, including my hero.

Larry continued, "Man, T.I. got a mean-ass connect, but he ain't tryin' to go nowhere with it. And Milt ain't gonna let him get but so far, anyway."

"So what you sayin'?" I was thrown back by Larry's knowledge of Terrance's connection. The identity of a drug connection is usually top secret. "T.I. is my blood."

"Naw man, I ain't talkin' 'bout knockin' T.I. out the box. He my man, too. He the only one that helped me when no one else would. Then you know how me and Suddar is—and you, too."

It was comforting to know that Larry felt that way. I would have moved against him without prejudice or hesitation had he suggested betraying my blood.

"I can do some things with you," Larry said. "I know you want money, not just pennies."

No truer words have ever been spoken. He definitely had my attention. But time was of the essence. I asked Larry to take me to the group home. I could not risk being late. He agreed, and I was grateful. He would have more time to tell me about getting real money, instead of the pennies Terrance was getting.

Inwardly, I felt that Larry was jealous of Terrance. In the brief time I had been working with Terrance, we had sold more than $20,000 worth of cocaine. If that was pennies, show me the money.

Larry still had his pretty silver-gray Cadillac with the red leather interior. I felt more special riding in it this second time. I was significant to him. Larry needed me to satisfy his goal.

"Tray, if you can fix it so I can get the room I need," Larry said to me as we drove toward the group home. "I can raise the money I need to get my old connect back."

"How much you need?"

"I need 'bout twenty more grand," Larry answered. "Then I can get shit back, and we ain't gotta keep eatin' outta Milt's hand."

I did not know enough about Milt and the deal he had with Terrance to make any commitment to aid Larry. However, I did believe in Larry enough to grant him as much room as I could.

I explained to Larry my situation, I had to attend school and report back to the group home at eleven o'clock each weekday night. I would be free on weekends. During which times, I would be free to be a full-time drug dealer. After I described Mr. Driver to Larry, he told me that he thought he knew him. Larry believed that he and Mr. Driver attended school together during their youth. Larry told me he would meet with Mr. Driver, and if that was the person he knew, he would have my restrictions lifted. I believed Larry would come through for me. After all, he did keep Mouse from testifying against me.

The Dance Continued

Chapter 30

I could barely sleep; I tossed and turned throughout the night. Larry had put a major burden on my shoulder. He was my hero, and I desperately wanted to help him and be a part of his fabulous plan. We were not going to be dependent on anyone, and we would control the narcotic commerce around our 'hood.

Larry had depicted Milt, Terrance's connection, as a controlling, manipulating homosexual with more money than he was entitled. He thoroughly convinced me that Milt was not a man I wanted to be associated with. All I had to do was keep the cocaine coming to Larry consistently until he raised the necessary capital to reconnect with his former supplier, some Nigerian cat, and we would be free from Milt. He assuaged my guilt about Terrance by assuring me that Terrance was not being crossed in the deal. Larry insisted that Terrance was the one mistreating him in their business arrangement.

"Tray, man," Larry had said to me. "I be ready to roll. I got shit set up whereas I can move three, four hundred grams a night, but T.I. won't give me nothin' past two hundred grams."

"Why he won't give you the shit?" I feigned naivete.

"That's that Milt shit," he angrily replied. "Don't let a nigga get past where you want him to be. He wanna control a nigga, and Terrance is gettin' just like him."

Larry went on to explain to me that if we were going to be out there on the front line throwing bricks at the penitentiary, we might as well seek all the financial gain possible. He made it clear to me that no nigga in the game should permit another man to tell him how much money he should be able to make. Terrance and Milt were of the same cloth. They felt that if you were associated with them, under their employment, they should regulate how much money you made. If they felt that you were growing too fast or getting too large, they did dumb shit like hold your package up for a few days or dilute your product so that you would have an inferior product to sell. Larry expressed to me that working for Terrance for the past two weeks had been an exasperating experience.

I could not tell Larry that Terrance not only distrusted him, he disliked him as well, The only reason Terrance supplied him was because of his relationship with Suddar. Terrance was grateful to Larry. Terrance believed Suddar's legal situation played a critical role in bankrupting Larry. A lot of folks had to be bribed into not coming to court. The victim himself and two innocent bystanders who were shot had to be paid off. There were those expensive attorneys' fees, too. Also, Suddar was high-maintenance while in prison. It cost plenty of money to keep him satisfied. His girl came by damn near every day to pick up a package of drugs to keep his addiction going, and he had to keep money on his books. Larry had been there for Suddar before Terrance was able to pick up the slack. Terrance was grateful; otherwise, Terrance would not be fucking with Larry. I kept that information to myself. It would have been an absolute betrayal of my cousin to disclose the contents of his heart to Larry.

"All you need me to do is keep hittin' you off without holdin' you up?" I needed clarity as to what, exactly, Larry required of me.

"If you can keep me on for 'bout three or four days consistent, the money will be right, and I can go on and do my own thing," Larry was pleading with me to understand his position. "Plus, you know T.I. don't like me. The sooner I can raise the twenty grand I need, the sooner I can get the fuck outta his way."

I could not contain my laughter once Larry revealed to me that he knew Terrance didn't like him. I was under the impression that Terrance's dislike for Larry was a secret. "What make you think T.I. don't like you?"

"The way how that nigga treat me," he jokingly responded. "Plus, he straight out told me, 'Larry, you know I can't stand your fat ass.'"

"Why is it like that with y'all?"

"I don't know, Tray," Larry was being honest. "When you start gettin' a little money, niggas gonna hate you for all kinds of reason. You'll go crazy tryin' to figure out why a mothafucka don't like you. And for real, what a nigga feel 'bout you ain't none of your business; how he treat you is."

When Larry dropped me off at the group home, I was convinced I would aid him in raising the money he needed. He was going to be my mentor in the game. I wanted him out of our crew. It didn't set right with my conscience to have the guru of heroin dealing under my command. However, I knew how stubborn Terrance could be. He was always a difficult person to deal with. Once he had his mind made up, that was it.

He had advised me to keep Larry on a short leash. He didn't tell me how much to supply him with, but I understood him well enough. He didn't want Larry to realize any goal as a result of his connection to us. Terrance told me that he supplied Larry once and only once per package. If Larry sold his supply before Terrance sold his, he would simply put him off until he was ready to get another supply from Milt. He was determined not to allow Larry to make a significant profit off a single package.

I had a lot to think about. If I aided Larry, would I be betraying Terrance? If I didn't aid Larry, would I be betraying the rules of the game?

• • •

Mr. Driver awarded me a weekend. He was impressed that I had been able to enroll in school so quickly. He appreciated the fact that my family actually had an interest in getting me out of the clutches of the juvenile justice system. Mr. Driver had once commented to me that he was saddened by the fact that so many other youths at the group home had no one. Several of the youths at the group home were there because they had nowhere else to live. Their families had simply abandoned them, making them wards of the state. I had a home to go to; therefore, Mr. Driver was going to let me go there as often and for as long as policy would allow. He simply cautioned me not to get into any trouble. If I caught a charge, if I was taken to the police station for any reason, I would be automatically returned to Training School.

When I hit the strip at about five o'clock Friday afternoon, Black and Wayne were out on the corner selling our cocaine. They had customers lined up. "'Bout time you got your ass down here," Black said to me as soon as I stepped out of the cab that brought me to the strip. "We been holdin' this shit down all day."

"I'm here now," I replied. "So we can hold it down all night together."

I could sense that Black was very pleased with his performance. He had never worked in such a lucrative business. When he was working with his cousin, Greg, they hardly ever sold more than $500 worth of dope in a single day. Now, he was moving $500 worth of coke an hour. I was determined to make certain that his pay for each day surpassed his previous employer's entire nightly gross.

I sent Wayne back to the stash house and I worked the corner with Black. I handled most of the runs to give Black a rest. When Terrance finally reported to Eager Street to see how business was going, it was nearing midnight. Black and I had nearly sold out. We had not taken a rest break like Terrance's former crew used to do.

We decided to close shop after the last of the product was gone so that I could go to the main stash house to learn how to dilute and package our narcotics. Black had already been shown the routine. He didn't have the time restraints that I did. But now that I had my very first weekend, I could learn the entire routine, too. I didn't have to report to anyone until eleven o'clock Sunday night. Mama might be a little angry with me for not spending any quality time with her, but as long as I was alive, she would be pleased. Kim would know where I was, or at least what I was up to.

Terrance phoned Charles and instructed him to come to Eager Street to pick us up. We needed a ride to Parkside Gardens Apartments. Terrance had rented an apartment there to stash the majority of our package. It was an ideal place because it was in a middle-class neighborhood with no open-air drug traffic nor a constant police presence. The quiet community with its tree-lined streets and manicured lawns offered us a sense of security.

"Drop us off at Moravia and Sinclaire Lane," Terrance ordered Charles. "I'm gonna call you in a couple hours when we get finished."

Charles drove us to our destination and asked, "You want me to come up to the house or meet you right here?"

Terrance reached into his pocket, pulled out a wad of cash, and gave it to Charles. He then instructed, "Meet us here at about three."

Terrance, Black, and I made our way the two or three blocks to the apartment on Bowleys Lane. We walked in silence. I guess because we didn't want to disrupt the silence of the wee hour in that peaceful neighborhood. What we needed to do required absolute privacy and secrecy. No drug-dealer ever wanted to be caught at his main stash house by the police or the stick-up boys. It would be a great tragedy. Therefore, it was important that we employ extreme discretion in making our way there.

No one seemed to be following us. The streets were completely empty, as expected. It was about one o'clock in the morning, and it was very cold out. "Yo," I exclaimed the moment we safely stepped into the apartment. "This spot is tight."

"I know it," Black said. "I told T.I. that when I first came out here."

Terrance bolted the door shut once we were inside. He instructed Black to wait in the bare living room while he took me into the apartment's only bedroom. The furniture in the place consisted of a single queen-size bed, a kitchen set—a small table with four chairs—and an elaborate entertainment center—a forty-inch television set and a stylish musical system. The apartment had wall-to-wall carpet and appeared to be the home of the average bachelor.

Once in the bedroom, Terrance shut the door behind us, went over to the closet and pulled up a floor board. He pulled out a clear plastic bag that contained more cocaine than I had ever seen in my life.

"I just got this the other day," he announced as he held the package in the air so that I could see it fully. "It's a key."

I wanted to contain my excitement, but couldn't, "Damn nigga, we large sure 'nuff."

Terrance was rather cavalier, "I told you, I buy five hundred grams and yo front me the other five."

"I know," I contained myself. "I just ain't never seen that much shit at once."

Terrance tossed the coke onto the bed and told me that he generally cut the coke up two ounces at a time. He informed me, "This shit takes a three, but I only put one and a half on it. I put a two on what I give to fat ass."

Terrance reached underneath the bed and pulled out a triple beam scale and a bag full of empty clear medical capsules. He turned the scale on, then poured cocaine onto it until the numbers at the top read fifty-six. Terrance then wrapped the larger quantity of cocaine up and instructed me to watch carefully as he placed it back where he kept it hid. He gave me a key to the apartment and impressed upon me that I would have the task of packaging the narcotics for street sales, or wholesales, depending upon the situation.

Terrance and I exited the bedroom carrying the two ounces of coke Terrance had measured out along with a bag full of empty capsules. We went to the kitchen to find Black sitting at the table with the necessary paraphernalia to package our product.

"We ought to be able to get at least two hundred pills outta this," Terrance said. "How much scratch do Wayne and 'em got down there?"

Black answered, "They should have twelve grand; we sold three hundred pills."

That seemed about right. We were doing real good business. Our product was the best around, and we were going to make sure that it stayed that way.

I was fully oriented. I only had to meet Milt, and run down on that nigga who took our shit, Blackface. I felt sure I could accomplish that before I returned to the group home Sunday night. No problem! Hell I could even manage a few hours with a lovely lady, or as I preferred, a freak bitch. There was no one to monitor my behavior. I didn't have to concern myself with any curfew. It was already concluded that I was "a bad ass little nigga."

Bad Boys Are Too Busy

Chapter 31

Terrance, Black, and I decided that it would not be a good idea for all three of us to travel together with illegal narcotics on our possession. So I collected the cocaine we had packaged for sale and went to meet Charles where we had agreed to rendezvous. He was there before me, parked at the corner of Moravia Road and Sinclaire Lane. I slid into the passenger seat next to Charles.

"Where's T.I. and Black?" Charles had to know that if I sat up front, Terrance was not coming.

"Take me down the hill—to Wayne's house," I saw no need to answer his question. I was nervous and anxious to get all the drugs off me. "I'm dirty as shit. If the police try to pull us over, keep goin' until I can ball out."

Charles understood the program; he had been driving Terrance to and from the main stash house since the beginning. In fact, it was Charles' idea that Terrance rent the place. Charles was three or four times my senior; he had forgotten more about dope-selling than I would ever know. The only reason he was no longer a triple-beam nigga, pushing weight, was because he violated the cardinal rule on dope selling: he fell hopelessly in love with his own supply.

He provided Terrance and me with sound advice on matters involving the operation of our business, but he could not be more than our chauffeur. He was too old to face the possibility of prison time and too hooked on drugs to get close to the money or the product. Terrance and I loved our cousin, Charles. We hated some of the things he did to himself, but respected his right to do it.

"Did y'all hook me up?" Charles always got a few grams of cocaine before we diluted it.

"Yeah, man, here," I tossed him the five grams Terrance had measured out specifically for him. Charles could be quite demanding when it came to his blast. "Get me down to Wayne's."

"You got to be patient 'bout things, Tray." Charles was offering his sage advice. "There is always more than enough time to do everything you gotta do."

I really didn't want to hear Charles' advice. I had 200 large capsules of cocaine in my possession. I would be buried under the jail if I got caught with all this stuff. I had no illusion as to who would do the time if I got caught in the car with the drugs. Charles definitely wouldn't take the charge. He was fifty-five years old with a thirty year drug addiction. If he got arrested, he would spill his guts about everything he knew as soon as the first signs of withdrawal manifested itself. Charles used to insist that Terrance and I not talk too much around him, or any other dope-fiend. He impressed upon us that a key police strategy was to arrest a drug addict, place him in a cell until his withdrawal symptoms began to show, then start the interrogation. Any dope-fiend would sell out his mother as opposed to face the pain of withdrawal.

Charles took me to the corner of Monument and Wolfe Streets. He told me that it would be too risky for him to take me any closer to Wayne's house. One black man in an expensive car at that time of the morning, in that neighborhood, was likely to get pulled over by the police. Two black men in an expensive car, in that neighborhood, at that time of morning, were certain to get pulled over, searched, have shit planted on them if no illegal contraband could be found, and carted off to jail.

I made my way through the alley until I reached Wayne's house via the back door. It was close to four o'clock in the morning, but I wasn't disturbing anyone's sleep. Wayne and Kirk were awaiting my arrival. They were wide awake and entertaining themselves with two neighborhood dope-fiend freak bitches. The whole house smelled of their orgy.

"Where y'all get these funky bitches?" I asked as soon as I saw Kirk and the girls that he and Wayne had lounging around the living room partially dressed.

"Fuck you mean, 'funky bitches,' nigga?" The red-bone freak was offended.

"Why is what I said so hard to understand?" I responded. "Y'all bitches stink."

"Fuck that nigga," Wayne said. "He just want some pussy. He just got outta jail."

Kirk took a deep breath, as to smell the air, "Damn, Tray ain't lyin'— these bitches do stink."

We all burst into laughter. Kirk's brutal honesty diffused what could have been a tense situation.

"If you want some of me, all you gotta do is ask," the red-bone offered. "I'm nasty and easy."

I must admit, I was very tempted. The girls didn't look all that bad. One of the two had a light complexion with a nice body. The other had brown skin with an even better body. The girls appeared to be rather young, in their early to mid-twenties. They were drug addicts, no doubt, but they were far from their bottom. They still possessed some of their former attractiveness.

If I was not so intent on business, I would have been interested in participating in the orgy. But Terrance was specific in his instructions: tell Charles to come back to the apartment to pick him and Black up, go to Wayne's house and get the money from the day's take, leave the new inventory with him, and take my ass home to get some sleep. We had a full day coming. Therefore, I just satisfied myself with a few looks and touches.

"Where the loot at, yo?" It was time to count the money.

"Upstairs," Wayne was going to stay with the girls. "Kirk know where it's at. Y'all can get it."

Kirk begrudgingly got up from the couch, where he had been lounging, puffing on a joint and having his penis caressed by the red-bone. "This shit better not take long, or I quit."

Kirk was my nigga, no doubt. I have always felt a special affection toward him. He and his family had always been kind to me. His mother, Ms. Boo, would become my Mama Boo.

"Fuck dem broads, nigga," I told Kirk as we headed up the stairs to Wayne's bedroom. "It's payday, if y'all ain't fucked up the money."

"Shit, you know we fucked up some money," Kirk said. "You know dem bitches downstairs didn't come free. They was cheap, but definitely not free."

"How close to twelve gees you got?"

"I won't know until we count," Kirk honestly responded. "But I don't think we fucked up more than a couple hundred dollars.

The money was under Wayne's bed in a shoe box. Not an ingenuous hiding place, but no one ever accused Wayne or Kirk of being great intellectuals. It was generally accepted that Wayne and Kirk were quite slow. School records will support that judgement. Wayne is the only child I know to have failed kindergarten, and Kirk was so dumb it took him an hour and a half to watch "Sixty Minutes." But they were my niggas, my childhood friends. I loved them both, though there were times when I didn't like either one of them very much.

Kirk was on point with the money count. A couple hundred bucks were missing. But that didn't affect me. Terrance had instructed me to only keep ten thousand dollars. Wayne and Kirk were supposed to get a thousand dollars each. I counted out the ten gees that Terrance instructed me to bring to him, and left the remaining eighteen hundred dollars or so with Kirk. I instructed him to give Wayne his half. After clear and careful calculation, Kirk concluded that half of eighteen hundred bucks was six hundred for Wayne. Kirk reasoned that Wayne wouldn't notice the difference since he was so dumb.

I got home to my grandmother's house at about dawn. The sun was rising in the sky. My grandfather and grandmother were sitting at the kitchen table eating their typical breakfast of eggs, grits, bacon, and coffee.

"Where you comin' in here from?" Mama asked me.

"From the group home," I didn't have to lie, but I assumed Mama would be hurt if she knew that I had neglected to come visit her on my first day home. "I wanted to see you first. You know I love you."

"Yeah right," Mama knew I was lying. I could never pull a quick one over on her. "You want something to eat?"

I was famished. Other than a few snacks from the corner store, I had not eaten anything. I accepted the hot grits, eggs, and left-over biscuits Mama set before me. After I finished eating, I went upstairs and got into Kim's empty bed. She had stayed out all night, too. I was pleased about that; otherwise, I wouldn't have had anywhere to sleep. All the beds at Mama's house were occupied. I would have to hook up the basement, perhaps design it like Terrance had designed his. I was certain I would have the money to afford the decoration. The $10,000 I was carrying gave me confidence.

• • •

"Man, get up," Black was shaking me awake. "We down there waiting on you."

"What time is it?"

"Little after nine," Black answered.

It seemed like I had just gotten into bed ten minutes before he came to wake me. Oh well, I had slept for about three hours, more than enough time for a poor boy to sleep. Once I got rich, I would get a lot of rest. I collected my consciousness, went to the bathroom to wash up, got some clothes out of the closet where Daddy-Pain had put them, went to the basement to hide the $10,000, and went out to Eager Street. Black had agreed that we would sell at least 200 pills every day. We had committed that we would not go anywhere until we grossed $8,000 dollars. We figured that if we maintained that level of business, we would both be able to purchase the cars we desired by summertime.

I was too young to drive, but I still wanted my own car. I would get me a driver like Terrance had. I was going to live ghetto large. But first, I had to start selling the coke. We had a large inventory, and it wasn't going to get sold with me laying around the house.

The weather was nice outside. It was uncharacteristically warm for a January morning. Our shop was up and fully operational by noon. Wayne and Kirk were on point and our clientele was responding well to the superior product we had prepared for them. Terrance had stopped by briefly to see how things were going. He also wanted to get the $10,000 I had collected from Wayne. I told him that I had left it at my grandmother's house. I gave him the specific details as to where I hid it in the basement. He went to pick it up, and Black and I continued to sell our product.

By the time nightfall came, Fat Larry had summoned me to come up to his house on Montfort Street. I was eager to meet with him. I didn't take offense to his sending an underling to me, "Larry said come up to his house. He's ready for you."

I informed Black that I would be gone for a couple hours. He was totally familiar with the arrangement that Terrance had with Larry. He didn't feel that I was leaving all the corner work on him. Besides, he could have Wayne or Kirk come out of the stash house to aid him with making the runs.

I caught a cab to Larry's house. When I got there, he treated me gracefully. His wife, Ada, a beautiful woman, offered me orange juice and cookies. She was the perfect hostess, warm, gentle, and genuinely kind. I knew from the moment we met, she and I would have a special relationship. She was not being used by Larry as Vivian had been used by David. Ada was too noble a woman to allow herself to be used in such a manner. The affection and courtesy she showed me were not part of some business deal. She genuinely liked me, and I genuinely liked her. The fact that she was gorgeous was insignificant. I did not look at Ada in a lustful manner. She was to become the mother I never had. Her tender nurturing and warm affection would comfort me on many occasions. I thank God, to this very day, for blessing my life with Ada. Her love and concern for me manifested itself in many forms. She even told me once, "Why don't you get the fuck away from Larry's sorry ass. You are too good for him."

Larry and I were seated at the kitchen table; Ada had just finished clearing the table of the dishes Larry and I had used. As soon as she finished, she left the room so that Larry and I could talk in private.

"Tray, I need for you to cover for me for 'bout a week," Larry began. "I been talkin' to my people and I can get back on by next week if I have all the money."

"What's all the money?"

"Seventy-five grand," he said. "I got sixty now. If you keep hittin' me, and hit me hard, I'll have it all."

I asked Larry whether he had the $6,000 he owed Terrance. He did, but he had to be assured I was going to give him a significant package before he could pay it. He didn't want to disrupt the financial timetable he had himself on. I didn't want to disrupt it, either.

"I'm gonna give you 300 grams tonight," I informed Larry. "If you knock that down tonight or tomorrow, I'm gonna give you 300 more."

"That'll get me where I need to be on time."

I knew I could manage that. Terrance was going to be mad as hell, but I felt that it was my call. The money would be straight. I was just going to allow Larry to make a larger amount of the profit than Terrance, Black, and I. Instead of Black and I selling 200 pills a day, we would sell 100. Terrance would see us out there working the package while he vacationed. He did tell me that it was my shop. He only wanted a small portion of the profit. I would handle everything. Terrance had assured me that all the business decisions were mine to make. I decided to get Larry out from under me. He would be of greater value to both Terrance and me if he was not under our domain.

Larry had a hotel room out on Route 40 that he had rented for the purpose of packaging narcotics. He gave me the address, and we agreed to rendezvous there at midnight.

It was still early. I had a few hours to kill before Larry and I were scheduled to meet. I lounged around Larry's house for awhile talking to Ada and getting acquainted with Lacrisha, Ada's fine cousin. I was enchanted by her beauty and proper manner of speaking. I wanted her dearly, and I didn't hide my desire.

Ada was amused at my attempt to seduce Lacrisha, and Lacrisha was annoyed. Initially, Lacrisha was flattered by my romantic overtures, but after awhile, she became annoyed by my aggressive tactics.

It became apparent that I was getting nowhere with Lacrisha. I left. I went to Terrance's house to meet up with him. I needed to gauge the degree of control I would actually have over the operation.

When I got to Terrance's house, he was preparing to leave. He was going to Odells, a local disco spot frequented by all the hustlers.

"I caught you just in time," I said to him as he stood in the living room adjusting his coat. "I just got finished seeing Larry. He's ready to get on."

"I don't care," he replied. "I told you, this is your thing now. Just make sure you got $22,000 when it's time for us to re-up. And you got to have a nice cut from the profits for me. I'm tired of this shit."

"What 'bout the $10,000 you got outta Mama's basement?"

"That's from the old package," Terrance said. "I'm keepin' that. You and Black get y'all's from the shit we got now. I ain't even gonna help you move it. You got the key to the spot, you know where everything is. Plus, Larry owe you $6,000. I'm takin' a break."

I had the clarity I sought. I left Terrance so he could go out to the disco. I went back to Eager Street to see how Black was doing. I was shocked to discover that he was not out there. I went around to Wayne's house, which we had been using as a stash house since Terrance relieved Ronnie of his duty.

Kirk and Wayne were there drinking beer and smoking weed. No business was being conducted, and I was mad.

"Why ain't nothin' happenin'?" I asked. "Where is Black?"

They informed me that they had sold out of everything, and every penny was accounted for. Wayne asked me, "Where'n the fuck you been?"

"I had to take Kattie-Mae to the hotel to wet that ass," it had been a long time since Wayne and I had played the dozens. "You know how your Mama gets when she don't get that dick."

"Yeah, she worse than Leola," Wayne was thoughtful enough to shoot back at my grandmother rather than my mother. "Last time I didn't fuck your grandmother, she called the police."

Wayne told me that Black had gone home. He would be there waiting for me. I instructed Wayne and Kirk to hold onto the money until I returned with the new supply. I had to go back to the table.

I went around to Black's house. He was there with Melissa, his girl-friend. "Black, we gotta go to the table," I told him. "You know we ain't got nothin' left."

"Let me meet you out there in 'bout an hour?" he begged.

"If I ain't gettin' no pussy," I replied. "Ain't nobody gettin' none."

I expressed myself in a joking manner, but I was serious. I had not had any time to spend in recreational matters since taking over the drug operation. I had only had three or four hours sleep, and I still had a lot of stuff to do before eleven o'clock Sunday descended upon me. When Black tried to entreat me to take a break, I firmly reminded him of our goals. I took him off to the side, where Melissa could not overhear our conversation, and told him, "Man, I gotta re Larry up. Plus, we gotta hook up some more caps."

I told Black that we would take it easy the next day—go take in a movie, spend some time with our girlfriends, and spend some money. I thoroughly mollified him. But Melissa was another matter all together. She became enraged when it became apparent that Black would be leaving with me as opposed to staying in the house with her.

"I won't be here when you get back," Melissa yelled at Black as we left the house. "Fuck Tray in his ass the next time you want some."

"We goin' to a hotel," I shot back to her. "I might give him some. You know I love him."

I put an arm around Black's shoulder and kissed him on the cheek. I looked back toward Melissa, and she angrily slammed the door. Larry was right; folks get mad at you for some of the most trivial reasons imaginable when you are in the dope game. Melissa didn't speak to me for months afterwards.

The Thug Rise

Chapter 32

Black and I decided not to open shop at all Sunday. Blackface had been shot multiple times and was presumed dead. People assumed that Black and I did it because we had been circling the neighborhood for days looking for him. It was no secret that Blackface robbed Kevin, someone in our employ.

Terrance was pleased that Blackface was presumed dead. He appreciated the fact that others in the game attributed Blackface's death to our crew. If a drug crew is unable to flex its muscles every now and again, they would be prey for every predator around. Blackface had strong-arm-robbed two of Terrance's dealers without any consequence. It would have been only a matter of time before others came to relieve Terrance and his crew of all that they possessed. Once I became a member of Terrance's crew, people immediately stopped robbing the crew. I was not having it, and I would imagine that is why Terrance handed me the reins. I had been nurtured to be a criminal.

I cannot recall what Black and I went to see, but I do recall we stayed downtown at the movie with our girlfriends all day, he with Melissa and I with Annette. We felt that if we avoided the neighborhood for a couple days, the police would not apprehend us nor question us about Black-face. He was only a black dope-fiend. The law would invest little time and resource into solving his murder. None of us was worth the effort. If witnesses did "step forward" rather than "fall from the sky" and people in the community did not complain about a person being murdered, the police would not pursue the case. Blackface and his assassins were non-persons. It was perfectly acceptable for them to murder each other in broad day-light, in the middle of the street. It meant very little. They were all entrenched in the narcotics trade; they were filth. Just stay away for about a week or two, and all would be forgiven when you returned. Perhaps your crime would be pinned on someone else if you have not become an annoyance to local law enforcement.

Black and I were fresh, still up-and-coming. The law had no need to lock us up. We went off to the movie with our honeys. We had plenty of money and the product was set up for sale. Larry would move most of the cocaine. He would realize the greatest profit from our package. He would make his goal of $75,000 to reconnect with his Nigerian heroin connection, and I would have the $22,000 for Terrance plus his nice little profit. Everything was looking pretty damn good.

At about ten o'clock that night, Black and I decided to part. He wanted to go home with Melissa, and I had to go to my grandmother's house to pack some clothes and make my way back to the group home. If a cab would stop for me quickly, it was quite possible I would be able to get with Annette. I envied Black for being able to spend the night with his girlfriend. I had to race the clock. This group home shit was really starting to get on my nerves. I thought I would have plenty of time to do everything I desired my first weekend home, but I didn't even get a chance to do the nasty. A number of girls and women alike had offered themselves to me, but I was too busy playing grown-up games. I had no time to spend with my grand-mother or any other family member. I had no time to do anything other than sell cocaine and secure my crew's place on Eager Street.

When Annette and I got to Mama's house, she was there waiting for me. She knew I would stop by to get some clothes to take to the group home. She wanted to take some time to speak with me.

"Tray, where you been all day?" Mama asked me as soon as Annette and I walked in the house.

"I went to the movies with Annette," I replied.

"How you doin' Ms. Leola?" Annette spoke to Mama.

"I'm doin' all right," Mama answered. "Would you excuse us for a min-ute, baby?"

Annette went into one of the back rooms, leaving Mama and I alone to talk. I wanted to tell Mama that I was really pressed for time, but I couldn't manage the words. My grandmother truly loved me. We had been very close at one point in my life. We were inseparable during my earlier childhood, and I suspected she missed me—as I did her.

"I love you, Tray," Mama said to me. "Whatever you need me to do, whatever you need me to be, I'm here for you."

I was humbled by Mama's announcement. It had been quite some time since anyone told me that she loved me, and I don't recall anyone ever telling me that she loved me with such intense sincerity.

"I love you, too, Mama," tears formed in my eyes as I embraced her, and I was grateful that she and I were alone. "You know I gotta get back to the group home."

"I know," Mama said. "I put your stuff in the suitcase. Go check it to make sure I ain't forget nothing."

Mama had packed my stuff perfectly. She always knew what I needed. I really miss her. She was the best, and I don't think I will ever stop mourning her death. I lost much when she passed on.

I phoned Charles, like Terrance always did, and instructed him to come pick me up. I was his new boss and it was time I demonstrated it. I was feeling better than I had in my entire life. I was a part of something important and I was important myself. Terrance and Larry truly needed me. I was not just an add-on to their lives. I was essential to them. Terrance needed me to fill his shoes; they were far too big for him. Fat Larry needed me to bail him out of a life of drug-dealer servitude.

I loved my life as a drug-dealer, and I had no incentive to do or be anything else. No longer was I made to feel as if I was an annoyance or bother to anyone. Mama and Kim would have reason to love me and adorn me with their affection and concern. I was going to pay some bills and put some food on the table. I was their "golden child."

Charles came to get me, per my instructions. He seemed a little annoyed about being summoned, but I gave him a hundred bucks and told him that I would instruct Wayne to give him a supply of cocaine. That appeased him. He took me to the group home, and then took Annette home.

Warren and Tony were quite pleased to see me. They were curious to know about my weekend. They launched a million questions at me. Did I fuck my girl, Annette? Did my rich cousin buy me any more new clothes? Could they hang out with me next weekend? I answered truthfully; I was an important man now. I didn't have to lie to build myself up. The truth of my importance would be hard enough to believe.

"I ain't really have enough time to lay up with no bitches over the weekend," I responded to their question. "I was too busy at the cuttin' table and movin' my shit. You know I gotta get my paper first."

"Nigga," Warren told me, "ain't nobody too busy gettin' money that he can't get some pussy."

Tony added, "Man, as fine as Annette chocolate ass is, I'd burn that thing up every chance I could."

I offered them some sage advice, "Pussy is always gonna be there. A nigga gotta have his money right first. I'm runnin' a major shop; bitches be throwin' themselves at me all day. But I gotta chase dem dollars."

I unpacked my suitcase, sat around and conversed with my two group home best buddies for awhile, took a shower, and went to bed. I wanted to be well-rested for my first day of school. I had promised Mr. Earls I would do well in the eighth grade, and I really wanted to keep that promise.

I got up the next morning, just like all the other youths at The Boys' Group Home, and readied myself for school. I truly felt jubilant. I would he able to leave the group home at seven-thirty in the morning, as opposed to staying there cleaning floors, toilets, dishes, and whatever else needed to be cleaned. I had to go get an education.

I went to North Avenue like everyone else awaiting transportation to school. The only difference for me was I flagged down a taxicab as opposed to waiting on a bus. I had to meet my partner in crime before I made it to Hampstead. The bus would eat up time.

Black was in bed sleeping when I got to his house. His sister, Valanda, let me in. She knew that Black and I were closer than brothers and that it was perfectly all right to allow me entrance to his bedroom without first alerting him to my arrival.

"Man, get up," I was shaking Black awake. "What the fuck you doin' sleep this late?"

Black looked up at me as if I was crazy and simply said "'Cause I'm tired."

I informed Black that I had to go to school. I told him that I did not think it was wise for him or me to work the corner that day. The shooting death of Blackface was still too fresh. Black agreed with my observation, and we decided our best course of action was to allow Wayne to work the corner for us. We had to maintain our shop. Fat Larry would be selling the majority of our product and reaping the greatest profit from it. However, we still had to get something.

Black assured me that he would see to it that our interests were looked after while I was at Hampstead getting an education. I didn't have to worry about anything. I could trust Black with my life. I went to school and allowed him to go back to sleep.

I made it to school on time my first day. I reported to Mr. Earls' office and his assistant showed me to my homeroom class. I was introduced to my homeroom teacher, a kind, middle-aged white woman, Ms. Rose. She showed me my class schedule and wished me good luck. My "dog," Ronald, was in my homeroom class, and he was going to show me around the school. I was not going to have any problems attending Hampstead Hill Junior High School. All my childhood friends attended there. Wayne, Black, and Kirk were too busy selling cocaine to attend school regularly. Ronald, Melvin, Buddy-Clyde, and Kent were there. They attended regular classes and would make my stay there pleasant.

I benefited greatly from having Ronald in all my classes. He could read much better than I, and he got me through most of my classes. He and his girlfriends helped me cheat on nearly all my class assignments, quizzes, and tests. His good looks and quick wit got me into the girls' lavatory on many occasions. I loved Ronald; our friendship endured many years. I am grateful to God for blessing my path with him. I came to prison too soon in life to fully bond with him in the way I would have liked, but his genuine and sincere nature allowed us to have a friendship that withstood the tests of time—and prison walls. I would not have been able to make it all these years behind prison walls without the loving support Ronald gave me. I owe him a debt I can never repay. He got me through the eighth grade and many years of prison. I will forever mourn his death.

I Only Took What Was There

Chapter 33

Two weeks had passed since Blackface's murder, and Black and I were back out on Eager Street slinging our product. Larry had tendered his resignation; he was no longer under my dominion. He had paid off his debt and was being supplied by the Nigerians again. He was moving heroin in the 1900 block of Eager Street while Terrance, Black, and I were moving our cocaine a block away, in the 1800 block. The drug traffic was heavy. Fat Larry was directing his abandoned cocaine clientele to us. That's why Terrance had to come out of retirement. Business was booming and the money was coming in by the bundles. No one was threatening us. The shooting death of Blackface had apparently sent a strong message.

I was doing great in school. I was making it to all my classes and Ronald and his corps of girls were helping me pass. I was determined to get a good report for my upcoming court hearing. I even made sure I obeyed all the group home's rules. I made curfew every day and attended all the four o'clock weekday meetings. I paid Tony or some other dude at the group home to do whatever household chore I was assigned. None of the house parents cared who did what; just make sure your chore was done. That was the only requirement.

I spent a lot of time at Larry's house with Ada and their son, Lamar, during my hibernation period. It was not cool for Black and me to hang around Eager Street. After I got out of school at 2:30 in the afternoons, I went to the group home for the ten minute four o'clock meetings and then made my way to Larry's house. He and Ada had adopted me. I became a part of his family.

I couldn't tolerate hanging around my grandmother's house for any lengthy period of time. I was ashamed of her alcoholism and I was embarrassed by Kim's heroin addiction. There was nothing in that house for me other than shame and embarrassment. I simply stopped by periodically to make sure they were all right with money and food. I hardly ever stayed long. I preferred the peaceful and wholesome atmosphere at Larry's home. I became attached to Lamar. He was the baby brother I never had. He and I would play Pac-Man, Galaxy, or some other game he had. Lord knows, he had every electronic game a child could want. I also enjoyed answering all the innocent questions Lamar's five-year-old mind could come up with. In addition, he was helpful in aiding me to seduce girls. The honeys thought it was so sweet that I would take my little brother almost everywhere I went.

Lamar was an ideal baby brother. He was hard! I taught him how to properly use profane language. I showed him how to shoot craps, and I explained to him where babies come from. I recall one evening Lamar and I were up in his room playing Galaxy. His Aunt Wilmer, Ada's sister, was at the house visiting, and she was pregnant. Lamar asked me, "How did Wilmer get a baby in her stomach?"

I answered, "Her boyfriend put it there."

"How?"

"He touched her on the butt," I explained. "And she liked it, and the next thing you know, she had a baby in her belly."

Lamar was satisfied with my answer. He appreciated my wisdom so much he never doubted the value of any of my answers. From that moment on, he took to patting girls on the ass who he wished to bear his children. I love that little nigga. The night the news reached me of his death, I wept uncontrollably. I had given him a lot of bad information. I had set such a poor example for him that the guilt will eat at me for the rest of my days.

"Black, we gonna have to get some help." I was growing increasingly tired of running all day. "I done made at least a hundred runs already."

"I know exactly what you mean," Black said. "I done ran 'bout two hundred times myself."

"How many runs Terrance made?" I asked.

Junior burst into laughter and could hardly get a response out, "I ain't the best with math, but I can count to two—and I know that fat mothafucka ain't run no more than that."

Black, Terrance, and I had only been back to full time drug-dealing for about two days, but it was obvious we would have to hire additional personnel to handle the volume of business we were conducting. Larry was a major distributor, and now that we had his full clientele along with our own, we would have to employ one or two others.

"Terrance ain't gonna want to put nobody else down," Black warned me. "You know how he is."

"Fuck how he is; we run this."

I would not have made such a comment about Terrance to anyone other than Black. He would not construe my remark as a prelude to mutiny.

"If we tell T.I. that we can't handle the runs by ourselves he gonna wanna bring Wayne back out here," Black advised. "And then all the stick-up boys will be on our ass."

Black had a point. But Terrance had given me the shop. It was unfair to me that he was taking it back now that I had solidified our corner. Fat Larry was no longer a concern, and Blackface and niggas like him were not preying on our dealers, taking our shit every day. I had some leverage. Plus, I was Terrance's blood and most trusted ally.

Black and I decided that we would talk to Terrance about hiring someone immediately after we closed shop at ten o'clock. We also agreed that we wanted Goodie, Black's cousin. It was best we kept things in the family. Besides, I suspect Black felt out-numbered by Terrance and me since Terrance and I shared an actual bloodline. He wanted a blood relative included. He certainly deserved it. He was essential to our success. If he wanted Goodie in our crew, then I wanted him in our crew.

"T.I., I'm gonna bring Goodie in," I announced as Terrance, Black, Wayne, Kirk, and I sat around Wayne's kitchen table counting the day's take. "We can use another runner out there."

"Bring Wayne out," Terrance said.

"Told you," Black blurted.

"I wanna stay in here," Wayne knew Black didn't want him out on the corner with us—and that I would side with Black—and Terrance would ultimately side with me. "I keep the count straight. Plus, Miss Boo ain't gonna let Kirk's fat ass hang but so long."

Miss Boo, Kirk's mother, kept periodic checks on him. Kirk could not be a full time drug-dealer and continue to live in her house. Wayne was the primary stash holder. Kirk was simply his assistant. We knew that Wayne would keep the money straight. He was in the best position for him. His passive disposition would attract the stick-up boys and, therefore, he would be a liability to us out on the corner.

"T.I., Goodie is a good bet," I was presenting Goodie as an ideal addition to our crew. "He can run shit with Black after I roll. Plus he know what he's doin'."

Terrance didn't have to be convinced of Goodie's merits. Goodie grew up with us. We all knew him to be Black's cousin and a fellow hustler.

Terrance conceded, "Cool. But he get paid from y'all end."

"Ain't that a bitch," I protested. "I already pay everybody else from my end. You get half the profit off the top and we split the rest."

"Shit, you and Black split the rest," Wayne corrected. "Me and Kirk get what y'all decide to give us."

We all laughed. The money was coming in fast and heavy. We all put at least $200-$300 into our pockets each night. I was pocketing about $500 a night and so was Black. Terrance was averaging about $1,000. But the $200 or $300 hundred bucks Wayne and Kirk were getting was far better than either was accustomed to. Since we threw Kevin away, there was a bigger cut to be divided. Goodie would carry his own weight. He would likely add to our revenue by serving more folks since we would be able to expand the hours we remained open for business.

Black had the honor of informing Goodie that he had been drafted into our noble crew. I wasn't present when Black told Goodie that he could hustle with us, but Black later informed me that Goodie was as happy as a homosexual going to the penitentiary. Goodie was struggling selling marijuana. He was not getting much money, so the prospect of making thousands of dollars per week was hard to resist.

Goodie would not be told about the apartment at Parkside Garden. He wouldn't know anything about our overall package and profit margin. He would simply handle the corner runs and get paid at least $200 a night. It was a great deal all the way around.

Goodie proved to be a good help to us. We were able to keep our business open until two to three o'clock each morning. Our daily gross went from about $10,000 to $15,000 a day. Terrance, Black, and I made even more money after Goodie came on board. Moreover, Goodie's bright and lively sense-of-humor added to the excitement out on the corner. There was never a dull moment when Goodie was around. He brought raw energy to our crew. He would make 100 or 200 runs and not utter a complaint.

Fat Larry was proving to be a great mentor. He was teaching me things about drug-dealing and the nature of the folks I would encounter in the trade. I confided in Larry about my home situation. I told him about my grandparents' alcoholism and Kim's heroin addiction. I expressed to him that I hated going there and that there was no room in the house for me.

Larry intimated to me that his upbringing was very similar to mine. He expressed to me that that was why his home was so comfortable. Larry said to me, "Tray, when you live like we do, you got to make a comfortable home for yourself."

"We out here duckin' the law, the stick-up boys, and dealing with all the dope-fiend games a nigga can bring to a nigga. We gotta have a home to come to at the end of the day that's comfortable and peaceful. So you know you gotta take care of home, keep the bills paid, keep plenty of grub in the 'fridge, and take care of your women. 'Cause if your woman and home ain't taken care of when you in this game, you ain't gonna have nowhere to find peace. But above all, Tray; don't ever bring dem narcotics where you lay your head at night."

Larry offered me that sage advice one night when he was driving me to the group home. He then said to me, "I got an extra room at my house. You can stay with me. Ada and Lamar is in love with you—and I kinda dig you myself."

I told Mama and Kim that I was going to move in with Fat Larry. I gave them the phone number and address. If the folks from the group home or my probation officer came looking for me, it was important that they know how to reach me. We had to keep up the façade. Master Goldstein would never release me from his court controlled-commitment if he knew I was living with a reputed drug-dealer. Hell, Master Goldstein wouldn't release me if he knew I was becoming a reputed drug-dealer myself. Mr. Lawrence, my probation officer, and Mr. Driver knew I was dealing in drugs. But I doubt that either cared. I was wearing a lot of fancy clothes and jewelry in their presence, and Charles and Larry were driving me to and from the group home each day. I kept a pocket full of money. All the tell-tale signs were there. Mr. Driver even commented to me one day, "You better be careful out there, young man. You get jammed up by the law, I can't save you."

I told Larry about Mr. Driver's comment, and Larry told me that it appeared that Mr. Driver was fishing for information. He decided that he would meet with Mr. Driver on my behalf—to see if he was receptive to a bribe. Larry already suspected that he knew him.

Johnny Driver wasn't the man Larry knew. However, he was receptive to bribes. For a $1,000, I would not have to report to any more ten-minute meetings at four o'clock in the afternoon after school. I would get a weekend pass every weekend, and I would get a flattering report to the court from the group home when I went before the juvenile master for my review in May. There was no getting past the eleven o'clock weekday curfew, but I no longer had to have any anxiety attacks if I was running a little late. Mr. Driver was the director of the Boys' Group Home; he could award me an extended time-frame some weekday nights. But it was not advisable that I take advantage of it. It would appear too suspicious.

I was set; I was living in a beautiful home where I was welcomed. I was circumventing the criminal justice system, and I was "ghetto rich." I was getting more pussy than I could handle—and nobody, and I do mean absolutely nobody—told me what to do.

It was during that high period in my life that I met, and fell hopelessly in lust with the insatiable Darlene. A fine honey-complexioned woman with a flawless, petite body. She had the prettiest smile I had ever seen. When she flashed her pearly whites at me, with the champagne-glass-imprinted gold teeth, I should have run for my life. I knew the bitch wasn't any good, but I couldn't help myself. I had to have her.

It was around late April or early May, I was standing out there on Eager Street with my whole crew. Terrance, Black, and Goodie. We were selling a lot of coke and the weather was beautiful—very sunny out. I had on a short black leather jacket, designer jeans, expensive jogging shoes, and expensive jewelry. I was looking good and prosperous. I spotted Darlene standing on Inky's step talking.

I was acquainted with Inky. I had known her for quite some time from living in the 'hood. She and I were fairly close. I abandoned everything I was doing and went up to introduce myself to Darlene.

"Hey 'dere miss lady," I spoke to her, ignoring Inky entirely. "My name is Tray and I wanna be with you."

I was bold with women, and now that I was getting money, I was even more bold. When Inky and Darlene burst into laughter at my highly irregular introduction I was not discouraged.

"Miss, I know a lot of older guys be tryin' to step to you, but ain't nobody gonna treat you as good as me."

"Darlene, take his young ass for his money," Inky instructed. "Tray, you know you ought to be somewhere with Annette or one of 'em other girls your age."

Darlene remained silent. She just kept staring at me and smiling. I was captivated. I didn't care that she seemed to be much older than I, and I cared even less about Inky's remark.

I directed my attention solely to Darlene, "So your name is Darlene?"

She finally spoke to me, "Yeah, that's my name," then she asked me rather curtly. "How old are you?"

The sound of her voice was like a sweet melody to my ear. I couldn't lie to her too badly, "I'm fourteen, but I'll be twenty-one my next birthday."

Inky offered, "His bad ass is already twenty-one. Look at all that cocaine dem niggas over there sellin'!"

Darlene looked over toward where Terrance, Black, and Goodie were standing; a large crowd of about twenty to thirty coke-heads were standing around waiting to be served.

"Damn, Inky, a nigga gotta eat," I was proud of my shop. "Why you puttin' me down in front of your friend?"

"I ain't puttin' you down," Inky laughed. "Shit, me and Darlene want some of that good-ass coke y'all got."

Darlene indicated to me that she did, indeed, want some cocaine. I told her that I would treat her and Inky to some coke if she provided me with her phone number and address, and a future date. She agreed; I went off to Wayne's house to get my next sexual conquest a generous dose of coke. I wanted to make a great impression upon her. I grabbed ten forty-dollar capsules from Wayne and poured them into a single package. Darlene was worth the $400 dollars. Terrance and Black could crack as many jokes as they wanted to about my trickin'. I had to have this woman.

When I returned to Inky's house with the package of cocaine, they were still standing on the front step where I had left them. I was invited into the house with Inky and Darlene, and we went up to Inky's bedroom. I poured the coke onto an album cover and told the ladies in grandiose fashion, "This is my treat to y'all. Enjoy yourself."

I told Darlene to expect my call real soon. I really wanted to get with her. I then exited the room and Inky's house, leaving the ladies to their vice.

I joined my crew, and we continued to sell coke until ten o'clock, my time to start making my way back to the group home.

I was going to wait until Friday, when I could stay out all night, before I contacted Darlene. A woman that fine would required an all-night stand. I would have to hold her in my arms after I made love to her. No quickie for Darlene. I had just given her four hundred dollars worth of cocaine. I would savor her essence and bask in all her feminine glories.

I told Terrance and Black what I had done, and Terrance immediately attached the moniker "Trickin' Tray" to me. I was Richard Griffin's grandson, no doubt.

Arlando "Tray" Jones

A Hustler Can Be Loved

Chapter 34

Friday took forever to come. I wanted to see Darlene desperately, but I did not want to seem anxious. I met her on a Monday or Tuesday; I wanted to allow a few days to pass before contacting her. Otherwise, I would have appeared to be some inexperienced adolescent, a true lame. I had experience with older women, none of whom were as physically appealing as Darlene. Still, I had experience enough to know what kind of image I had to project.

I had been bragging to all my friends that "I just scooped a new bad-ass bitch." I couldn't let her know that I was absolutely and utterly enchanted by her. She would have become too expensive.

I hurried home and went directly to the phone once I left school on Friday afternoon. I didn't bother to exchange pleasantries with Ada or inquire about Lamar's whereabouts. It was Friday and I was going to contact Darlene. I invested $400 into that project; it was time that I receive some return.

I dialed the number Darlene had given me as soon as I got to my bedroom and felt secure behind a closed door. My "mack" was top secret. I needed privacy for this call, and I hoped Ada would not disturb me. She was downstairs in the kitchen cooking and probably didn't even notice me come in.

"Hello," I spoke to whoever picked up on the other end once I dialed Darlene's number. "Let me speak to Darlene, please."

"Who's callin'?" A grown man's voice asked. How dare this bitch have a boyfriend living in her house, answering her phone. "Tell her Tray on the phone."

I heard this guy yelling for Darlene, and when she answered him, he told her that someone named Tray wanted her on the phone. It seemed like an eternity passed before I heard her lovely voice say to me, "Well, it took you long enough to call."

"I ain't gettin' you in no trouble with your boyfriend, am I?" That was the only way I could ask about that guy who answered her telephone without appearing to be a lame.

"My boyfriend ain't here," Darlene jokingly said. "That was my brother, Donnell. My boyfriend won't pick my phone up anyway. He don't pay no bills here."

"So you got a boyfriend?"

"Yeah—and a nigga I'm fuckin'," she was being brutally honest. "And ain't neither one of 'em shit. That's why I'm in here all by myself. Glad you called."

I told Darlene about my legal situation. I let her know that I was in a group home and that I had delayed calling her because I wanted to spend my entire weekend with her. I expressed to her, in the least ambiguous terms possible, that my time was valuable and that she must not prove to be a disappointment to me. Darlene told me that she was a lot of things, but she wasn't a disappointment. She assured me that she was fun to be with.

"Want me come out to your house?" I asked her.

"No, I was comin' in town tonight," she replied. "I can meet you down on Eager, at Inky's 'round nine o'clock."

"I'm cool with that," I wanted to meet with her immediately, but I had to maintain my cool pose. "I got a few things I gotta take care. But I'll definitely be there."

I felt exultant. Darlene didn't impress me as a "good girl." She gave me every indication that she was the type of woman that didn't have a moral issue with screwing on the first date. She had a wonderful sense of humor. She kept me laughing the entire time we were on the phone.

I went downstairs to the living room and Ada and her cousin, Lacrisha, were lounging around listening to music and conversing. Lacrisha saw me coming down the stairs before Ada, and she spoke to me, "How you doin', Tray?"

"I'm straight."

Ada was shocked to see me, "When you get in here?"

I checked my watch before answering, "'Bout an hour ago."

"Larry was just here lookin' for you," Ada spoke in a matter-of-fact tone. "He asked me was you here. I ain't know you was here so I told him, 'I ain't seen you.' He acted like it was something important."

I had been living with Larry, Ada, and Lamar for two weeks, long enough to know that Larry had a way of making everything seem like an emergency. "Do you think it was really an emergency?"

"You should've let me know your ass was in here," Ada snapped at me for the very first time. "Then you would know for yourself what he wanted."

I was truly a part of the family. Mama Ada was concerned about my whereabouts. She launched into a diatribe about my being completely selfish when I didn't let anyone know where I was. "I waited up all damn night for your ass to come home last weekend," she shot at me. "You could've least called to say you wouldn't be home."

All I could do was stare at Ada. I had no idea that she cared about me to that degree. Larry had told me that she was in love with me, but I didn't take him seriously. But there it was: Ada genuinely loved me. I would call her in the future if I decided to stay out all night.

If Darlene acted right, I would be calling Ada tonight to inform her that I would be staying out. It really felt great to have Ada demonstrate concern and care for me. Kim was no longer showing much interest in me, and Mama was too consumed by alcoholism to be a meaningful emotional factor in my life. I needed Ada; I was lost to Kim and Mama. Kim still gave me an affectionate kiss on the cheek on the rare occasions I stood still for her, but that was not significant. I suppose I desired so much feminine attention and affection to make up for the abject neglect I received from my actual mother.

I was getting a lot of sex, but hardly any true feminine affection. In fact, Annette was the only female I was having sexual relations with whom I moderately liked.

I was out there on Eager Street, holding my spot down...Black, Terrance, Goodie, and I. We were all out there selling our coke, as usual. I had let everyone know I would not be selling drugs all night. I had a date with the lovely Darlene. My crew was happy for me. I had dedicated all my time and effort to our business. I had virtually no personal life. I occasionally went off to have a "quicky" with a freak broad, and I took in a movie or two when the police redoubled their effort to rid the community of drugs and drug-dealers. But I mostly hung out on the corner selling cocaine when I wasn't in school or at the group home on lock-down.

Terrance, Black, and Goodie were envious when Darlene came up to me, looking better than any woman on the block, and asked me, "Waiting for me?"

"Sure you right," I had responded to her. Then I announced to my crew, "I'm out, y'all."

Darlene took hold of my hand and we walked away from the corner. When she told me that she wanted to take a long walk, I let her know that I had a chauffeur. Darlene messed my head up when she told me, "Let's take a long walk so we can talk. We might not even like each other." I never did that kind of stuff. We didn't have to walk anywhere. Darlene insisted. It was warm out, a perfect April or May night.

We walked and talked forever. We ended up in downtown Baltimore, near and around the Inner Harbor. She told me that she was twenty-six years old, her birthday was on August 14th. She was a Leo, the lion, just like me. We discussed our interests. We talked about the many things each of us liked and disliked. It was the very first time I had had an intimate conversation with a woman I surely wanted to screw. It was great; I was really enjoying the experience. I felt truly content with holding Darlene's hand, and I felt an awesome sensation when she leaned her head over and placed it on my shoulder as we walked down the city streets. It felt so natural.

My favorite moment was when Darlene and I stopped at the War Memorial in front of City Hall. We seated ourselves on a comfortable bench and embraced the beauty of the area. We allowed ourselves to be engulfed by the city lights and calmness of the night. Darlene rested her head into my chest and looked up at me and asked, "Can I kiss you?"

There was no need for me to respond with words. Our lips met. I experienced the sensual sensation of her tongue insinuating itself into my mouth. My libido was raging out of control. I wanted Darlene right then and there, in full view of downtown Baltimore.

Darlene became special to me at that very moment. I wanted her exclusively for myself, "You have a boyfriend, don't you?"

"Not really," Darlene answered. "I'm seeing this guy name J.B. but he's married and ain't nothing serious goin' on with us."

We sat there in silence for awhile. I didn't want the moment to end. This was the first time I had ever experienced intimacy of this nature. I didn't want to lose it—ever.

"I don't want you to see J.B. anymore," I finally said. "I want to be your man."

"Do you know what you're gettin' into?" she asked.

"I don't care, I want you."

Darlene burst into laughter, "Nigga you want some pussy. And I'm gonna give you some, too. But you don't want me."

"True, I do want to do it to you," I found the humor in the moment and joined her in laughter. "But I want to be the only one."

"Let's go to the Matador," Darlene abruptly switched the subject. "I feel like dancing and partying."

"Okay, but I'm gonna call Charles," I said. "I don't feel like walkin' all the way to The Matador."

We walked around to The Block—downtown's red light district. A plethora of prostitutes stood out on the corners selling their commodity. Ordinarily, I would have been intrigued by the bright lights and scantily-clothed women, but Darlene dominated my thoughts. She did suggest she was going to give me some pussy. I had no need to look anywhere else.

I found a telephone booth outside of McDonalds and called Charles. I told him that I was downtown and that I needed him to come get me. Darlene and I decided to go inside to get something to eat. We learned through our discussion that we both were crazy about Big Macs and chocolate milkshakes.

If Charles felt disgruntled about me summoning him again, he didn't let on. He simply asked me, "Is a half hour good?"

I told Charles that a half hour was perfect. I told him, "Nigga, I'm feelin' so good I'm gonna give you a special treat."

Charles' timing was near perfect; when he walked into the McDonalds, Darlene and I had just finished eating our order of Big Macs, french fries, and chocolate milkshakes. I told Charles that I wanted him to take me to the apartment at Parkside Gardens. I wanted to get him a nice piece of raw coke, to show him my gratitude. He was always in place to drive me wherever I wanted to go. I also wanted to get Darlene a nice treat. I suspected she would be less sexually inhibited if she was under the influence of cocaine. Niggas around the 'hood swore that "women do it best when they got that coke in 'em."

I directed Charles to drop me off at the corner of Moravia and Sinclair Lane. He was to drive around with Darlene for about fifteen to twenty minutes, then meet me at the very same place. I needed the time to measure out his bonus. My instructions were followed to the letter. It took me about fifteen or twenty minutes to go to the main stash house and measure out three grams of raw coke for Charles and five for Darlene. By the time the night was over, she would be convinced that I was the only man she would ever need.

"Here baby-boy," I handed Charles the coke as soon as I gathered myself in the back seat, behind Darlene. "Take us to The Matador."

"Somethin' hot goin' on down there tonight," Charles informed us. "T.I. and Black said they was goin' there. Somebody havin' a birthday party or something."

Darlene knew about the whole event, "Yeah, Roosevelt; his wife givin' him a birthday party—invitations only."

"How we gonna get in then?" I was curious.

"Nigga, you Tray," Darlene reminded me. "He ain't gonna turn no hustlers away at the door."

"Tray know he ain't gonna have no problem gettin' in the Matador—or no other place like that," Charles added.

All this was new to me. I had never given much attention to my reputation. I had attended Odell's and other haunts for hustlers, but I didn't think much of it. No one ever asked me to produce any identification. I was fourteen, so what. I was in a big-boy game doing big-boy things. My bank roll was just as large as the next fellow's and my pistol roared just as loud. Something as trivial as age should not prevent me from attending the bars, disco spots, and gambling pits that my peers frequented. My age certainly was not going to keep me from Darlene. I was going to get her even if it required bankrupting my crew.

"Here, Darlene, hold this," I passed her the five grams I had measured out on the triple-beam for her. "I know you gonna want your Shirley shot, too."

"You damn right," she gratefully accepted the package. "I was hoping you ain't forget me."

We pulled up to The Matador, and the first thing I noticed was a huge sign hanging over the door's entrance that read: "Private Party; Invitations Only!" There was a large crowd gathered around the building and many of the club's patrons were disgruntled about being denied entrance into the disco. I was not certain whether or not I would be granted access. I told Charles, "Give us a few minutes before you roll out. I don't want to get stuck without a ride."

"Nigga, you gonna get in," Charles insisted. "Give me some money so I can buy some dope to come down off this coke. I don't want to be up all night."

I went into my pocket, pulled out a wad of bills, and counted out $100. I gave it to him and told him that he was expensive. He assured me that he was worth it, and I had to admit that he was. Darlene and I went directly to the front of the line. She dragged me there. I was going to stand in line like the others. I asked for Roosevelt as soon as we reached the front. I was vaguely acquainted with him; he was a fellow hustler. But there was no need to disturb Roosevelt, he was enjoying his birthday party. The attendant at the booth knew me.

"Go 'head on in Tray," the tall, muscular doorman said to me—and Darlene. "You know Roosevelt, he enjoying his party. Larry and T.I. already in there."

I tipped the doorman with a twenty-dollar bill, and Darlene and I made our way up the stairs and onto the disco floor.

The spot had a modest crowd. The music was loud, but not too loud. They were beautiful hip-hop tunes. I saw Black, Terrance, and Fat Larry, but, I declined to hang out with them. I wasn't going to separate myself from Darlene for any great length of time. I had invested much into her. I had romanced her, and I would be damned if some other man would take her to bed that night. I was the one who had her prepped for a fuck.

I drank beer, smoked weed, and danced through a few songs with Darlene. I even went to the basement of the club and joined some fellow hustlers in a friendly high-stakes craps game. I was grateful when Darlene wrapped her arms around my waist and asked me, "You ready to go home, baby?"

"Yeah, I am," I answered, and kissed her full on the lips. "Your place, mine, or the hotel?"

"I wanna go home, and I want you to come with me."

I was grateful for that answer. I didn't feel that Ada or Larry would approve of me bringing Darlene into our home. She was far from the ideal girl for me. Larry was adamant about not bringing "around the way girls" into our home. And Darlene was definitely an "around the way girl." The five grams of coke she had accepted from me attested to that.

Terrance and Black were exiting the club. It was three o'clock in the morning—time to go home. "T.I." I yelled to Terrance as I spotted him and Black making their way to the exit. "I need you to take me somewhere."

Terrance had just purchased a brand new car, a silver-gray 1983 Nissan Maximum. It still had the dealer's tag on it. He loved driving. I knew he would have no problem with taking me to Darlene's house.

"Where y'all goin'?" Terrance asked.

"Highlander Ridge," Darlene answered.

"Come on," Terrance said. "You better not hurt my little cousin."

Terrance, Black, Darlene, and I drove the short distance to Darlene's house at Highlander Ridge. Terrance and Black took pot-shots at me throughout the drive there. They teased me about being with an older woman and warned me about the perils of being "pussy whipped." I told them that they were just jealous because neither of them had a woman as fine as Darlene to go home to. Darlene held her own. She told Terrance that she wouldn't hurt me. She let him know that she would be gentle with me—not to worry. She let Black know that he could not find a woman nowhere as fine as she if his life depended upon it.

We all had great laughs on the drive, and parted on good terms. I told Terrance and Black that if I didn't show up on Eager Street later that day, not to come looking for me. But Terrance reminded me that "business is always before pleasure."

No one was awake at Darlene's house when we finally got there. It was totally dark and silent. She turned on a light, and we sat down on the sofa in the living room, I expressed to her that I desired her, and I had been anxious to be with her since the moment I first laid eyes on her. She kissed me, then went to dim the lights, came back to me, and kissed me again.

I slipped my hand under her blouse and began caressing her breast while I nibbled at her neck. It got very heated. Suddenly Darlene got up from the sofa, and said to me, "Let's go upstairs. I don't want my son to come in on us."

She guided me up to her room, and I was impressed at how neat and orderly it was. The whole house, from what I had seen, was neat and orderly. But Darlene's bedroom was extra neat—and very feminine.

Darlene told me to make myself comfortable while she went to the bathroom to freshen up, and I suspect, take a blast from the cocaine I had given her.

I took off my shirt and loosened my belt buckle, but I didn't get undressed. I had learned from Tina the previous year that a man was supposed to allow his woman to undress him. And that's exactly what Darlene did to me. When she returned to the bedroom, she was wearing a red teddy—and nothing more.

In a seductive tone, she said, "I just got on this little thing, and you got on all those clothes. Get comfortable, baby. I ain't gonna hurt you too bad." She begun undressing me—and I did nothing to resist.

Whipped and Happy About It

Chapter 35

When I awoke Saturday at around noon, I felt blissful. Darlene had made love to me. I felt like a man—or at least what I thought a man should feel like.

I didn't know where Darlene was; I was laying in bed alone. I recalled her being in my arms when I fell asleep, but she was no longer there. I heard a lot of voices coming from other rooms throughout the house. I could not distinguish Darlene's. Intuitively, I knew that she would be back soon. She wouldn't leave a naked man in her bed, I hoped.

I had to go to the bathroom, but I was hesitant about getting out of bed and finding the bathroom. I was naked, and though I was feeling quite blissful, I felt a little vulnerable. I was in a strange house with strangers. I wanted to call for Darlene. But I didn't have to; she came into the room just then. She was wearing an extremely large, dark blue terry-cloth bathrobe that subtly hid her gorgeous physique. I could only see her face, hands, and bare feet. She was carrying a tray of food: eggs, bacon, toast, and orange juice. She was smiling from ear-to-ear. She had had a terrific time, too. Damn, I was good.

"I gotta go the bathroom," I announced

"Go 'head," Darlene was grinning, "I ain't stoppin' you."

The bathroom was adjacent to the bedroom; I had no problem finding it. I leaped out of bed, snatched one of Darlene's gowns to cover my nudity and rushed to the bathroom.

I closed the door behind me, but that didn't stop Darlene from following me in. I was making use of the facility when she came up behind me to nibble at the back part of my neck. Darlene gave me a brand new toothbrush and washcloth to freshen up. She urged me to make haste because she didn't want the food to get cold. It was important to her that I knew she was a good cook, I suppose.

I freshened my breath, washed my face and hands, and joined Darlene in the bedroom. I sat in a cozy chair she had in the corner while she sat on the chair's arm and fed me the meal she had prepared. It was a sensual moment, and she intimated to me that she really had had a fantastic time. She told me that I was a good lover and that with further instructions I could be a perfect lover for her. Darlene beseeched me not to allow our first sexual time together to end as a "one night stand."

Suddenly, Darlene got up from where she was seated next to me and went over to the dresser and withdrew from its drawer a door key, "Here's the key to my house, and my heart," she said. "I want you to have it—and think about it."

There was nothing to think about; it was a no-brainer. I didn't heed Terrance's warning. I wanted to be with Darlene and damn the consequence. I would bear her burdens along with my own—just as long as she remained sensuous, sexy, and affectionate. I had never had a steady girlfriend before, and Darlene seemed ideal. She was funny, smart, older, and drop-dead good looking. Damn near as fine as me. Annette was okay, but she lacked the maturity that I desired in a woman. She was still a girl.

I accepted the key Darlene offered me. When she left the room, I hurriedly got dressed and phoned Larry. I had to share the great news with my hero.

"Hello," it was Ada's voice on the line.

"Ada, I'm sorry—" The click interrupted my pseudo apology. Ada had hung the phone up on me. She was mad. I should have called to let her know that I was staying out.

I dialed the number again, and after about four or five rings, Larry answered, "Yeah."

"Yo, Larry," I was too excited and overcome with joy to allow Ada to rain on my parade. "You gotta come pick me up. This honey is the bomb, nigga."

"Where you at?" he asked.

"I'm out Darlene's house," I informed him. "You know that chick you saw me with last night. I been tellin' you about her all week?"

"Oh, yeah," he remembered. "The bowlegged girl that be with Inky and 'em."

"Yeah, her."

"Man, that bitch ain't bowlegged," Larry retorted. "She be fakin'. Her ass pigeon-toed."

"Whatever," I said, Larry's humor was infectious; I couldn't resist the laugh. "Come get me. I got a story to tell."

I gave Larry the directions to Darlene's house; he told me that he would be there within the hour. I assured him that I would be awaiting his arrival. But before he hung up, he told me, "Ada gonna get you."

"Man, won't you handle Ada for me?"

"I'm leavin' that alone," Larry was solemn. "I got my own shit to deal with."

• • •

Darlene entreated me to come downstairs to meet her brother, Donnell, and her friend, Terry. I told her that I was waiting for Larry, and I only had a few minutes before he arrived.

"Just come and say hi," she pleaded. "They think I'm hidin' some lame up here I'm ashamed of."

That was all I needed to hear. I was at the top of my game; no woman needed to feel ashamed about being my girlfriend. I went downstairs to meet Donnell and Terry. They were cool folks, very pleasant. Donnell and Terry looked familiar. Donnell had patronized my illegal establishment on Eager Street a few times. When I asked him whether or not he and I had met before, he told me that he had done business with me in the past. He knew of me, but we had never been formally introduced. Terry was a similar case, we had met at a disco before. I tried to seduce her one night—came damn close, but she went home with my cousin, Terrance. Fate had operated perfectly for me; had I been successful and freaked her that night several weeks ago, Darlene would not have even considered taking me to bed.

I appreciated the conversation I had with Darlene, her brother, and friend, but I was anxious to see Larry. When he pulled up to the door and blew the car's horn, I casually kissed Darlene full on the lips and excused myself. I told them that I would likely see them later. Darlene secured a commitment from me to come back later that night.

Larry had a broad grim on his face when I got into the car, "Ole Darlene worked you over!"

"Man," I said to Larry as we drove off, "she hit a nigga's spot. I kept bustin' nut after nut. Every time I tried to stop, she'd rub my joint 'cross her cheek or over her tittie. I couldn't stop even if I wanted to."

"Sounds like you got whipped."

"Whipped," I uttered. "I waxed that ass. I fucked her up so much she gave me the key to her house."

Larry slammed on the brakes; the impact of the car's sudden stop jerked me forward. He said to me, "You damn fool, you better take that mothafuckin' key back."

"Man, drive!" I thought Larry was being overdramatic. "I can handle this thing."

"Look, Tray," Larry said as we started to drive on. "When a broad give you her door key, that mean you gotta start payin' bills at that crib."

I was silent. I could not grasp what Larry was trying to impress upon me. He said to me while we were paused at a traffic light, "You been played, and you gettin' ready to get used up."

"Well, if gettin' played and used up feel like it did last night, then I'm for it."

Larry, in his infinite wisdom, concluded that it would be futile to try to convince me to return Darlene's door key. I was pussy-whipped. I would have to experience the heartache and hurt that come with trying to turn a whore into a housewife.

"What you gonna do about your court situation?"

The question caught me completely off guard. I had not thought about my impending court hearing. Ever since Mr. Driver had accepted my $1000, I was not feeling the pressure of being at the group home.

"I'm gonna take my ass to court," I replied after a brief moment of silence. "And hope the judge cut me loose."

Larry informed me that he had taken the liberty of hiring Ronald Kirkland to represent me. He felt that my chances of getting out of the clutches of the juvenile justice system would be better if I was represented by private counsel.

"The public defenders ain't shit," Larry insisted. "Them mothafuckers work for the state, get paid by the state, and will keep your ass locked up for the state."

I thanked Larry for watching my back, protecting my interest. I also assured him that I would go downtown first thing Monday morning and meet with Mr. Kirkland. My court appearance was scheduled for the following

Wednesday. The lawyer would have less than forty-eight hours to prepare for my case.

We pulled up to the front door and I got out the car and went into the house. Larry was not going to come in; Ada was on the war path. I would have to face her without him.

"How you doin', Ada?" I asked as soon as I stepped through the front door and saw her sitting on the sofa watching television and waiting for me.

"Don't you 'how you doin', Ada' me," Ada barked. "Didn't you tell me you would call if you was gonna stay out all night?"

"I'm sorry," I cuddled next to her, preparing to employ all the charm I could to assuage her anger. "I was with this girl, Darlene, last night, and the time just got away from me. By the time I remembered to call, I couldn't get to a phone."

"You was out there fuckin' with one of 'em old-ass High Hats girls?" Ada barked.

"You know I been locked up, Mom," the smile on Ada's face let me know I was forgiven. "I gotta get my man. A brother gets backed up and need a little sumtin-sumtin'."

"That ole-ass woman gonna fuck 'round and give you worms," Ada said. "You need to stay with girls your own age."

I wasn't about to discuss the complexities of what attached me to Darlene. I kissed Ada on the cheek, excused myself, went upstairs to take a bath, and got dressed for the day. I wanted to play Lamar a couple games of Galaxy. The last time we played, he had beaten me. I wanted to get even. But above all, I missed my little brother and wanted to see him.

I was mildly disappointed that he was around at his friend's house playing. I wanted to tell him about my new girlfriend, even take him to meet her. I had no doubt that he would want to pat her on the ass.

The Occupation

Chapter 36

Ronald Kirkland proved to be an effective attorney. He impressed upon Master Goldstein that I was a terrific child who had made some poor decisions in the past. He made the court aware of my excellent progress report from the Boys' Group Home. He highlighted the fact that I was passing all my courses at school. Kim was seated in the courtroom neatly dressed in a dark blue suit and high heeled shoes, per Mr. Kirkland's instruction. I wore a simple white dress shirt, blue jeans, and tennis shoes. I didn't wear any jewelry. I had to capture the "reformed criminal look." Mr. Kirkland was adamant about presenting a particular image.

The court was impressed with my progress; over the state's attorney's strenuous protest, Master Goldstein ordered my immediate release from the group home. It served no rehabilitative purpose to maintain me at The Boys' Group Home. My family was prepared to accept me at home, and based on all the evidence provided to the court, I was receiving adequate adult supervision. The state attorney reminded the juvenile master of the serious nature of the crime that brought me into custody. Master Goldstein wasn't impressed; he told the state attorney, "If the court remembers correctly, the victim disputed the state's claim that Arlando shot him."

It went well for me. The only reason I was being maintained at the group home was because the court had found me delinquent for not attending school and not having any visible adult supervision. Based upon everything offered to the court, I was now a well-managed child. At the group home, I had said my good-byes earlier that morning. I was assured by my attorney, Mr. Kirkland, that I would be released. I left Tony and Warren my clothes to split as they chose. I gave my radio to Tony since Warren already had one.

I thanked Mr. Kirkland for getting me out of the group home. I took Kim out to lunch after the court hearing concluded. I can't recall where Kim and I dined. It was probably some fast-food placed like Wendy's or Mc-Donald's, nowhere spectacular. I recall Kim being really anxious to get away from me. She told me that she had to go pay some bills and check on some outfits for Kieshawn's and Yalanda's summer wardrobe. I gave her a few hundred bucks to contribute to her effort, and I went home. I wanted to let Ada know that I would be home more permanently.

Mr. Kirkland had already called Larry; Ada knew of the court's decision by the time I reached home. No big deal; I still had to call home to let Ada know if I was going to stay out all night. I needed to find someone to share my excitement. I was totally free from the juvenile justice system. I could sell cocaine all day and fuck all night. I could wake up in the mornings in the comfort of a woman's arms as opposed to having to wait until the weekend for that pleasure. I had no more supervision, and I had a pocket full of money. I was absolutely free to destroy my life—and others' lives as well. I went to Eager Street to find Black. I knew he would share my delight. He seemed to always be on the same page with me.

Black and Goodie were standing on the corner of Rutland Avenue and Eager Street when I spotted them. It was not a big deal, but it seemed odd that they would be a half block away from the corner we had established. It was very early in the day, about three o'clock in the afternoon, and it didn't appear as if the narcotic squad was harassing the local dealers. It was a beautiful day out, a perfect spring day. The streets were crowded with people. Attractive "around the way girls" were out and about in their spring dress; I couldn't understand why Black and Goodie had abandoned our spot. It was prime real-estate.

"Why y'all down here?" I asked my crew members as I approached.

Black shrugged his shoulders and replied, "Dem mothafuckin' New York Boys crowdin' our space with that dope. Our corner hot as a mothafucka since they been there."

I had known for the past week that the New York Boys' encroachment on our territory was going to become a problem. Black and Goodie knew, too. When we brought the matter to Terrance's attention, he brushed it aside. He said, "They sellin' dope; we sellin' coke. They ain't no problem to us."

Larry had voiced his concern about the New York Boys selling product on our corner, too. Larry had casually said to me just two days prior, "Terrance gave dem niggas a pass to sell dope down there just to annoy me."

"No, he didn't, Larry," I defended Terrance. "Dem niggas just moved in and started rockin'."

"Well, they gonna just have to rock their ass somewhere else."

I sensed that a corner war was inevitable. The New York Boys had a crew of about seven or eight in its core, and they were taking money out of Larry's pocket. Larry could not compete with their product. However, they were not positioned on Larry's corner. They were on our corner, a mere block away from his domain. If Terrance, Black, and I didn't protest to the New York Boys' presence, Larry had no right to. He would look like a monster for demanding that the New York Boys leave. Besides, Larry was still in the process of rebuilding. He could not carry out a street-corner war without our support. He only had three runners in his entire crew, and not much money in reserve for possible bails and hiding-out.

If we told the New York Boys to move their operation, there would definitely be a war. No drugs would be sold during that time. No money would be made. Only blood would be spilled and bodies dropped. The neighborhood would be under siege while we shot at each other on the city streets until one crew or the other was destroyed, or convinced to move its operation somewhere else.

Black, Goodie, and I knew that we would side with Fat Larry. I didn't appreciate Terrance's growing relationship with Greg and Victor, the leaders of the New York Boys. I understood how naïve Terrance could be in matters concerning big boy games, but he was going a little too far with his naïveté this time. Black and I had told Terrance that he was making a bad move by associating with the New York Boys. He ignored us. Now it was my place to scold him.

Black, Goodie, and I sold our product from Rutland and Eager. I told Goodie and Black that I no longer had to report to the group home on weekday nights, we would have the time to resolve our crisis together. We would endure the indignity of allowing our corner to be occupied by the New York Boys for the time being. We had to give Terrance the opportunity to break off his ties with Victor and Greg before the hostility began.

Terrance finally came down to the strip at about nine or ten o'clock that evening. I took him off to the side so that I could speak to him in private. I told him, "T.I., Victor and his crew is outta control. Dem niggas got shit so hot down here we had to move from our spot. The crowd dem niggas bring 'round here keep the police comin'.

"Terrance, they gotta get the fuck away from 'round here—with a quickness." I spoke in a tone that was matter-of-fact, and left no doubt that my mind was made up. There was no room for compromise.

Black and Goodie came up to us, and we all stared up at our corner. The New York Boys were standing there with about forty to fifty heroin addicts lined up awaiting service. My beloved Aunt Kim was among the crowd.

"You handle it, Tray. I'm gonna leave it alone," Terrance knew that I was right. The New York Boys had to go.

I went home at about midnight. I wanted to discuss the matter with Larry before I confronted the New York Boys. He was there lounging around with Ada. I told Larry that I needed to speak with him in private. Ada got up from the sofa where she had been enfolded in his arms to allow us the opportunity to talk shop.

"Larry, I talked to Terrance and Black, and we decided to move dem New York niggas."

"I already decided on that," Larry said. "I just need 'bout a week or so to knock down the rest of the shit I got. I'm gonna tell all dem niggas they don't belong down there. They gotta pack their shit and roll out."

"When was you gonna let me know you was cleanin' house?"

"Man, you know I wasn't gonna let that shit last down there," Larry told me. "I build Eager Street up. I was gone for a minute, but I build that spot up. I'm the one who ran the stick-up boys away and all dem other niggas that fuck up the peace 'round there. I ain't lettin' that go."

I needed clarity as to exactly who Larry intended on driving out. So I asked him pointedly. He answered me in like fashion. He explained to me that it was important that we not allow folks to sell drugs in our neighborhood who don't live there or have any roots there. Larry informed me that if we allowed folks to sell drugs in our neighborhood who don't live there or have an established root there, they would disrespect the old people in the community by conducting open air drug markets in the places that have always been safe havens for our parents, grandparents, and young children. There were places in our neighborhood where children played touch football in the middle of the street safely. There were places where folks could sit out on the front steps free from the conflicts and other ugliness associated with drug trafficking.

Larry admitted, "We do enough fucked up shit in our own 'hood. We don't need no outside help in fuckin' it up."

Larry instructed me to delay confronting the New York Boys for another week or so. He advised me to keep running my shop as I had been. We needed time to buy some automatic guns and hire gunmen. The New York Boys were a powerful crew and known to be ruthless. We had to amass our forces and make a smart, strategic move against them. We were playing a "big boy" game; lives would be lost. There was no doubt about that. We stood out on the corners and laughed and joked with each other, but when disputes arose over territory and money, we settled the matters through the ends of gun barrels. We couldn't petition the court to settle antitrust violations. I can't imagine how a judge would view a petition that read: Now comes Fat Larry and Little Tray, petitioners, praying upon this honorable court to compel the New York Boys, defendants, to sell their heroin in a location other than on Eager Street. They are putting far more heroin in their fifty dollar bags than their competitors are able to…[and therefore] are in violation of antitrust codes established by the Federal Government…. (See Bill Gates Vs. Other Software Companies.)

The decision was made; we would wait. I called Darlene to ask her if I could spend the night with her. It had been two days since I had seen her last, and I was missing her.

"Darlene," I had her on the phone. "Can I come spend the night with you?"

"You ain't gotta ask," she spoke to me softly and lovingly. "That's why you got a key."

This was the perfect opportunity for me to explain to her why I had not used the key she had given me, "Well, I think its still best I call before I come by. I might be fucked up if I came over and caught J.B. or one of your boyfriends there."

"Well, if you would've came 'bout an hour ago, you would've caught J.B. over here," Darlene's honesty was inciting my jealousy. "That nigga came over here and took his VCR back and some other shit."

Ada and Larry were sitting in the living room with me while I was talking on the phone with Darlene. I sensed they were tuned in to everything I said. I asked Larry to hang up the phone once I got into another room and onto another extension.

"Darlene, you still there?"

"Yeah, I'm here," she confirmed.

I yelled into the other room to instruct Larry to hang up the phone. He replied that he had hung up the phone. I distinctly heard the click of the phone hanging up. I wanted to make certain Larry didn't overhear what I had to say to Darlene.

"Give that nigga back all the shit he ever bought you," I told her. "I'll replace it with better shit."

There was a moment of silence, and then she finally said, "Okay. You comin' out?"

That was a no-brainer, of course I was going to come. Since Darlene had made love to me, I could hardly think about anything other than her making love to me again. I assured her that I would be en route to her house as soon as I hung up the phone. I gathered my jacket and an overnight bag and went back into the living room where I had left Ada and Larry.

They were snuggled on the sofa smiling up at me when I walked into the room. "Tray, she gonna say J.B. bought her everything. You just left yourself wide open for the kill. She gonna break your ass."

I came over to the sofa and kissed Ada on the cheek. I informed her that I would not be staying home that night, not to wait up for me.

"My baby is pussy-whipped," Ada laughed at me. "And you gonna catch the worms."

"It is messed up y'all eaves-dropped on my phone call," I said. "You goin' back out Larry?"

He was, so he agreed to take me to Darlene's house. I knew he would tease me non-stop about Darlene during the drive. That is why I was very tempted to call Charles, but I didn't give in to the temptation. I loved being with Larry. I would make the most of every opportunity to spend time with him. He was like the father I never had. I admired everything about him. He spoke to me in a language that I could appreciate, and he represented everything I wanted to be. Above all; he opened his home to me and provided me with a comfort I had not known since Daddy died.

The Corner War

Chapter 37

The summer of 1983 was in full swing. I had turned fifteen. Larry had forged an allegiance with Andrea Poole and his associates from Murphy's Homes Project—Murder Incorporated. We had amassed a remarkable arsenal, a couple of submachine guns that fired sixty 45mm rounds and an assortment of handguns. My Uncle Derrick and Cousin Terrell had recently been released from prison. They were added to our employ. Larry was operating a 24 hour a day heroin shop in the 1900 block of Eager Street and Terrance and I were doing likewise in the 1800 block with our cocaine. The New York Boys had become a profound annoyance competing with us. They had started pushing coke, too. Our profits were nowhere near where they should have been. It was time to tell the New York Boys and the other crews that were selling narcotics up and down Eager Street to pack their operation and move somewhere else. The eight-block area that encompasses the two-thousand block of Eager Street down to the seventeen hundred block, bordered by Washington Street and Broadway up to Ashland Avenue, was our territory. No crew other than Larry's and mine would be allowed to sell drugs within that area.

It was time to implement the excellent strategy Larry had designed in his diabolical mind. We waited for Victor, the primary leader of the New York Boys, to separate himself from his crew. He was en route to Chapel Street to visit a local girl he was having relations with. We had discovered through our observations that around midnight, every night, Victor left his crew to go visit Sheryl's house. We instructed Andrea and Blue, members of Murder Incorporated, to kidnap Victor on his next sojourn to Sheryl's house. We wanted him gone. We reasoned that the New York Boys would be lost and completely disarrayed without their primary leader.

I got a phone call at the phone booth at about two o'clock in the morning. It was Larry, "Victor taken care of, handle 'em other niggas."

I hung up the phone and per previous instructions Black, Mississippi, Derrick, and I armed ourselves and rounded up the remaining New York Boys.

Mississippi casually walked up to Greg and slapped him across the face with the forty-five automatic he had armed himself with while Black, Derrick, and I drew our guns on the four other New York Boys who stood around in disbelief.

"Bitch, get on the wall," I pointed the submachine gun at the stunned New York Boys. "You mothafuckas know y'all ain't got no business 'round here no way."

The small crowd of addicts who where standing around on the corners waiting to be served by whatever crew they patronized stood back in complete surprise as we lined the four New York Boys against the wall. Greg turned to face me, with blood spilling from his head, "What's this shit 'bout, Tray? I thought we was cool."

Black stepped up and hit Greg across the face with the barrel of the gun he was wielding. The blow was thunderous and the impact of it knocked Greg to his knees.

"Bitch, we ain't cool with none of you niggas," Black bellowed, and then kicked Greg in his ribs. "Y'all takin' food off my table."

"Y'all ain't sellin' no more shit 'round here," I declared as the adrenaline flowed through me, affording me a sense of power I had never known. "If I see any y'all 'round here sellin' shit I'm gonna kill you."

I don't know if it was nervousness or sheer stupidity, but one of the New York Boys jumped from the wall and attempted to run away. The sudden move caught us all by surprise. The shots rang out. I fired about twenty rounds from the machine gun and Mississippi, Black, and Derrick fired their weapons as well.

No one can say with any certainty who shot whom, but two of the New York boys lay dead after the smoke cleared. The war had begun.

Black, Mississippi, Derrick, and I fled the scene. We knew the police would come around to investigate the situation and remove the dead bodies. We would have to lay low for awhile. Terrance, Larry, Terrell, and Goodie would have to continue selling our product. We had to keep a cash flow. It was agreed that we would merge our operations during the war.

Terrance and Larry and a few others within our crew were to stay out of the actual shooting. Terrance and Larry would tell the unwanted drug-dealers encroaching on our territory to go some place else. If they refused, Black, Derrick, and I—with the help of Murder Incorporated—would kill them.

No one refused to move their operation. The surprise annihilation of members from the New York Boys' crew set an awesome example. Fat Larry's crew and Terrance's crew were the only two crews that would sell drugs on and around Eager Street. If anyone felt like challenging our claim, he or she would have to raise a ghetto army.

• • •

I went to Darlene's house after I fled from the scene of the double murder. I had let Darlene know that I would be involved in a very hostile situation. It was important that she not let anyone know I was staying with her. In fact, the only ones who knew I was staying at Darlene's house were Fat Larry, Terrance, and Black. We all had a special place to hide until the heat blew over.

Fat Larry approved of my decision to stay with Darlene.

I had been quite generous with her since I promised to replace all the things J.B. had given her and wanted back. I bought her brand new furniture for every room in her home and maintained her on a $300 per-week allowance. I didn't want her to share herself with anyone. She was all mine, and I didn't care about the dollar value.

Darlene was a rare woman. She was honest, gracious, and beautiful. She was not a woman of pretense. She had three children and no time for game playing because she enjoyed nice things and understood how demanding life could be.

Larry assured me that Darlene was the perfect hustler's girl. She would follow my instructions and she wasn't naïve. He told me when he was driving me to her house one day, "Darlene ain't a bad girl. You ain't gotta worry 'bout a nigga trickin' her to play you outta position and she ain't gonna be followin' you all around town worryin' 'bout where you been.

"If you come in four or five o'clock in the mornin', or don't come in at all, she'll be cool with that. She understands a hustler's schedule. She won't go through your pockets seachin' for phone numbers. She's a hustler's girl. Plus, she ain't bad lookin'."

Larry was totally correct about Darlene. She was a hustler's girl. If my business kept me out all times of the night, she didn't complain. The only demand she ever placed on me was to stay still long enough to eat a decent meal.

It took about two weeks for the smoke to completely clear. The police had asked a lot of questions about the shooting, but they didn't have any suspects. Larry, Terrance, Black, and I were communicating by phone for the most part. We all had pagers and a special code for emergencies. Terrance and Larry made sure that Black and I got respectable portions of the profits from drug sales. It was because of our bravery and brutality that we had a monopoly.

The remaining New York Boys were never spotted again. Rumor had it that they had gone back home to New York. Mississippi, Andrea Poole, and the rest of Murder Incorporated went back to West Baltimore—Murphy Homes. We maintained a business relationship with Andrea and his associates. It was vital to our interest—and theirs.

I slowly came back out onto the strip. I wasn't in any particular hurry. Darlene was treating me wonderfully. She satisfied me sexually every night, and she was a joy to hang out with. I loved going to various places with her. Her beautiful features and shapely body commanded much attention and was a source of my pride. Darlene had a lot of interesting friends and family members. I took a special pride in the way Darlene introduced me to her friends and family. She was proud of having snatched me up. My age was not a problem for her. When folks would make an off remark about the difference in our age, Darlene would simply laugh and say, "He easier to train."

When she first made that comment about me, we were at her mother's house visiting her sister. I got mad and snapped at her, "Bitch, what you think I am—a puppy?"

She soothed me by wrapping her arms around me, placing her head in my chest, and softly whispering, "Tray, you the best man I ever had. I love you; I didn't mean to hurt your feelings."

I was thoroughly mollified. Darlene wasn't the kind of woman who apologized for the things she said. She was a remarkably smart and calculating woman. She was very observant, and seldom misspoke. I wish I had listened to her when she told me, "Leave Larry's sorry-ass alone! You don't need him; he need you."

I was hurt when she spoke ill of Larry, but she didn't offer an apology. She meant every word. Whenever I think about Darlene, and I do that quite often, especially when the weight of my life sentence and Larry's betrayal begins to overwhelm me, I am reminded of just how naïve I was. Darlene tried to enlighten me, but my human frailties and limitations would not allow me to accept guidance from a woman who didn't love me exclusively.

Ain't No Fun When
the Rabbit Got the Gun

Chapter 38

The summer of 1984 was almost perfect. I was living with Darlene on a part time basis. I was infamous, the bad-ass nigga I always wanted to be, and the money was rolling in faster than I could spend. I wanted no more than I had. I gave no thought whatsoever to the future. All I had was the present, and that is all I wanted. The pain, suffering, and filth of the ghetto didn't disturb me. I was accustomed to it. Dope-fiends with their hollow and empty eyes were a constant. I was completely immune to the suffering and hardship that surrounded me. Things were how they were, and I was powerless to effect a meaningful change. I was simply fortunate enough not to be one of the many who went to bed hungry or forced to sleep in the street.

I would imagine my soul ached at some incidents that occurred. It troubled me to witness small children go hungry because their dope-fiend parent or parents spent all their money on drugs. It was troubling to me when houses burned down because candles had to be used for lighting and some drunkard or dope-fiend mishandled the flames and small children died in the ensuing fire. Too many tragedies occurred around me. I grew immune to them. I couldn't be compassionate to everyone. What little compassion I had went to my family—who desperately needed me.

I was only sixteen years old, but I had many people depending on me. Kieshawn and Yalanda needed me. Mama, Kim, and Daddy-Pain needed me. Darlene and her three children needed me. But above all, I had a crew of about six or seven, and they needed me, too. I couldn't let them down.

There was absolutely no time for me to experience a childhood or waiver in my choice of a career path. The police were seeking to place me in prison, rival drug crews were seeking to encroach on my territory, stick-up boys were targeting my stash house, and the New York Boy Greg had resurfaced. He wanted revenge.

Larry and I were driving down Milton Avenue; once we reached the intersection of Milton Avenue and Madison Street, Greg and two of his associates opened fire on the Cadillac Larry and I were driving in. It was my very first, but not last, near-death experience.

The temperature was hot and muggy that August day. We had paused at a traffic light and bullets flew into the car windows. I felt the bullets whistling past my ear. I saw Larry duck his head below the car's dashboard, and I followed his example. Larry slammed his foot on the accelerator and the car lunged forward into thick traffic. I was terrified.

We hit a parked car, but fortunately not head-on. It was a side swipe. Neither Larry nor I was injured. Larry yelled for me to hit the door in order for us to escape the car. He was blocked in from his side.

I obeyed on impulse. I threw the passenger's door open and leaped out into the traffic. The other cars on the road were attempting to go around us or back up from the scene. Folks were running in all directions, and I rushed to join the crowd. Instinctively, I knew that I had to get away from the targeted vehicle. I had no idea where the shots were coming from or who was firing them. I just knew there were many of them.

Larry and I got away from the car safely. We merged into the crowd. We saw Greg and two other men run away with guns still in their hands. The immediate danger was over; we came back to the car to assess the damage done.

It was riddled with bullet holes and the windows were shot out. The driver's side was badly dented.

I could not meet Larry's gaze. I kept my eyes fixed on the damaged Cadillac; I didn't want him to see the fear in my eyes. I didn't want Larry to think that I was a coward or a frightened little boy who was in too deep.

"That was that nigga Greg," Larry spoke to me in a hushed tone. "Wasn't it?"

The police were nearing the scene, and I was grateful. I didn't want to answer Larry's question. My voice would have betrayed my fear. I simply put my hands into my pockets to stop them from trembling, took a few deep breaths, and erected my nonchalant façade. I was going to feign the role of a bad ass nigga as best I could. I was going to answer the police's annoying questions with as much indifference as is expected of a true gangster.

"I be damned, Fat Larry and Tray," the police officer I knew as Officer Peanut was speaking in a spirited manner as he and his fellow officers approached us. "What the hell happened here?"

I leaned on the Cadillac next to Larry and fixed my eyes on my shoes. I was going to allow Larry to answer all the questions. I just wanted to get away from there. I wanted to go home to Darlene, Ada, Kim or Mama. I wanted to be comforted in a woman's arms. But that was not to be; some questions had to be answered. "So, who's trying to kill you?"

"Man, I don't know," Larry was angry. "We was just drivin' down the street, and somebody just started shootin' at the car."

"I doubt that they were shooting at the car," one of the officers declared. "They were shooting at you."

I didn't look up, I maintained my stare at my shoes. I wasn't prepared to allow anyone to look into my eyes. My confidence was not yet restored.

"Y'all fucked up somebody's dope or something, Larry?"

"Why you talkin' to me like I committed a crime?" Larry protested. "I'm the victim."

"Victim my ass," the police said. "You and this little fucker have killed more folks this past year than Hitler killed during the war."

I raised my head and spoke directly to Officer Peanut. He and I had a police-to-criminal relationship. "Man, I ain't tryin' to hear this dumb shit. I'm rollin'."

I lifted myself from my leaning position and endeavored to leave the scene. But I didn't get too far. One of the other officers pushed me back onto the car, in a less than gentle manner, and shouted at me, "You ain't goin' nowhere 'til we're finished."

I mumbled, "These motherfuckers gettin' ready to start this harassment shit," and settled in for the long haul. I just knew that I would spend the night at the police station. Every time I came in contact with the Baltimore City Police, I went to jail. I had experienced nothing good with them.

"If y'all got more questions for me," Larry announced after fending off some rather biased questions, "put them to my lawyer."

Larry walked away, and I joined him. The police stood there and watched us leave. None of them endeavored to stop us. I was truly impressed with Larry. The police were even afraid of him, I thought at the time. "What about the car?"

"Fuck that car," Larry snapped. "I'll get another one. Might get two. Right now, we gotta get that nigga, Greg."

There was no doubt that I would have to keep a gun on me or near me at all times. Larry and I were lucky not to have gotten severely wounded. Seventy-eight rounds had been fired into the car. It was a miracle that we were not killed. God was watching over us, but I was not going to depend on His continued vigilance. I arranged to be fitted for a holster in order to carefully conceal my snub nose .38. I initially selected a .45 automatic to carry around for protection. But Larry advised me that automatic guns were not reliable. They could jam at the most inopportune moments. Larry told me, "Tray, the only time you roll with an automatic is when you are goin' straight at your hit. Otherwise, keep a revolver with you."

I was concerned about getting caught with a loaded handgun during a random police search, but I was scared to be caught without it if I came across Greg again. In ghetto logic, it was better to be caught with it than without it.

Word spread quickly that I was a marked man. A lot of acquaintances who had enjoyed hanging out with me at the park, out on the corners, or wherever, began shunning me. Folks with Uzi submachine guns were out to kill me, and I to kill them. Darlene didn't mind me not coming home. In fact, she encouraged me to stay away from her and the children until I settled my conflict with the New York Boys.

I called Darlene later that evening to inform her about the incident. But word had already reached her. She told me, "Tray, dem niggas want you dead. They was even out here waitin' on you."

"They came to my house?" I asked.

"No, Greg and this other guy was parked across the street earlier," Darlene spoke in a nervous tone. She was intimately aware of the deadly conflict between the New York Boys' crew and mine. "They looked like they was waitin' on somebody. Now, I know."

I told Darlene I was going to settle this matter before I came back to her house. She was afraid for her children. However, she still loved me and wanted our relationship to continue. I told Larry about Darlene's observation, and he told me, "Man, that bitch ain't see nobody parked nowhere. She just scared and don't want you 'round for awhile."

I challenged Larry's wisdom on that matter, but he offered a strong argument.

"If dem niggas knew where you been laying your head, you'd be dead. They would've come up in that mothafucka to get you."

Larry thoroughly convinced me that Greg's attack upon him and me was opportunistic. At our strategy session, we reasoned that Greg and his associates had probably just surfaced again and were driving around and happened to spot us. It was probable that they had only followed us for a few blocks.

The core of our entire crew, Black, Terrance, Goodie, Terrell, Derrick, and I met up at one of our stash houses to discuss the matter. We decided that we would keep our guns out on the corners with us. Hide them behind car tires, in trash piles in the gutter, anywhere that would allow quick access. It was also decided that we would all keep our eyes and ears open for information as to Greg's whereabouts. We would pay anyone a substantial sum of money for information relating to Greg's location.

It was a very tense period for our crews. Terrance suggested that Larry had started all this shit for no other reason than ego and greed. Terrance even told me one day while we were out on the corner conducting our business affairs, "You gonna have to stop hangin' out with that fat mothafucka so much—or I'm gonna cut you off."

Terrance didn't stay for my response. He avoided me. I told Black what Terrance had said to me. Black simply shrugged his shoulders and said, "Fuck Terrance. He just scared right now."

I accepted what Black said. However, I was still disturbed about what Terrance said to me. He had threatened to fire me, and Terrance rarely spoke a word he didn't mean.

I loved my cousin dearly. But I loved my lifestyle, too. He was threatening to take it all away from me. But he couldn't, I had built up his crew. It was my crew, or at least ours. It was true that Milt was his connect, but it was my distribution line. I was the one who initiated the effort to establish a monopoly for our product. It was me who kept the stick-up boys at bay. I was an intrinsic part of everything. Terrance couldn't possibly consider cuttin' me off without cutting his own throat.

I presented the matter to Larry during the wee hours. We were at our home on Monford Avenue packing up furniture and clothes preparing for the move to our new home. Ada and Lamar were in their beds fast asleep. "You know T.I. told me that I had to stop hangin' out with you or he gonna fire me."

Larry burst into uncontrollable laughter. "Boy, I knew that was comin'," Larry eventually managed to say. "That's that Milt shit."

"It can't be Terrance," I said. "I'm the one that's been doin' most everything."

"Tray, get the fuck away from that bullshit before you and Terrance get somewhere y'all don't wanna be," Larry advised. "You and T.I. family. Y'all love each other. But he gettin' ready to start that game playin' shit with you that Milt be puttin' him up to."

"I got bills," I cried. "I ain't just gonna throw away everything I put together. I built this shit we got."

"Ain't no money worth what you and T.I. got," Larry was emphatic. "Plus, it ain't like you gonna starve. Let him run that shit. He need you, you don't need him."

Larry had a tremendous influence over me. He rarely offered me advice or guidance I questioned. But in this instance, he was advising me to abandon Terrance and what I had built with him. I knew that Black would leave Terrance's crew if I left. Black and Terrance were too much alike in personality to get along well together without me. Besides, Terrance's closeness and preference toward Wayne, whom Black despised, would present an insurmountable problem. My Uncle Derrick and Cousin Terrell would stay with Terrance. Goodie would go with Black and me. Terrance would have no buffer between his crew and the stick-up boys if I was to leave. Terrance and I had to have a conversation.

Terrance avoided me for a couple days, and I permitted it. I was not anxious to have what I knew would be an ugly discussion. Besides, my primary concern was to locate Greg. The matter with Terrance was definitely important; however, it could be put off for a day or two. Terrance couldn't remain under the impression that he could fire me if I didn't do exactly what he instructed.

I was informed that Greg and his crew had opened their business on Jefferson Street. I hooked up with Mississippi and Andrea Poole to seek him out. Larry advised me that it would be best if I kept Black as far away as possible from the situation. I wanted to give Terrance as little as possible to complain about.

Black spotted me getting into a car with Mississippi and Andrea late one afternoon, and he approached me to ask, "Where you goin'?"

"We gonna handle this New York Boy shit."

Black attempted to get in the car with us, but I told him, "Let us handle this one. You lay down here and look after things."

In a single instant, Black understood why I was distancing him from the situation. Terrance was blaming all the violence surrounding our crew on my association with Larry. "If we wasn't fuckin' with Fat Ass, the stick-up boys wouldn't be on us so much," Terrance had proclaimed during our last nightly count at Wayne's house. "Before we hooked up with that nigga, we ain't go through all this shit." He conveniently forgot about Blackface.

My Uncle Derrick had been pistol-whipped and robbed of jewelry, a leather coat, and a few hundred bucks moments before we all had assembled at Wayne's house, and Terrance was seething with anger. He knew that we would have to address the matter. We had so much stuff happening on so many fronts, and Milt was pressuring Terrance to stop all the violence surrounding us. It brought on too much attention.

It would have been useless to try to explain to Terrance the nature of our business. I didn't really understand it well enough myself to articulate it. The more money we generated, the bigger our clientele got, the more violent we would become. In the narcotics trade, things don't get better the longer you stayed in the business; they get worse. We all knew that on some level, but the game prevented us from looking beyond the moment. The future was for suckers to ponder.

We searched earnestly for Greg, but it was to no avail. He was nowhere to be found. In frustration and anger, Mississippi, Andrea, and I kicked in the front door of a house we believed to be Greg's stash house. We terrified the two occupants inside, two young women, and eventually set the house afire.

We had boldly come through the front door wielding our weapons. Mississippi had kicked the door ajar, and we rushed into the house, catching the two women by surprise. "Please don't kill us," one of the frightened women begged. "The money and dope is right here."

Mississippi went over to the couch, where the young, relatively attractive woman pointed, and lifted up a pillow to expose a small quantity of narcotics and money. He announced, "Bitch, we ain't here to rob you; where Greg?"

Andrea Poole and I made a quick canvas of the house. It was important that we know who was there.

It was a typical two-story red brick row house structure in the five or six hundred block of Collington Avenue. It was in the late evening, about ten or eleven o'clock, and it was doubtful that the police were called. We had time to search the house and leave a potent message. I took charge, "Get the basement, 'Drea," I instructed. "Keep your eyes on dem bitches 'Sip."

I raced up the steps. It was empty up there. Nothing or no one was there—other than a single bed in the master bedroom. It was a typical stash house. No one actually lived there.

We all assembled in the living room. The two women were relaxed. It was made clear to them that we were not interested in them. We wanted their boss, Greg. The older of the women, who was about twenty-five to thirty, swore to us that she didn't know where Greg was or when he would show up. She informed us that Greg hardly ever came around to that house to collect the money. "Some young boy they call Blood come get the money and re us up all the time," she said.

I believe she was being sincere. When Andrea slapped her across the face with the barrel of the .45 automatic he was carrying, I felt pity for her. I knew the vicious blow would leave an ugly scar on her face. "She ain't lyin'," the assaulted woman's friend exclaimed. "Greg don't come here. Please don't hurt us no more."

I didn't know why she said, "Don't hurt us," for no one had assaulted her. Her friend was the one laid out in the floor bleeding profusely from the head.

"Both you bitches get up and get outta here," I instructed. "And tell your boss Tray was here lookin' for him."

The woman that Andrea had struck in the face with his gun was aided to her feet by her friend, and they both started for the front door. But Mississippi blocked their path and asked Andrea and me, "Do y'all wanna have some fun?"

"Let the girls go," I was adamant. I was many things, but I wasn't a rapist. I would never prey upon vulnerable women or children.

The Break-up and Go Down

Chapter 39

Terrance insisted that I discontinue my relationship with Larry. He felt that the violence surrounding Fat Larry and me was too much and would bring us all down. If I live to be a hundred years old, I will never forget the hurtful words Terrance and I exchanged.

I went to Wayne's house early one morning to collect the money, only to be told that Terrance had picked it up. I was thrown aback because Terrance never picked up the money during the day-time hours. Black or I generally collected the money during the day.

I asked Wayne, "Why T.I. come get the money?"

"I don't know," Wayne spoke hesitantly. "But you need to see him because he told me not to give you the loot no more."

I was stunned. I hurried to Terrance's house. I was determined to confront him. We had avoided the matter long enough.

"Where Terrance at?" I asked Fatty-Poo, Terrance's sister, when she opened the door to allow me into the house.

"I believe he down in the basement," Fatty-Poo replied. "Ask him what he want to eat."

"Fuck what he wanna eat," I mumbled as I rushed past her and down the steps into the basement, into Terrance's haven.

Terrance was laying across his bed napping when I entered the room. He was completely oblivious to my presence. He was truly naïve. He was attempting to take away my livelihood, yet he was fast asleep with me in the room with him.

"Terrance," I bellowed. "What the fucks goin' on?"

The sound of my voice brought Terrance out of his sleep. He slapped his hand across his face twice, rather hard, in an effort to wake himself. "Don't come down here hollerin'. You ain't on the corner."

I was truly angry. Terrance had instructed Wayne not to give me anything when I should be able to take whatever I wanted, and now he was admonishing me about my tone of voice. This nigga had a lot of nerve. Good thing he was my family; otherwise, I would've killed him.

"Terrance," I lowered my voice to a conversational tone. "Why did you tell Wayne not to give me anything?"

"Man, you bringing too much heat on me," Terrance was sitting up in bed and his head was completely clear. "I told you last week to leave that fat mothafucka alone."

"Since when did you start tellin' me what to do?" My anger was apparent. "If it wasn't for me, we wouldn't have shit."

Terrance leaped from the bed as if he was going to attack me, but I knew intuitively that he would not. He was simply excited.

"Nigga, I don't need you. Your broke ass need me," Terrance was so close to my face I could smell his horrible breath. "You didn't have shit when I brought you in."

"You and 'em faggot-ass niggas was gettin' robbed every day before I started fuckin' with you and still would be if I wasn't with you now," I shouted.

Fatty-Poo came into the basement and stood between us. I had called Terrance some nasty names, and he had called me some in turn. It is probable that he and I would have exchanged blows had Fatty-Poo not stepped between us.

"Fuck you and this shit," I said to Terrance in exasperation. "I'm tired of dealin' with your punk ass anyway."

"Well, keep burnin' down houses and shootin' niggas for that fat sorry mothafucka and you ain't gonna have to deal with nobody but the police, anyway," Terrance offered that nasty retort as I left the basement and the house.

Fat Larry was absolutely right in his assessment. Terrance was marching to whatever orders Milt gave. I was just as angry with Milt as I was with Terrance, and I didn't even have a relationship with Milt. He was just a nigga I knew from afar. He was just another one of my many puppeteers.

I went to the main stash house at Parkside Garden and measured out 112 grams of raw cocaine on the triple beam scale. Four ounces of coke plus the $4000 I had at my grandmother's house seemed like reasonable severance pay.

I stashed the coke I took from Terrance and went in search of Black. I found him at Melissa's house.

"You know Terrance fired me," I told Black. "I got four ounces and four gees. If he don't like it, he can kiss my ass."

We were sitting on Melissa's front steps watching the cars and pedestrians pass. Our mood was rather gloomy. Our great times of prosperity and harmony were coming to a halt. Black and I both knew that things wouldn't remain the same without me. Black could come over to Fat Larry's crew with me, but it wouldn't be the same. Larry had about twenty to thirty dealers. Boo, Ada's younger brother, was Larry's lieutenant—his second-in-command. While there was room in Larry's crew for me at the top, there was none for Black. We both had to have leadership roles.

"I want you to stay with T.I.," I entreated Black. "You know he gonna need you more than ever with me gone."

"You and Terrance gonna be all right. Y'all just mad with each other right now."

"When he find out I got all his shit, he really gonna be mad," I offered. Black and I laughed. We both knew that what I took only amounted to a day's take. I was worth that and much more. Terrance would only mention the theft of such a small quantity of drugs and money if he desired to aggravate the already tense situation.

"Tray, you know what?" Black seemed serious.

"No, I don't know what, tell me." I wasn't being sarcastic. I really wanted to know what Black had to tell me.

"Melissa is pregnant," he informed me. "I need a break from this shit for awhile, anyway."

I was genuinely happy for Black—and for myself. I was going to be an uncle. Melissa had finally given me a reason to like her. She and I had never gotten along very well. We fought all the time—never physically, but we exchanged a lot of insults. When she came to the Maryland House of Correction to visit me, after I had already served nearly fifteen years in prison, the warmth of her embrace necessitated that all be forgiven. Otherwise, her trip all the way from North Carolina to visit was for naught.

I called Darlene to inform her that I would be making a clandestine trip to her house. I wanted the comforts of her loving. I had four ounces of cocaine to simply blow. I wanted to share it with her. It was about time I actually knew what brought the drug addicts out in scores to purchase our product.

I knew that I wasn't supposed to ever sample my own product. There is no sin greater than a dealer getting high on his own supply. I was well aware of that fact, but I was truly upset over the situation between Terrance and me. Everything I did shortly after our bitter argument was motivated by the anger I felt toward him. At sixteen, I wasn't wise enough to know that whenever you acted from anger, frustration, and shame, the consequences would be disastrous.

The situation between the New York Boys and my crew was far from resolved. I had burned down one of their stash houses less than forty-eight hours prior to contacting Darlene. I had shot Hank several times, leaving him for dead, for robbing my Uncle Derrick. I should have been amazed that Darlene would welcome me to her home. I was a marked man. Folks with a reasonable degree of intelligence maintained a respectable distance from me. Even my beloved grandmother and Aunt Kim encouraged me to stay away. Every other day someone was shooting at me or I was shooting at someone. I was living in various hotel rooms—not sleeping at the same place for more than a single night. Larry was doing likewise. We had purchased a new home, but it still wasn't safe for either him or me to stay there until we settled our conflict with the New York Boys. Until that issue was totally resolved, I was a walking target. Darlene understood that, but she obviously missed me—or was low on cash, and needed to see me.

I was too paranoid or cautious, depending upon one's perspective, to tell anyone the exact time I would be at any given place. I appreciated the fact that men like me were often betrayed by our girlfriends and other trusted associates. I liked Darlene a hell of a lot, but I wasn't going to give her the exact time of my arrival. Had she asked, I probably would have felt that she had sold me out. There was no doubt a price was on my head. The intense violence surrounding me was significant enough to cause Terrance, one of my strongest allies, to distance himself from me. There was no predicting what else was likely to happen. I was living in constant fear, but I had to hide that emotion. I was Tray; I had an image to protect.

It was well after midnight when I finally found myself at Darlene's house and in the comfortable confines of her bedroom. After leaving Black at Melissa's house, I had hooked up with Mississippi and Andrea Poole to seek out the New York Boys. We didn't locate Greg, the principal target, but we did manage to shut their operation down for a day. We terrorized a few of their dealers by forcing one of them into the car with us, and then firing a barrage of shots at their place of business as we drove away.

It was now time to relax. I had been consumed with the conflict I was involved in; however, I had to find some time to settle down. Darlene was perfect for the situation. I brought a nice piece of raw cocaine with me, at least a half ounce. I was going to try some of it myself. Andrea and Mississippi had been proclaiming all week that "coke keep a nigga dick hard." They told me that it was not as good as heroin, but the sexual euphoria was better.

Mississippi had advised me, "Look man, sprinkle some coke all over your body, and just let a bitch lick it off you. Man, all your shit gonna be stiff as shit."

Andrea agreed with him. He only added, "Bitches go nuts when you got that coke in 'em and in you, too."

I expressed concern over getting addicted, but Andrea informed me that cocaine wasn't addictive. "Man, you ain't gonna catch no habit off of Shirley. Now if you start fuckin' with dope, that's where you can catch a habit, if you got a weak mind."

Armed with that foolish advice, overwhelmed by frustration and anger at Terrance, I snorted cocaine for the first time in my life. Darlene had set up everything perfectly. She was dressed in a black negligee. She had the gold-plated straw laid out, and the based lines evenly drawn. We had smoked some weed, drank some wine, kissed and caressed each other's bodies. It was great. The cocaine had rendered me completely uninhibited.

When I announce to her that I wanted her to lick coke off my body, she challenged me, "You first."

"Come on, Darlene, you know I can't eat nothing that's gonna get up and walk away."

"I ain't gonna walk away," Darlene was tantalizing, spreading cocaine over her body. "Taste me baby. I taste good."

I started licking the powdery substance from Darlene's body, but she kept pushing my head toward her vagina. "I ain't eatin' no pussy, baby," I spoke in a passive manner.

Darlene looked me directly in the eyes, kissed me tenderly upon the lips and said, "Tray, I need you to make love to me like I make love to you. Taste my body like I taste yours."

The first time I snorted cocaine marks the first time I performed cunnilingus. Darlene had convinced me that licking her pussy was a measurement of my manhood and the affection I felt for her.

Shame ate at my soul. I had snorted coke, sucked pussy, and I was afraid for my life. I could share those secrets with no one. Larry and Black would frown upon me for snorting drugs. Larry would appreciate the fact that I had finally performed cunnilingus, but the snorting drugs and being afraid were unforgivable. Black wouldn't understand any of my transgressions. He would ridicule me for being afraid for my life and eating pussy, but he would whip my ass for snorting drugs. I had created an awesome hole for myself. There was no escape. I was imprisoned by my image.

"You know," I confessed to Darlene as we laid in each other's arm. "I ain't never did none of this shit before."

"Shit, as good as you were?" She didn't believe me. "You been hangin' for awhile."

"Baby, honestly," I insisted. "I ain't never sucked no pussy and sniffed no coke before."

"Whatever," Darlene said as she began exploring my body with her tongue—taking me to another state of ecstasy. Forget it, she didn't have to believe me. It was probably better for me that she didn't believe she was my first anything. I couldn't control my passion toward her. I didn't need her armed with dangerous information concerning my emotional attachments and other vulnerabilities. Let her think I had sucked pussy before, let her think I had used cocaine before. Darlene was witnessing me at my weakest moment and didn't even know it.

A Tough Time for Love

Chapter 40

I was truly a victim of nihilism. I had absolutely no prospects for the future. My current life was my future and the only value system I had was the ghetto code of ethics. Traditional values were nil. I was prepared to catch a few bullets in my head at any moment. I existed as a typical drug dealer.

Terrance and I were barely speaking. He had shut down the operations at Eager and Durham for all intents and practical purposes. He and Black were selling weight or wholesale cocaine to those who sought to sell retail. I was working for Larry full-time, but there was very little for me to do. Boo was handling the daily operations. I was a trouble-shooter. I warned other drug dealers about encroaching on our territory and I avenged any offense committed against our crew. If someone robbed one of our twenty to thirty dealers, I saw to it that he would not do it again. I was also responsible for picking up our large supply of heroin from the Nigerian connection. Boo and his friend, Kevin, were responsible for diluting and packaging the product for street sale.

Larry and Greg had met and come to peace terms. Greg had agreed to buy Larry a brand new Cadillac. He also agreed not to sell his product beyond Madison Street. He would stay on Jefferson Street.

The peace between the New York Boys and us didn't make my life much safer. I was still a target for other drug dealers who felt offended by me telling them that they could not deal narcotics on Eager Street. I had shot several stick-up boys who likely wanted revenge. But Greg was my most feared enemy, and it was less tense after he and Larry had reached an accord. I was able to walk down the streets without always having to carry a gun. I just had to have one nearby. I could also stay at home on consecutive nights, attend neighborhood sporting events, and engage in other social activities without the threat of gun-fire erupting around me.

It was during this semi-peaceful time that I met the girl who I thought would be the love of my life, Joy. She was by far the most beautiful girl I had ever known. Her personality was warm and inviting. She appreciated laughter. Joy epitomized her name. For she was an absolute and complete joy.

I was visiting my cousin, Melvina. I was low on weed, my drug of choice. I made all my personal purchases from her. We were gathered around Melvina's living room. Melvina, my cousins Mark and Boodie, and I were watching a video and listening to some soft music and enjoying conversation, when a knock came on the door. Melvina got up from her seat on the couch next to me to answer it.

This beautiful creature walked in. She was five-foot-six, her complexion was light and her smile bright. She was wearing a pair of tight blue jeans that accentuated her youthful, shapely figure. I wanted her, and I couldn't wait for an introduction.

"Hey 'dere," I spoke to her in ghetto fashion. "Who you be, miss lady?"

She laughed along with everyone else in the room. It was obvious I was enchanted by her. I even got up from my comfortable seat to make her acquaintance. My super-ego and arrogance rarely allowed me to do that at that point in my life. Women sought my affection and attention. I was Tray—that nigga. But I had to know this girl. I had to win her affection and attention—and love.

"Boy, you a trip," Melvina chastised me. "This is my friend from school; her name is Joy."

I told Joy that I was pleased to meet her. But I wanted to get to know her a hell of a lot more. I inquired into her love life, and she informed me that she had a boyfriend. I wasn't dissuaded by that. I had a girlfriend myself. In fact, I had a few girlfriends and a woman whom I was living with—Darlene.

I convinced Joy to join us as we drank beer, smoked weed and socialized. After some time passed, I asked Joy more about her boyfriend, whom I envied.

She told me that his name was Paul, and that he was away at Job Corps. Great, while the cat is away the mouse can play.

"Joy, let me call you sometime," I implored. "Perhaps we can go out to the movie or whatever; I'm a good guy to know."

She was hesitant, but Melvina entreated her, "Give my cousin some play, girl!"

Joy gave me her phone number. I didn't write it down, from habit. Guys in my profession remembered numbers; we hardly ever wrote them on paper. Anyway, Joy was convinced that I would forget her number because I didn't write it down. I assured her that I was not going to let her get away from me that easily. I was determined to win her affection.

I didn't win her affection away from Paul, but I did establish a lasting, very complicated and loving relationship with her. In fact, Joy stands as the only girl to ever make me cry from a broken heart.

Black didn't like Joy. He felt that she was just another girl using me for my money. But I know that wasn't the case. I had to force gifts upon Joy. She wanted me to abandon my lifestyle. Joy assured me a thousand times that if I had no money, she would still enjoy my company. She always maintained a part-time job to keep her own money.

One day Black, Joy, and I were on Monument Street shopping for a leather coat for her. The only reason Black tagged along with us was to ensure that I didn't spend a ridiculous sum on her. Black knew that he couldn't stop me from spending my money any way I elected to, but his ridicule would have influenced me.

We were about to enter a clothing store on Monument Street when suddenly, Joy separated herself from Black and me.

"What's sup?" Black asked.

"That's Paul," Joy said as she went over to join her boyfriend.

I was emotionally devastated and profoundly embarrassed. Black knew it; therefore, he did the most appropriate thing. He looked at me with utter amusement and asked, "Yo, you gonna let that bitch play you like that?"

I walked away; I knew Black would get loud and draw attention to the situation. I didn't want to get Joy in trouble with her boyfriend. I considered her interests above mine.

I endured Black's ridicule and criticism over Joy's disregard toward me. However, I continue to maintain that befriending Joy was one of the best things I ever did. The devastated emotions I eventually experienced from our relationship was a consequence of receiving life imprisonment. Judge Davis, not Joy and I, destroyed what she and I could have established.

My troubles with the law came upon me soon after Joy and I started a meaningful relationship. She had invited me to attend her Junior Prom, but I was arrested on the night of the event. One of our stash houses had been robbed. I went there to investigate the matter. No sooner had I come through the door of the house than it was raided by Baltimore's finest. A large quantity of packaged heroin was found, and I was arrested with three others who were on the premises.

I was returned to The Maryland Training School for Boys. At a subsequent hearing, I was waived from a juvenile offender to adult status. The state presented to the court that I was a reputed drug dealer and that the juvenile justice system had nothing to offer me. The judge was impressed with what the state presented. He waived jurisdiction and set my bail at $25,000.

Terrance was present at court with me. He had come along with Mama, Kim, Black, and Joy. He gave me a tentative hug and assured me that my bond would be paid within the hour. All was forgiven between us. The heated argument and ensuing split between us was forgotten in that instant. Blood was thicker than water and far more potent than the green ink used to print money.

I hurried home once the sheriff released me from custody. I wanted to take a luxurious bath, put on some fresh clothes, and see Joy. I was profoundly sorry for ruining her prom night. I would see Terrance later to thank him for putting up my bond. Larry was prepared to pay it, but Terrance had beat him to it. I was grateful that I didn't have to wait in jail an additional hour or two. I had already been locked up for two weeks awaiting the hearing for waiver of jurisdiction.

Joy was at home doing her chores; she couldn't spend any quality time with me. Her curfew simply wouldn't allow it. Therefore, I called Darlene to let her know I had been released from jail, and I wanted to be with her. It had been a long time.

Eventually, I caught up with Joy. We coordinated our time so that we could be together. I made it up to her for ruining her prom, and she showed me that she had forgiven me by giving herself to me fully.

After a great movie and dinner at a fine restaurant at the Inner Harbor in downtown Baltimore, we consummated our relationship. We checked into a Holiday Inn on Moravia and made passionate love. My night with Joy was perfect; the only blemish was that she mistakenly referred to me as Paul while I was deep inside her. That was a forgivable error. Women often called me by others' names—Jesus, God—Apostle Paul was a first. Darlene was the only sexual partner I had at the time who couldn't afford to call me by another man's name. Jesus was an exception, of course.

I was deeply entrenched into my lifestyle. Joy was a good girl; she did her little scandalous shit, but her lifestyle was saintly compared to mine. There was no place in my life for good girls—or good people. I had chosen a path that led to a premature death or a lengthy prison term.

It was not a great surprise to me when Ada called me to pick up the phone early one morning to speak to my hysterical grandmother.

"Tray, baby, the police are lookin' for you," Mama was truly upset. "They say you killed somebody."

"Be cool, Mama." I was calm. The police had accused me of killing someone or another in the past. "You know the police is always sayin' I did something."

"Baby, it's different this time," Mama wasn't going to allow me to trivialize her concern. "They tore the house up. They had their guns out and everything when they came in here this time. They said for you to turn yourself in or they might kill you."

I was still in my pajamas and barely awake, but my head was clear enough to know that Mama was a veteran with us criminals. If she was hysterical, there was need for concern.

"I'm gonna get with my lawyer to see what's happenin'," I endeavored to assuaged Mama's concern. "Don't worry 'bout me, Mama."

I hung up the telephone. Ada was standing right before me. She wanted to know what had my grandmother so upset.

"The police tore my grandmother's house up lookin' for me for a murder," I offered. "She scared."

"Me too," Ada solemnly replied.

Larry wasn't home. I paged him. When he responded I informed him that a warrant had been issued for my arrest for murder.

"Get out the house," Larry instructed. "They will probably come there lookin' for you next."

I hurriedly got dressed and went to a friend's house to hide out. I didn't want to be seen by anyone until I discovered more details about the warrant. I felt, intuitively, that I was in more trouble than ever before. I thought about contacting Darlene; she had always served as my best comfort at times of stress. But that was a thing of the past. She had betrayed my heart and trust. I had vowed never to deal with her again. She had slept with Greg, the New York Boy, during the time he was trying to kill me.

Larry had suspected that Darlene was sexually involved with Greg. The grapevine had reported it, but he didn't reveal it to me until he had proof.

Greg disclosed the treachery during the truce meeting. He was trying to use Darlene to trap me somewhere.

Darlene denied her relationship with Greg. She said that Larry had concocted the story because he wanted her for himself, but I believed Larry. If Larry wanted to fuck Darlene, he would have simply asked, "Tray, can I fuck Darlene?"

I was sixteen years old and on the run for murder. I had to avoid vengeful stick-up boys and the police. I had nowhere to go. I was tired of driving around the countryside and sleeping in different hotels. I often solicited sexual favors from various women for comfort, but I missed the stability of home. I wanted to see Joy, Mama, Kim, and my sisters. I was lonely, but I suspected the police had my loved ones under surveillance. I had to run and keep on running.

It was a great emotional release when the police finally apprehended me. I had spoken to my attorney, and he had assured me that he would represent me with diligence. Gangland slayings were difficult to prosecute, my lawyer boldly confided in me. The longer it takes to bring you to court, the more difficult it will be for the state to get a conviction. That was the legal advice given me. Thus, I avoided the law for as long as I possibly could. I didn't kill Cam. He had been my friend at one time. The wrong man was being sought. But that was not the issue. A murder warrant was serious business, and since I was who I was, it would be difficult to convince anyone I didn't murder Cam. There had been some tension between he and I when he popped up dead.

A Wretch Like Me

Chapter 41

I was tired of running; I wanted to have all my legal troubles over and done with so that I could enjoy the upcoming summer. I called my Aunt Kim Friday night to notify her that I would appear in court the following Monday, May 28, 1985. I was out of jail on bond for a previous arrest and that was the day I was due in court. I didn't want the bail bondsman searching for me, too. I told Kim that I would most assuredly be apprehended when I appeared in court. The police were conducting a fierce search for me. They had come to my grandmother's house on a number of occasions in the two weeks that I had been avoiding capture. The bail bondsman had even contacted Terrance to ascertain whether or not he would lose out on the bond he had posted on my behalf. He did not feel comfortable coming after me. Larry and Ada also felt that it would be best for me to surrender myself. They felt that the charges would not stick. I didn't kill Cam; we felt that Baltimore's finest were just trying to shake me for some information or get me off the street for a little while.

I met up with Kim and Terrance on Monday, May 28,1985, outside of the Eastern District Courthouse at approximately nine o'clock in the morning. That was the date and time that my subpoena commanded that I appear in court. It was a beautiful day, and I was hesitant about surrendering myself. The last time I had done that, I had had a horrible experience. I stayed in custody longer than I felt I should have stayed.

Like a fool again, I submitted to everyone's fear. Mama and Kim feared that I would be shot and killed by the police if I continued to evade capture. Larry and Ada feared that I would eventually bring the police crashing through their front door, and the bail bondsman feared that he would lose his $25,000 bond. I was getting pressure from all sides to turn myself in. No one wanted me around. I was feeling completely isolated, like I had leprosy or some other feared disease.

"You ready, baby?" Kim asked me as we stood on the top step, near the entrance to the courthouse.

"I gotta be," I spoke with a confidence I certainly didn't feel. "It's a small thing."

Terrance put his arms around my shoulders, and we strolled into the courthouse. We went into the courtroom where I was scheduled for a preliminary hearing and sat on the front row to await the bailiff to call my case.

The bailiff never got the chance to announce my case; several police surrounded me. I was quickly and smoothly handcuffed and escorted from the courtroom. My attorney, Mr. Kirkland, was entering the courtroom as I was being escorted out in handcuffs. Several bystanders offered a curious glance in my direction, for it was not unusual to see a black teenage male handcuffed and taken from the court.

"Hey, Mr. Kirkland," I said to my attorney as I was being dragged pass him. "Come on and holla at me."

"I'll be right there, Arlando," Mr. Kirkland said. "Don't talk to anyone until I get there."

There was no one to talk to other than a few drunks locked in the cell next to me, and they were sleeping off their drunkenness. I wasn't interviewed or fingerprinted. The police just tossed me into an empty cell and left me alone.

The cell I was placed in was subtly different from the isolation cells I had inhabited at Training School. In some respects, the cells at Eastern District were more comfortable. There was a toilet and small basin in the cells there. At Training School there was no toilet, wash basin, or running water in the cells. There were bars on the cells at Eastern District; at Training School, there was a steel door that prevented any human contact. At Training School, in those cells, it was not possible to know if it was day or night outside.

The squalor at Eastern District was extreme. The open-face toilet and wash basin smelled horrible and the hard wooden bench with the screws protruding from its base offered no comfortable place to sit or lay down.

The forty square-feet of space was restricting. But at sixteen years of age, I had already experienced worse living conditions—and that was the greatest tragedy of all.

On the advice of veteran criminals, Herb Johnson and Eggie Scott, to name only two, I had hidden two grams of cocaine in one shoe sole and two grams of raw heroin in the other. It was going to be a lengthy ordeal. I wanted to numb my senses. I didn't want to experience jail's inescapable suffering with clear consciousness. I got my drugs out and inhaled the death while the turn keys were toward the front of the cell block and the drunks in the cell next to mine were asleep. I had absolute privacy and solitude. I was free to destroy myself as I had been for quite sometime.

When Mr. Kirkland finally came to see me, after several hours had elapsed, I was high. I had inhaled a substantial amount of the heroin and cocaine I had smuggled into the holding cell. If anyone notice my intoxicated state, he didn't mention it. The turn-key just came to retrieve me.

"Jones, Arlando," a tall white police officer said to me, "your lawyer is here to see you."

My cell door swung open and I was escorted to a small conference room where Mr. Kirkland was waiting for me. He was sitting at a small conference table with papers spread out in front of him. I sat across from him, and as soon as the police exited the room, affording me privacy with my attorney, I asked, "How much trouble am I in?"

"I don't know, yet," Mr. Kirkland answered. "They're playing this one very close to the vest."

"You gonna get me a bail?"

"I will most certainly request one, but this is a capital case," Mr. Kirkland expressed doubt. "The state is going to fight hard against it, and they probably will prevail at this stage."

Mr. Kirkland had explained to me several days prior that I would likely have to stay at the Baltimore City Jail until I went to trial, if a trial occurred. My question was merely an exercise in futility. I knew the process; Mr. Kirkland and his partner at the law firm had explained everything to me when Larry and I first contacted them about the warrant for my arrest. The only surprise I received from my attorney was when he asked me, "Who is Eric Hunter?"

The euphoric effects of the drugs I had consumed wore off in the instant Mr. Kirkland asked me about Eric Hunter. Suddar, or Eric Hunter, is my cousin. He had recently been released from prison and had vowed to go straight. He was not associated with our illegal activities. He couldn't possibly know Cam. The closest to our operation Suddar came was to work for Larry at the beauty salon Larry owned. Cam was at the very bottom of our organization's hierarchy; niether Suddar nor I dealt with him. The only reason I knew Cam was because we grew up in the neighborhood together and crossed each other's path from time to time. Cam was too inconsequential to our business to come into contact with Larry or me.

"Why is Eric Hunter being mentioned?" I inquired.

"Well, I just discovered, just before coming down here to meet with you, that he is being sought as your accomplice," Mr. Kirkland answered. "I don't have any significant details. I won't know much of anything until I get the state's disclosure. You know all this, Tray. We've already discussed it."

I expressed to Mr. Kirkland that Suddar had absolutely nothing to do with our operation. I wanted to make that abundantly clear because I felt awful for him. Suddar had done his dirt, shot and robbed folks. He had even sold dope for Fat Larry at one point. He didn't want to go back to prison. He was engaged to a lovely woman, Kathy, and they had a beautiful child. It was killing me inside that he was being associated with our dirt.

Suddar was my favorite cousin, and I loved him deeply. He was trying to pull me away from criminality. He would seek me out after his work day at the beauty salon and endeavor to instill in me a fear of my future.

I recall Suddar saying to me one day, soon after he was released from prison, "Tray, you gotta stop this shit. You gonna end up in prison forever—or one of these niggas is gonna kill you out here."

Suddar would sometimes have tears in his eyes when he would try to dissuade me from criminality. I think he felt a strong degree of responsibility for my life choices. Suddar had been my idol and he knew it. I wanted to be just like him in some respects.

Suddar was tall and very muscular in build. All the women loved him and wanted to have him. The men envied him or simply feared him. He was deadly, and he could fight extremely well. If given only a little more time, I probably would have accepted the extreme shift he had made.

"Mr. Kirkland, this is real fucked up," my voice was solemn. "Me and Suddar ain't do this shit."

He told me to take care of myself and that he would see me the following day at my bail review hearing. I didn't have to worry about being questioned by the police. He had already let the state's attorney and investigating officers know that I would not answer any questions.

Mr. Kirkland left me alone in the conference room. After a short time, two Baltimore City Police came into the room to get me. They took me to an area in the police station to fingerprint me. They asked me a few routine questions such as my name and address. I simply said, "My lawyer told me that y'all wasn't gonna ask me questions; so I ain't answering none."

The officers respected the fact that I wouldn't answer any of their questions. They just fingerprinted me and escorted me back to the filthy cell I was initially placed in. My hands were covered with black ink, and when I asked for soap to wash them. I was told, "Fuck off, Jerk."

Back in the cell, isolated and depressed, I snorted more of the drugs I had brought with me. My mood became relaxed and my fear subsided. I talked with the others who were in the cell block with me. I was amazed at all the familiar faces. In the hour or two I had been away talking with my attorney and getting fingerprinted, several others had come in. I had plenty of company to party with, and since I decided to share my drugs, I became the life of the party.

My first night in custody is a total blur. I didn't sleep. The drugs and the uncomfortable jail conditions wouldn't allow it. I looked a mess when I appeared before the district judge the following morning. My attorney told me bags were under my eyes. I smelled terrible from not bathing or brushing my teeth, and my clothes were wrinkled. I was nodding from the effects of the drugs, and my posture demonstrated the contempt I felt for the court. I knew I was going to be denied bail, so fuck the court and the judge. I didn't kill Cam and the police knew it.

When I was first informed by Mama that I was being sought for killing Cam, it wasn't a big deal. Cam was employed by us. He was murdered. The police needed to hassle someone to gather information. I was reputed to be Fat Larry's trigger-man. It wasn't surprising that I would be a suspect. It was just a typical police ruse. I had rationalized my panic away. But they were involving Suddar with this shit; it was a set-up. I was mad, and with my limited education, I couldn't adequately express the depth of my pain, confusion, and outrage. I had so positioned myself that I could hardly convince anyone that I didn't do what I was accused of doing. My dream had come true; I was finally known and accepted around the 'hood and by the police as a bad-ass nigga. Suddar was my predecessor, and that was his only crime. After my bail hearing, I was returned to my cell to await transportation to the Baltimore City Jail. My destiny awaited me. I was not afraid. I was nothing.

The officials at the jail treated me just like they treated all the other suspected criminals who crossed the jail's threshold. I was thrown into a crowded bullpen to join the ranks of the downtrodden. I answered the annoying questions the intake officials at the jail asked. I underwent a tedious physical examination and was finally placed in another filthy cell with a filthy wino. All my drugs were gone. I had to experience the dismal conditions of jail with a clear head. I prayed to a distant and obscure God to help me have victory over my enemies and to give me insight. I was suffering a great deal, and I didn't have a clue as to why. I was loyal to my family and friends and I followed the code of ethics instilled in me. Some folks even qualified me as kind, warm, and generous; why was I suffering? Why was I in so much pain? I needed insight.

God definitely answers prayer. Well, at least he answered mine. I didn't understand it immediately. It took me some time to discover that my prayers were answered. While at the jail, I learned how truly ignorant I was. I learned that my greatest enemy had been me, and that I was the principle cause of my suffering. I got truly acquainted with myself. I learned that God was in me. He wasn't some obscure or distant being. He was clear and never away from where I was. God existed all the time, in all situations, and in all people. I was suffering because I desired to suffer. I had used my divine qualities to create pain and suffering.

Alas, my legal situation went funky. The state presented a completely fabricated case against Suddar and me and we were convicted and sentenced to life imprisonment. I felt utterly devastated, but thanks to all the blessings God had sent me, I pushed on.

From Thughood to Manhood

Chapter 42

Suddar entered the city jail a month after I did. He wasn't angry with me or embittered by the circumstances. Suddar assuaged my negative feelings about the situation by convincing me that we would be exonerated of the false charges launched against us. He encouraged the positive relationships I had with those individuals who were seeking to enhance my knowledge base and expand my horizon. Each time I reverted back to ghetto practices, which I did often, Suddar would be among the first to chastise me.

I had learned how to smuggle illegal narcotics into the jail. I still felt a need to earn money. When Suddar discovered that I was still involved in the very thing that brought me to the city jail, he became enraged. He called Larry and Terrance and forbade either of them to send me drugs. He even jacked me up by my shirt collar and told me, "Look here, you little motherfucker, you gonna stop this bullshit. We in a 'nuff trouble as it is."

It was a good thing that we were in an isolated area of the jail's annex where others couldn't witness him man-handle me. Otherwise, I would have whipped his ass, or at least, tried my best to.

I didn't take heed to Suddar's threat; I continued to engage in the drug trade. I was using the stuff too. I had convinced Black and Boo to send me whatever I asked for. Suddar wasn't my father. He didn't tell me what to do. I just made my participation in the illegal trade less obvious, and I made sure I wasn't housed on the same floor of the annex as Suddar.

It wasn't difficult to keep my activities hidden from Suddar. He was too overwhelmed with our legal situation to concentrate his focus on what I was doing. While I concentrated my attention on smuggling heroin and cocaine into the jail, Suddar busied himself in the jail's legal library. I maintained a relationship with many of the girls I had met before. Suddar focused on getting back home to his fiancée and daughter. I read a few books and did some positive things, but my negative thinking and behaving caused my stay at Baltimore City's jail to be quite turbulent. There were a number of guys at the jail who hated me. I had brought much harm to a lot of folks, and it was time to pay me back.

I was walking to the dining hall one evening with my section. I was housed on the first floor of the jail's annex, the hopper section, a place for young suspected criminals. We had to enter the main jail and go over to its Southside to eat. This short, very stocky man came from nowhere and suddenly attacked me. He hit me with a solid blow to my head. The blow was so powerful it knocked me off my feet. I didn't know what had happened to me. I was semi-conscious, trying my best to regain my footing. Thanks to the unwritten code of ethics adhered to by the hoppers on the first floor of the annex, I was saved from any further punishment. My niggas Junebug, Sylvester, and Johnny Smalls leaped at my assailant's ass before he could follow up with another assault. In an instant, I gained my balance and joined my friends from the hopper section beat this guy into a bloody pulp.

Someone from among the crowd hollered, "Five-Oh" to warm us that the correctional guards were coming. Everyone scattered. I stayed; I needed to know the identity of the man who had assaulted me.

It was a dope-fiend nigga I knew as Roland. I had beat him with a baseball bat several months prior to coming to jail while Boo held a gun on him. He had purchased some drugs from us and had the audacity to complain about their quality. Moreover, he had demanded his money back. Roland just couldn't catch a break when it came to me. I was his nemesis, I suppose.

I was taken to the jail's segregation unit where I stayed isolated for six days. Captain Gilbert, who was in charge of the annex, told the warden that it was I who had been assaulted by Roland. My friends simply prevented me from being brutally beaten by a bigger, stronger, older inmate.

I don't know how Captain Gilbert came upon the exact details of what happened, but he had the exact story. He knew that the conflict started from the streets, a drug dispute that had absolutely nothing to do with city jail.

I was taken off segregation and returned to the first floor annex. Captain Gilbert said to me, "You got a lot of shit going on in your life. Half the jail's population probably wants you dead, and the other half don't care one way or the other about you."

I didn't wait for Captain Gilbert to invite me to a chair. I simply sat down in the only chair available in the tiny office and that was next to where Captain Gilbert sat.

"I gotta lot of drama in my life, Captain," I admitted. "People probably wanna kill me that I don't even know."

"You want protective custody?" Captain Gilbert asked me.

I felt offended that Captain Gilbert would think that I wasn't capable of defending myself. He didn't mean to offend me. He had seen much in his sixty years of existence and thirty-five years as a corrections officer. He simply wasn't about to take anything for granted.

"I don't need P.C.," I was adamant. "Whoever wanna bring it to me need P.C."

My comment caused Captain Gilbert to laugh uncontrollably. "I knew you would say something like that," he managed to say through his laugher. "You ain't nothing but a buck and thirty pounds soaking wet. How are you gonna fend against all those big ole niggas 'round here that's out to crush you?"

"Don't let my size fool you."

Captain Gilbert stood up from his chair, exposing his full six-foot-five, two-hundred-fifty pound frame, "I'm three to four times your age," he announced playfully. "And you can't beat me."

It was my turn to laugh. Captain Gilbert was probably correct in his assessment. He certainly was in great shape for a man his age. Captain Gilbert appeared to be a man who exercised regularly. The only way to know that he was an elderly gentleman was from the gray hairs on his head and face. If he dyed it, he could pass himself off for half his actual age.

"Captain Gilbert," I humbly submitted. "I ain't got no beef with you. Why you wanna beat me up?"

Captain Gilbert proved to be a great asset to me. He aided me tremendously while I was at the jail. He made me his clerk on the condition that I attend school and receive good grades. He felt that I needed an education. I suspect Captain Gilbert felt that the clerk job and school would keep me too busy to settle old scores. The less turbulence I had to face as a result of my past, the better off I would be, and the less trouble I would bring to his therapeutic youth program at the annex.

I became affectionately known as Captain Gilbert's son. I answered his phone, took messages for him, and typed memorandums that he wanted issued. It was a sweet job. It afforded me privileges that were denied other inmates. It was okay for me to work for Captain Gilbert, since he didn't keep snitches around him, and he forbade homosexuals entrance to the annex. Only stand-up men could command respect from Captain Gilbert. He was a man's man—a real nigga.

Suddar was satisfied that I was secure in the annex. The few known enemies who were in the jail with me had been effectively neutralized. Therefore, Suddar went into the main section of the jail. He hated staying in the annex.

One great contention between Suddar and me concerned who would represent me at trial. I was satisfied with my attorney, Kirkland. I felt comfortable with him. But Suddar wanted to be represented by Paul Polansky. I had no problem with Polansky representing Suddar; Polansky was reputed to be a great trial attorney. However, Polansky and Kirkland had some kind of civil action pending in court against each other. I had to dismiss Kirkland or Suddar had to dismiss Polansky; there was no alternative.

Suddar was smarter than I, and through Terrance's insistence, I dismissed Kirkland and secured the legal service of Attorney Diamond. I am not disappointed with Diamond's legal representation. I feel that he did a terrific job at representing my interest. But that sorry-ass Polansky left much to be desired.

The state attorney at the evidentiary hearing phase of our trial, presented Abraham Robinson as a witness against us. This no-good liar was supposed to testify against me for murdering Cam. But he offered details about another murder that was pending against me and kept confusing details about other cases the state was using him to testify in. Under Diamond's intense cross-examination, it was demonstrated that Abraham Robinson routinely offered testimony for the state's attorney to get out of his own legal troubles. He was a professional snitch. The court found Abraham Robinson to be so thoroughly untrustworthy that the judge refused to allow him to go before the jury.

Polansky's approach and attitude toward our trial were lackadaisical. He didn't believe in our innocence enough to provide a passionate and diligent defense. Polansky simply did enough not to be declared an incompetent attorney. A key eyewitness, Brenda Branch, came to Polansky's office and told him that she didn't actually witness Suddar and me kill Cam. The only reason she was testifying against us was because she was being pressured to do so by the state's attorney and the investigating police officers.

Brenda gave Polansky a sworn affidavit attesting to the fact that she lied to the grand jury about Suddar and me and that she was prepared to lie at our trial. But Polansky convinced us all that it would not be prudent to use that affidavit to impeach Brenda at trial. We had truth and innocence on our side. However, Polansky chose to use trickery as our defense. Diamond stuck with honesty; he believed in our innocence. But he didn't want to conflict with Polansky. It would have damned our defense.

We were damned anyway. The court that tried my case didn't care about judicial integrity. It permitted the state to present its fabricated case against Suddar and me, and we were ultimately convicted and sentenced to life prison terms for the murder of Cam. I was destined to go to the Maryland Penitentiary, and the very prospect of that frightened me.

The large Gothic structure that sat on Forrest Street was intimidating. The huge boulders that formed the structure resembled those that surrounded cemeteries. The place was called "Castle Grayskull" because it looked like the castle from the "He-Man" cartoon.

After the trial concluded, Diamond wrapped his arm around me and said, "You got a real bum deal here. I will file your appeal and do whatever I can to help you."

I have been incarcerated for well over twenty years, and Diamond has not done much of anything to aid me in securing my release. But I ain't mad at him. He didn't do anything to hurt me, either. And that is more than I can say for Polansky.

When I finally got to the Penitentiary, a whole new world opened up to me. I had moments of transgression. I spent a considerable amount of time on the notorious South-wing, the prison's segregation unit for inmates who violated prison rules and regulations. But it was at the Penitentiary, ironically enough, that I discovered freedom. In the belly of corruption, abysmal misery, suffering, and utter dejection, I learned how to love and be loved.

Mrs. Testerman, an elderly white woman, was among my first formal teachers at the Penitentiary. She afforded me patience and genuine compassion as she introduced me to literature and the fine points of English composition. She acquainted me with the works of Paul Lawrence Dunbar, Langston Hughes, Robert Frost, Longfellow, and scores of other classical and renaissance writers. Mrs. Testerman shared Biblical scriptures with me, and she showed me how a true Christian is supposed to behave.

I was out in the hallway one afternoon, in front of Mrs. Testerman's classroom arguing with Earl, an inmate who cleaned the hallways. I called him an "Uncle Tom ass nigga" and Mrs. Testerman came out into the hall and asked me to come into the classroom. I felt embarrassed about her overhearing me use foul language, but I said what I said and there was no taking it back. I had to own up to my words.

"Arlando, have a seat," Mrs. Testerman instructed me to sit at one of the empty desks in the classroom. "I heard you call Earl an Uncle Tom."

"I didn't mean for you to hear that," I said. "Earl made me mad."

"If Earl made you angry, why did you give him a compliment?"

I was thrown completely aback. I thought I had offended Earl. "What you mean?" I questioned her question.

"Uncle Tom's Cabin is about a slave named Tom who epitomizes Christian ideals. If you read the book, you will never refer to someone you dislike as an Uncle Tom."

Mrs. Testerman had a smooth and subtle way of chastising me. She never displayed anger or frustration when dealing with me or any of her other students. If I had a position different from hers, she would employ me to research the matter, as she would. It was never a matter of who was right or wrong with her. Mrs. Testerman taught me that ignorance was the greatest obstacle I would face.

Once I secured my high school equivalence diploma, Mrs. Testerman encouraged me to enter the college program offered at the Penitentiary. I didn't feel that I was college material. I had only learned how to read and write effectively two or three years prior. Surely, the curriculum of a college would be too challenging. I didn't want to set myself up for failure.

"I ain't goin' to college, Mrs. Testerman," I said to her as we sat in her classroom the day after I received my G.E.D. test scores. "That's a little too much for me."

"The only things you can't do, Arlando, are the things you decide you can't do."

I was humbled by Mrs. Testerman. She urged me on with her patience and strength of character. I love Mrs. Testerman and will forever be thankful for the lasting friendship I established with her. A large part of my academic success is due to her. I also owe Mrs. Testerman a huge debt of gratitude for making my personal relationships with women better.

I had confided in Mrs. Testerman about the estrangement I felt with my mother, who was long deceased; my grandmother, who was an alcoholic, and my Aunt Kim, who was addicted to heroin and not visiting me or accepting my phone calls. I confided in Mrs. Testerman that I couldn't trust any woman; they lack personal integrity. Mrs. Testerman made apologies for the women who had failed me during my development. She sagely assured me that my mother, grandmother, and aunt genuinely loved me, but their personal histories prevented them from giving me everything I wanted or needed. I had to forgive my mother for neglecting me and making me feel that I was an annoyance and a bother to her life. I had to forgive Mama and Kim for being emotionally unavailable to me, and I had to forgive myself if I intended to go forward.

I wanted to go forward. I forgave my mother, Mama, and Kim. I told Mama that I appreciated all the love she afforded me. I explained to her that I understood the many hardships she had faced trying to rear a hard-headed child who didn't care about life and sought only to be an outlaw. Mama and I shared the intimacies of our heart. We traded emotional secrets and cried in each other's presence. Mama stopped drinking and became the grandmother I always wanted. Unfortunately, I didn't get the opportunity to have a heart-to-heart with Kim. She died from a heroin overdose before I was able to let her know that I forgave her and needed her to forgive me. I wanted to tell Kim that I appreciated the fact that she had shared all that she had in food, clothing, shelter, and love with me. In my heart, I knew Kim did all that she knew how to prevent me from facing the hardships of a life of crime.

I became a man in the Penitentiary. I wasn't afraid to open my heart to permit myself to love and be loved. I was prepared to be with Joy. I didn't shy away from the vulnerability necessary to have such a sensuous woman in my life.

I kept no secrets from Joy, I expressed to her my fears at being in prison—in the Penitentiary. I told her all about the shame, anger, and confusion that directed my steps when I was in the streets. I told Joy that the reputation that I had built for myself was a shield from the shame and embarrassment I felt at simply being who I was.

It is a tragedy that no meaningful romantic relationship can last for me while I languish away in prison. Joy and I had a genuinely loving relationship, but she required far more than I could give. It pained me that our relationship had to end.

I still had to move forward. I graduated from college with honors, and I embarked upon more meaningful relationships. I met and befriended a guy named Drew Leder who came into the Penitentiary to offer a course in philosophy. I signed up for his class, and it resulted in my learning things that transformed me—making it possible for me to endure all that lay ahead with dignity and courage. Through the philosophy course that Drew brought into the Penitentiary, I learned to use my refined mind to see the world and incidents without blinders. I read the works of Heidegger, Nietzsche, Siddartha Gautama, Jesus, Ghandi, and scores of other great thinkers who have given wisdom to the world.

I traveled the world through Drew's class and learned to appreciate the different cultures, races, religions, and attitudes. I escaped my self-imposed prison of ghetto logic and reasoning. I went beyond Eager Street and fellow felons and realized a freedom that no court of law can grant—or withhold. I became a man worthy of liberties and the loving affection of Francine, the woman I married and divorced.

In Walks Francine

Chapter 43

A function was being held at the Penitentiary, an event when the inmates could have extended visitation and contact with their family and other loved ones. I didn't want to attend the event. I had no one to invite. My grandmother was dying from brain cancer. She was bed-ridden, and not expected to live much longer. Joy and I were no longer involved with each other in a meaningful way. She seldom visited me, and I stopped calling her. Our once beautiful relationship was at an end. Terrance was dead; he had been fatally shot in 1992. Black was serving time in the Federal Prison System for narcotics violations. I had absolutely no one to accompany me to the prison's function, and I was okay with that. I was acquainted enough with the accumulated wisdom of the ages to cope with my loneliness. I wasn't depressed. Things simply were what they were. I didn't want to be at the function where others would be hugged by their respective loved ones—enjoying good food and good music while I sat alone in a corner.

My friends Warren, Brother John, and Richard, good men whom I had met during my time at the Penitentiary, convinced me to attend the function.

Brother John said to me, "Tray, man, bring your monkey ass to the function. You might meet somebody. Besides, you have to be there for Project T."

I was the Operations Director for Project Turnaround, a prison group that dedicated its efforts to deterring youths from crime and the inevitable consequences. We, the members of Project Turnaround, were sponsoring the function. I had to be there, and Brother John, Warren, and Richard insisted that I attend.

I put on the best outfit I had and went to the affair.

I made a speech about our organization and entreated everyone present to support our effort. I acknowledged everyone who supported our efforts, passed out certificates and then found myself a seat in the corner of the dining hall after the formal ceremony had concluded. I wanted to get away from everyone.

Dorsey-Bey, a fellow prisoner, brought me a plate of food and a beverage. While I was enjoying my repast, a woman came over to me and asked, "Aren't you Tray from around Eager Street?"

This beautiful sister looked vaguely familiar. She posed no threat to me; I doubted that the prison officials would have allowed her to bring a gun into the place. If she was someone who wished to hurt me, she would not have been able to, for I could whip her. She was only 5'4", and a 130lbs if she wore an ounce.

"Yes, that's me," I answered honestly. "Who are you?"

"I'm Francine," she replied. "You don't remember me?"

Then, I remembered her. I had stood her up many years ago. One day, back in '84 while I was out there on Eager Street, managing my illegal drug operation, I had introduced myself to Francine, and after some discourse, I secured her address, but I never followed up. How I regretted it. Francine was looking quite desirable in her tight fitting brown slacks and sweater. Her honey-colored smooth skin and radiant smile made her rather alluring. I could do nothing about the past; it was done. There was no need to remind her of the stand-up. I just said, "Of course, I remember you. It's been a long time."

"How long have you been here?" She inquired.

"About ten years."

"Damn!" Francine exclaimed. "I asked everybody about you. I was told that you were sent to the Feds."

Francine sat down at the table with me, and we talked about some mutual acquaintances. I told her that I no longer associated with many of the folks from my past. She was pleased to hear that. She was a practicing Jehovah's Witness and didn't deal with folks of the criminal element anymore. I told Francine that I had graduated from college, Coppin State, with a Bachelor's Degree in Applied Psychology and was currently studying graduate-level philosophy. I wanted to impress her. She informed me that she had gone back to school also. But she was having problems with English Composition.

After a considerable amount of time passed, I asked Francine, "Who did you come here to see?"

"Oh, my Cousin Jamie," she answered. "Do you know him?"

"Yeah, I know him," I replied. "I don't deal with him, though."

I hoped like hell that Francine wouldn't ask me to join her with her cousin. He was reputed to be a sissy, and I didn't want to damage my image by hanging out with a sissy in the Penitentiary. I had matured in many respects; I was no longer caught up on reputations. But a man of my criminal stature simply couldn't afford to be associated with prison homosexuality. And everyone in Jamie's circle of friends bore that stigma.

"Why don't you come hang out with me?" The feared invitation.

"Naw, I'm just gonna sit here and chill," I was not going to disclose my true reason for not joining her crowd.

Francine was concerned about me being alone. She asked me about my guest; I told her that I didn't invite anyone. The only reason I had attended the function was because my organization was sponsoring it. I assured her that I was all right. I successfully entreated her to go enjoy the remaining time she had with her cousin.

It was a heart-breaker when I saw Francine hug and passionately kiss Ronald Cummingham as the function concluded. I envied Cummingham. But if you snooze you lose. I gave no credence to the matter. Francine had obviously misled me about who she had come to the function to be with, because she wanted me. I was a handsome, intelligent, and enchanting man. Francine would have preferred to be with me rather than Cummingham. I thoroughly satisfied my ego.

Days had passed since the function. I was outside in the prison's courtyard, taking my daily forty-five minute jog. Jamie made it a point to catch up to me to let me know that Francine had been asking about me. She wanted to talk to me on the phone. Jamie invited me to come down to the phone room within the next fifteen minutes so I could speak with Francine. I continued my jog, and once I felt that fifteen minutes had elapsed, I went to the phone room.

It was relatively crowded in the phone room. Inmates were standing all around G-Building, the prison's phone room area, playing cards and ping-pong, and shooting pool. I felt self-conscious about joining Jamie to share a phone conversation with a mutual party. He must have sensed my hesitancy.

"Here," Jamie handed me the phone and got up from the chair he was occupying. "You go 'head and talk to her. Just tell her I'll call back later."

I was relieved. My homies would probably have wanted to check my pedigree to see if I was still their dog, a real nigga, if I hung out with Jamie. Prison etiquette can be quite complex, to say the least.

"How are you, Francine?" I spoke into the phone. "I hear you've been asking about me." Francine informed me that she was doing well. The reason she had been asking about me was simple; she had the hots for me. I asked Francine about her relationship with Cummingham. She told me not to concern myself about that, Cummingham was simply a friend who her cousin, Jamie, had paired her with for that function. She wasn't interested in him.

"The way how you and Cummingham were hugged up kissin'," I expressed my doubts, "looks like y'all got something serious goin' on."

Francine insisted, "That was only a friendship kiss."

I told Francine that Cummingham was a dear friend of mine. He and I had spent a considerable amount of time together on lock-up on the South-wing and at the Supermax. I felt uncomfortable about establishing a romantic relationship with his girlfriend. I had a bond with Cummingham. If it was anyone else, someone whom I had not befriended, there would be no problem.

Francine understood my dilemma. She told me that she would clear up my doubts concerning her and Cummingham. She wanted to embark upon a love affair with me. I concluded my phone conversation with her and went out into the courtyard to search for Cummingham. I didn't want Francine to blindside him with her sudden change of heart. I also wanted to satisfy my own conscience. I had no moral issue with stealing another man's girlfriend if that other man wasn't my friend. In this case, Cummingham was my friend.

It didn't take long for me to spot Cummingham. He was sitting on the bench outside of the school building smoking a cigarette. He was alone, an ideal situation for the conversation I wanted to have with him.

"What's up, baby-boy?" I spoke to Cummingham as I approached him. "I got some words for you."

"I know what it is, too," Cummingham replied with his customary warm and generous smile that revealed his gold teeth. "Francine; right?"

"Yeah, I just got finished talkin' to her," I was bold. "You know she wants me."

"Knock yourself out. I can't do nothin' with the bitch."

I detected a little resentment in Cummingham's voice, but I did not know whether it was directed at me or Francine. I was determined to find out. I didn't want Cummingham to resent me; I genuinely liked him. I wasn't prepared to strain my friendship with him over Francine. I was between relationships; it had been awhile since I had a visit. I was quite lonely, but I felt confident I would have another girlfriend shortly. I was too fine, too intelligent, and too popular to be lonely too long.

"Cummingham, I'm not trying' to step on your toe," I said. "You my man! I just want you to know your girl is sweatin' me."

"I knew that the night of the function," Cummingham informed me. "When the bitch came back to the table, all she did was keep askin' 'bout you."

Cummingham's tone was friendly; he assured me that Francine could not come between him and me. He encouraged me to pursue a relationship with her. However, he advised me to pursue with caution. He had discovered, in his brief romance with Francine, that she was deceitful and self-centered.

Cummingham and I parted company when the officer announced over the speakers, "The yard is now closed; report to where you sleep for the security count."

I went back to my cell feeling rather ambivalent about the matter concerning Francine. If Cummingham felt hurt about Francine choosing me over him, he couldn't express that hurt to me. He would look and feel like a lame if he did. Cummingham had no alternative other than to encourage me to pursue Francine. Etiquette dictated it; etiquette also dictated that I get her to a function and have unauthorized but utterly enjoyable sex with her. It was not that simple. I was vulnerable to the unadulterated, genuine love and affection Francine had to offer me. The lessons about love, courage, pain, and suffering I was learning from my philosophy course opened my heart and soul to what Francine offered me. I couldn't trivialize her affection. Practicing certain meditation techniques and contemplating upon what certain great thinkers disclosed made me realize that I had never experienced true love from a woman because I never gave it. This was my opportunity to experiment with love.

Francine was extremely attentive to my every need. She visited me every visiting day, and allowed me to bask in all of her feminine beauty. I was able to be myself in Francine's presence. I was at ease with her; I didn't have to erect a façade to impress her. She saw me for who I was, and loved me anyway.

I had absolutely no one in my life whom I could depend on. Mama was dying from cancer. Black was serving a lengthy prison term in some Federal prison. Terrance was dead, and Suddar was in a prison separate from me. Joy was denying me any further contact. Our relationship had mysteriously ended. There were no bitter words exchanged between us. She just stopped coming to visit and accepting my calls. I was alone and lonely.

It was during that period in my life that Francine came along and assured me that I wouldn't have to be alone as long as there was breath in her body. All I had to do was be honest and lovable. I went out on faith and loved Francine with my whole heart.

Two years after that function, Francine and I were married. We have had our ups and downs—our highs and lows, but the love we share has been my constant sustaining source of comfort and growth. Before Francine came into my life and instilled love there, I was becoming empty inside. Life's miseries and sufferings were all around me, overwhelming me. Philosophy was aiding me with understanding the miseries and sufferings, preventing me from becoming embittered by it all. But it did little to eradicate it from my life. I was coming to the point where witnessing young boys get raped in the shower, or in other isolated areas of the prison, no longer offended my sensibilities. I was becoming so inhumane, hardened, that I wasn't repulsed by senseless murders. I had seen too many good people lose their precious life for the most petty reasons imaginable. The Penitentiary was beginning to harden me and create a coldness in my soul.

I am thankful that Francine's love warmed and humbled me. Genuine love is no longer a vague philosophy to me, an object for philosophical debate or discussion. I am now experiencing the love the philosophers pontificate about and the poets romanticize. I know that my troubles resulted from not loving genuinely and sincerely. I had always longed for sincere and genuine love, but I never gave it. I guess I didn't know how. Francine invoked my natural ability to love genuinely and sincerely. And that love opened my mind to true wisdom and my heart to true compassion—life's essential ingredients for success.

About the Author

Arlando "Tray" Jones

Arlando "Tray" Jones, III, is serving a life sentence in the Maryland State Penitentiary in Hagerstown. While in prison, Tray educated himself through a program offered by Coppin State University, graduating cum laude with a degree in Applied Psychology. He was one of the inmates featured in Dr. Drew Leder's book, *The Soul Knows No Bars*. He hopes his story convinces young urban people, especially young men, that life on the corner dealing in crime and violence is not glamorous, but a ticket to a life like his behind bars.

"Every man born will experience at least one great challenge. That challenge will have its ups and downs, highs and lows. No one can avoid life's inevitable great challenge. Therefore, no one is likely to be measured or judged by the challenge he faces. Each man is only measured or judged by the way he responds to his great challenge."
— Arlando "Tray" Jones

The future of publishing...today!

Apprentice House is the country's only campus-based, student-staffed book publishing company. Directed by professors and industry professionals, it is a nonprofit activity of the Communication Department at Loyola University Maryland.

Using state-of-the-art technology and an experiential learning model of education, Apprentice House publishes books in untraditional ways. This dual responsibility as publishers and educators creates an unprecedented collaborative environment among faculty and students, while teaching tomorrow's editors, designers, and marketers.

Outside of class, progress on book projects is carried forth by the AH Book Publishing Club, a co-curricular campus organization supported by Loyola Universtiy Maryland's Office of Student Activities.

Student Project Team for *Eager Street*:

Kristen English, '08	William "Mike" Tirone, '08
Francesca Knowles, '08	Margo Weiner, '08
John Likoudis '10	Elizabeth Watson, '08
Julia Sherrier, '08	

Eclectic and provocative, Apprentice House titles intend to entertain as well as spark dialogue on a variety of topics. Financial contributions to sustain the press's work are welcomed. Contributions are tax deductible to the fullest extent allowed by the IRS.

To learn more about Apprentice House books or to obtain submission guidelines, please visit www.ApprenticeHouse.com.

Apprentice House
Communication Department
Loyola University Maryland
4501 N. Charles Street
Baltimore, MD 21210
Ph: 410-617-5265 • Fax: 410-617-5040
www.ApprenticeHouse.com • info@apprenticehouse.com

Breinigsville, PA USA
22 December 2010
252001BV00002B/64/P

9 781934 074459